"The madness of retail will be perceived only by those who find no meaning in it. Whilst the essential retailers will be those that embrace the sense of it."

Published by Wordzworth
www.wordzworth.com

MEANING
IN THE
RETAIL MADNESS

*How to be an **Essential** Retailer*

TIM RADLEY

Tim Radley

Tim Radley is a retail consultant based near London. He brings to the table 30 years of being young in the industry.

He has worked with retail companies on a wide variety of strategic and operational projects, from back-end product development to front-end customer experience, and on most things in-between. His role has always been to introduce 'new' retail thinking and processes. To improve both the financial performance KPIs, and the human experiences of retail businesses. This has never been as important, as it is now.

He has been fortunate to work across the world of retail from Europe and Asia, to South America and the US. It has confirmed his view that retail people and customers are all 'cut from the same cloth,' yet are as diverse and wonderfully individual as the list of people he has worked with suggests.

Primark, Walgreens, Boots, Adidas, AllSaints, Ferrari, Luxottica, Ray-Ban, Nespresso, Bata, Halfords, Carrefour, Ladbrokes, Camper, Jack Jones, Marks & Spencer, Cortefiel, Sainsbury, Continente, Sonae, Otto Versand, BonPrix, World Duty Free, Sprinter, La Caixa, National Geographic, Real Madrid, KappAhl, Flex, Gruppo Vestebene, Alessi, Eroski, Gruppo Coin, OVS, Carrera, Aena, Heatons, Bally, Portaventura, Sony, Clarks, Benetton, Imaginarium, Dublin City Council, Porcelanosa, Northumbria University, Bialetti and Baltika.

In 2007 Tim set up VM-Unleashed to create a company that specializes in developing world-class customer experiences in physical and digital shops. He collaborates internationally as Director of Retail Experience at Ispira, based in Italy, and with agencies throughout Europe.

Tim is a popular and well-regarded speaker presenting at retail conferences across the globe. He regularly appears at the Retail Design Expo in London, the VM & Design show, and at In-Store Asia, the largest retail conference and trade fair in the Indian sub-continent. He is also a judge on the VM&RD Retail Design Awards panel for Asia, and has advised the LCF (London College of Fashion) on retail course content and structure.

Tim contributes articles for a variety of magazines and radio features, discussing retail issues as varied as the "Omnichannel Store of the Future" to the "Saving of the High Street."

For my meaning in the retail madness:
Gail, Alice, Sophie & Dominic

Contents

3. Excel in...
Astute Strategies

The Z to A of retail disruption   256

Businesses that are successfully disrupting the traditional ways of doing retail are creatively and commercially diverse, emerging from the worlds of imaginative new enterprises, and re-energised classic retail brands.

This book contains over 90 specific insights on how 'doing things with meaning' is now the only way to be 'essential' to customers in this brave new retail world.

Action Pages   258

How to make yourself into an 'Essential Retailer'

With such a myriad of opportunities available to join the retail revolution, it can be difficult to know where to begin and how to proceed.

This book contains 70 Action Plans, linked to every area of retail innovation and evolution, outlining the reasoning behind every disruptive initiative and offering step by step guidance on how to achieve your goals.

Introduction

> "This book draws on my many years working with retail best practice and is driven by the things that I have seen, and those I never wish to see again."

"It was the best of times. It was the worst of times." To paraphrase the words of Charles Dickens is to sum up the crossroads at which we find ourselves in the retail industry. Except that the revolution we face is not a work of fiction, it is real, and it is worldwide. It is however, being caused by a dissatisfaction of the masses, a growing groundswell of consumers with different buying priorities and product sentiments, and a system of mass production flooding the world with generic product beyond our needs and desires.

This worst of times has been brought to a head by the COVID pandemic. It has been the most brutal of encounters for the retail sector, but history will show that it was in fact the final poisoned cherry on the top of a crumbling retail cake that was for many well passed its sell-by date.

It is the best of times for disruption and innovation. Totally new businesses are being born from customer communities with the same concerns, and with a passion to approach the buying and selling of goods in a new way. These will flourish alongside existing retailers who have prepared for these times. Far sighted businesses that could see the storm approaching, have ridden it out, and are emerging as better and more commercially attractive propositions.

It is also the best of times to write, and I hope, to read this book. This has also been a time coming. A time with many businesses still persevering with the familiar misguided and destructive strategies. I have written this book for anyone who wants to consider the alternatives.

This book draws on my many years working with retail best practice and is driven by the things that I have seen, and those I never wish to see again.

This book encapsulates two defining pillars that I have believed from my earliest days in the industry, and from my travels and travails from Europe to Asia, South America to the United States. That retail knowledge should be for everyone, and that retail expertise must be broad and inclusive.

This book is for all those retail employees who continue to surprise and inspire me with their own enthusiasm and appetite to learn and improve. Employees young and old, from the boardroom to the stockroom.

The retail business is a joined-up process that requires an astounding diversity of skills, activities, and functions. Many people with different areas of expertise must connect and integrate as part of a wider plan, a cohesive strategy, and a defining vision. I know that successful retail stories do not happen by accident, but through the skillful collaboration of these many people, guided with simple and singular objectives.

Every individual skill is richer, every single task is lighter, every employee is wiser, when they can see and understand the wider context of their personal contributions.

Some non-fiction books invite the reader to "dip-in." You are very welcome to dip into the chapters and the parts of the book that you feel are most relevant to you. But I would also encourage you to read everything, and to read it in the order that it is written. This book is a narrative, a story.

Simply "dipping-in" has been the scourge of many retailers. Executives have "dipped-in" their influential but sometimes mis-informed opinions. Retail specialists have "dipped-in" their own expertise, ignorant to the wider processes. External agencies, creatives, and marketers have "dipped-in" their visions without understanding the everyday realities of a brand. I should know.

I hope this story reads well. The chapters are built around the familiar and enduring cornerstones of retail, the organisation, the product, the shops and channels, and above all, the people. I have sought to look through the eyes of retail people, the colleagues, and the customers. I have kept segmentation to a minimum, because the segmentation of functions and people serves no positive purpose.

Transversal issues such as technology, collaboration, marketing, training, ethics, and sustainability have been woven into the text wherever relevant. For progressive retailers, these topics must always be "in-mind," considered and included in every decision and initiative.

I have developed 'sketches' to help illustrate and explain the disruptive concepts I discuss. There are also numerous best practice insights that will bring life and illumination to the text. Above all, I hope this makes the content accessible and relevant to everyone, whether you are a small cog in a large business wheel, the only cog in your own entrepreneurial wheel, or an informed observer of the perpetually turning wheels of the retail industry. You are all welcome.

This book aims to communicate both breadth and depth of retail knowledge. A breadth of understanding across many functions of retail that allows precise initiatives to be taken with proper context. A depth of expertise that makes those initiatives both informed and actionable. To widen our horizons, to improve our surroundings.

This book is intended to make us think. Think as retailers, as customers, and for good measure, as part of humanity. In each of these guises we impact an industry that has lost its way.

Some will see the meaning in what I would like to say, others will discard it.

Ultimately, the madness of retail will be perceived only by those who find no meaning in it. Whilst the essential retailers will be those that embrace the sense of it.

I hope that you can apply the stories in this book to your own individual context. I wish you every success as you write your own story in this amazing industry. Successful retail must be built on pragmatism and processes, on the collaboration and the integration of its many facets, but without a story it really has nothing to say.

Without a story we all have nothing to say.

Here is my story. I look forward to hearing yours.

1. Flourish in ...

The Life & Times of the 'Essential' Retailer

What makes a retailer essential?

Our viewpoint of what is essential has been re-focused by the covid19 era.

Through degrees of concern and panic many of us now fully appreciate what is important to us. It has also made us aware of the things in life that are not.

Consumer goods were put into perspective within the wider social context. The people in our lives, and those who effect our lives, were recognised with a new clarity as being essential.

The existential threats and the exciting opportunities now emerging for many retailers have been growing for some time.

What the COVID 'emergency stop' has given us is a unique point of reflection in the otherwise endless dynamic of retailing.

COVID lockdown has ironically been a defining period of clarity to ask the question…'are we essential to the customer?'

'Are we an essential retailer?'

Our new lives and behaviours are markedly different from before the lockdown. Retailers who were just familiar or friendly, convenient or useful, were always walking on a tightrope of viability. These 'strengths' alone were never going to be enough to guarantee survival and growth, in any future retail landscape.

To be an "Essential Retailer" is the only way to be part of that landscape.

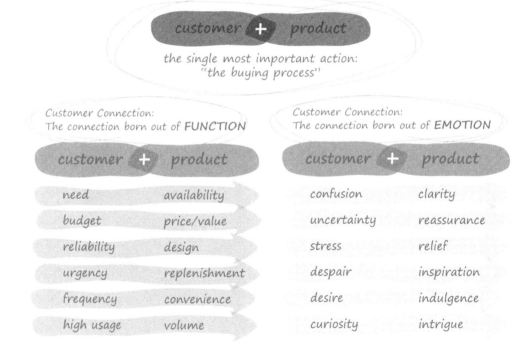

© 2021 vm-unleashed ltd.

Sketch 1   Functional & Emotional Customer Connections

The Functional and Emotional Relationship

We should never forget the fundamental buying process. The role of a retailer is to bring together the customer and a product. It is to bring them together functionally & emotionally.

A functional connection alone will rarely be enough to command customer loyalty. Equally, an emotional engagement can never compensate for a retailer who fails in the basic functionality of availability.

If a customer enters a shoe shop to buy a pair of size 5 black shoes, it is essential that they leave with a pair of size 5 black shoes. You are a shoe shop.

It is acceptable that a suitable shoe is ordered which will be delivered to the customer's home, or to the shop for collection the next day. It is also acceptable that the service team apologises for not having an appropriate black shoe and directs the customer to a nearby competitor who has.

In all eventualities, the customer did not fail. The retailer did not fail either. It made no sale on one occasion, but it enhanced its reputation with the customer who will make purchases there in the future.

What is a 'good customer experience?' A good customer experience is not to fail!

Successful retail connection is more than just selling a product. Retailers can be so much more than what they sell, and the customer now expects them to be so much more.

At every level of connection from product availability, through lifestyle engagement to supporting the well-being of the customer, the retailer must use every opportunity to be the 'essential retailer' amongst a growing world of 'essential retailers'.

© 2021 vm-unleashed ltd.

Sketch 2   The Spectrum of Emotional Customer Connections

The Focused Relationship

The emotional focus of a retailer depends on the demographics and lifestyle of its customers, as well as its own values and philosophies. These will vary considerably within the same sector and across any sector.

> *Retailers and customers naturally gravitate towards each other when they share the same values.*

For some retailers and customers, the relationship will be more ethical and philosophical. For others it may be about enjoyment and lifestyle or built on a common aesthetic taste and style.

The ultimate goal for every retailer is to generate a genuine relationship across all areas. These relationships must be meaningful and fruitful for both retailers and customers. They are at the heart of being an 'essential' retailer.

Retailer relationships most commonly focus on one aspect of a customer's personality. Ethical, Aesthetic and Enjoyment relationships can be personal and enduring.

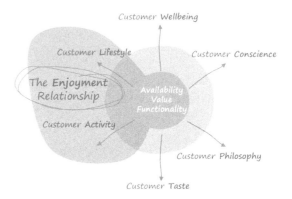

However, the deepest relationships allow the retailer to connect with the customer in different ways, at different moments and periods of their lives.

© 2021 vm-unleashed ltd.

Sketch 3   The Relevant Relationship

The Relevant Relationship

Recent history should have taught us never to be complacent about the "here and now." We are all reflections of the turbulent times in which we are living.

The needs of a customer never stay the same. They naturally evolve and mature, whilst they sometimes fluctuate sharply in response to social or personal upheavals. The retailer cannot communicate in a banal and blanket fashion but must respond in whatever way the customer needs, at any moment in their lives.

Sometimes the communication will be fun, frivolous and focused on impulse purchases. At other times it must be measured and appropriate, in response to the customer's need to buy products with more serious meaning and motives.

'Essential retailers' must be there for customers in the best of times, and the worst of times.

The Best in 'the Worst of times'

The responses of retailers in the COVID lockdown were genuinely astounding. We saw clearly the distinction between the generous and compassionate businesses and the self-centered and selfish ones.

We saw retailers who changed payment policies so that struggling small suppliers were paid instantly, and we saw retailers who hung onto their money for as long as possible.

We saw retailers who honoured their orders with suppliers and supported overseas factories and their workers, and we saw retailers who cancelled orders.

We saw retailers who ensured their staff felt safe and protected before re-opening, and we saw retailers who opened shops to make every possible available sale.

We saw retailers who furloughed their staff and supported their well-being, and we saw retailers who furloughed for as long as was financially beneficial.

We saw retailers that set aside shopping hours and online delivery slots for essential workers, and we saw retailers who delivered to those willing and able to pay for the privilege.

And we saw retailers who gave unsellable stock to charity and created gift boxes for health carers, and we saw retailers who mothballed their stock to sell at next year's prices.

In the darkest of times, we witnessed some remarkable and spontaneous gestures to customers, to colleagues and to suppliers. The lockdown was a showcase for retailers who developed 'essential' and long-standing relationships.

They became essential in supplying the basic needs of a variety of people, whilst rising to the emotional challenges of being empathetic, compassionate and generous.

The template for the essential retailer has been drafted. The rules for the 'essential relationship' have been written.

Marks & Spencer: school learning support

Brands both established, and relatively new to the market all rose to the challenge in many varied ways to support their colleagues and the wider community during lockdowns.

Marks & Spencer is a 'British institution.' It has a history of 137 years and counting, and despite increasingly difficult times it has maintained an enviable relationship with customers and the wider public, where it still commands a great deal of trust.

During the pandemic, many schools were closed for long periods of time. Alongside the best efforts of teachers and schools there was still the opportunity to support children further with remote lessons, to deliver the curriculum with more online materials.

Marks & Spencer has a huge archive of content relating to subjects as diverse as healthy eating, making clothes, financial awareness and sustainability. It coordinated its internal resources to curate the material and launch a range of free online learning modules for parents, carers and teachers of primary and secondary aged children to download at home.

The resources aimed to support skills in maths, science, art and design, and business studies. The resources were developed by education experts in collaboration with teachers and home-schooling coordinators for Key Stages 1 to 4. As well as offering learning resources the modules also gave children an opportunity to get a behind-the-scenes insight into the workings and processes of M&S.

Such COVID lockdown initiatives have only served to strengthen the reputation of M&S and its relationship with the public, as it re-aligns itself into a digital-first company implementing its 'Never the Same Again' transformation programme.

As businesses develop for the modern age, they should always guard against throwing away those traditional values that customers regard so highly.

The Entertainer: shop colleague wellbeing

The Entertainer is the UK's largest independent toy retailer, operating more than 170 stores across the country.

In the Christmas period during lockdown, when every physical shop retailer was trying to claw back as many sales as possible, it put its people first, before its profits. The Entertainer gave its staff more opportunity to be together with their families and loved ones, as it closed its shops from Christmas Eve until Monday 28 December, giving them three of the five days of the eased restrictions as holiday.

In theory The Entertainer is in a vulnerable market position, selling many of the generic toys and games brands that can be found on Amazon and any other online marketplace. But the Entertainer is thriving because of the powerful loyalty it generates from its colleague and customer community.

It is family owned, and more to the point it feels family owned. The business speaks through its actions. Its reaction to the COVID Christmas is entirely consistent with its broader philosophies and behaviour.

The Grant Foundation is The Entertainer's charitable wing. For many years it has donated hundreds of thousands of pounds to children's charities, including The Toybox Charity, a charity which supports street children in Guatemala.

The Entertainer is also an active member of Pennies, the digital charity box. It is available in all shops, allowing customers to round-up their purchases and donate the change to charity when paying by debit or credit card.

The retailer has also pioneered 'quiet hours' in its shops to create calm shopping experiences for children and adults with learning difficulties and conditions where quiet and peace are important for their wellbeing.

Gary Grant, alongside his wife, is the founder of The Entertainer. There are many interviews with him that you can find online. It is always worth reading his words. A man and a business with values.

The Z to A of retail disruption

Morrisons: caring for the community

Morrisons supermarket emerged as a real superstar during the COVID pandemic with a variety of responses & initiatives that cemented its role as a retailer from the community for the community.

The retailer launched a meal delivery service for primary schools who were feeding children having to self-isolate at home. The supermarket worked with schools to provide the meals for children who would normally be eligible for free meals with breakfast, lunch and snacks.

Developed in partnership with Morrisons company nutritionist, the Morrisons Kids Meal Pack included enough cereal, milk, bread, fruit, yoghurts, sandwich fillings, pasta and squash for seven days. The cost was covered by schools as part of the Government's free school meals programme.

Schools were able to order the packs directly from the Morrisons doorstep delivery team. Orders were then picked and packed by local Morrisons stores and sent to children's homes via its 'doorstep delivery' service.

Morrisons also extended its ongoing work with food redistribution charity 'The Bread and Butter Thing' in which it provides food for families in need. The initiative also means that the retailer significantly reduces food waste in its food making operations and supply chains around the UK.

After embarking on the partnership in 2016, Morrisons has already provided two million meals to the charity's members. During 2021, the retailer plans to redistribute surplus food to 30,000 families. The food comes from a range of Morrisons' food-making sites, distribution centres, and UK suppliers and includes fruit & vegetables, meat & fish, prepared food & bread.

Particularly within the food sector, the COVID lockdowns fuelled a renewal of respect for the frontline staff working in shops. The public saw people who were making great personal sacrifices to keep shops open and to supply customers with the essentials. In many cases colleagues went far beyond the basic requirements expected by customers giving them additional support and guidance.

Morrisons has a reputation for being a family business and was run by members of the original family until relatively recently. True to its business community heritage, it was not only the first retailer to announce permanent wage increases for all shop colleagues, but it committed to a permanent promise to pay every employee in their shops at least £10 an hour.

Whilst other brands have also made wage increases on the back of the lockdown, no one, to my knowledge, has matched the level of pay being offered by Morrisons.

Holland & Barrett: flexible wage payments

Health and wellness retailer Holland & Barrett launched a new scheme during COVID to give staff instant access to their wages. Its 'Earned Wage Access' service enabled its 5,000 UK employees to get earned wages whenever they needed them.

Holland & Barrett explained their commitment to the importance of making wellness accessible to all, including focusing on the impact of financial stability to their colleagues' mental health.

'Earned Wage Access' was a relatively new and innovative initiative across the sector. It promises to give business colleagues more protection from the financial pain and emotional strain of meeting unexpected expenses.

The Z to A of retail disruption

Boots: vaccination centres

Boots the health & beauty retailer used the medical expertise in its pharmacies and health services to set up Covid-19 vaccination sites at several of its locations.

The business has extensive knowledge and experience of mass vaccination (having completed over a million flu vaccinations in 2019) and was able to develop a model for Covid-19 vaccinations that was aligned with the required stringent safety, clinical and operational standards.

Superdrug: volunteers for hospitals

Superdrug, a competitor health and beauty retailer to Boots used five of its stores as vaccination hubs to aid the NHS with the rollout of the Covid-19 vaccine.

The retailer also has decades of experience in delivering mass vaccination services and has developed a team of highly qualified nurses and pharmacists. As well as working closely with the NHS to support its Covid-19 efforts, Superdrug nurses also volunteered in hospitals, the wider community and blood transfusion centres.

Amongst other retailer initiatives during the vaccination Waitrose donated its staff leisure centre at its HQ, to be repurposed as a temporary vaccination site for six months, with nearly 1,000 residents being vaccinated at the premises in its first two days in operation.

PureGym offered up space in its gyms, which were closed under government guidelines, to help with the vaccination effort, whilst Brewdog offered space in the pub chain's premises to store and administer the Covid-19 vaccine.

Dixons Carphone (Currys): relieving digital poverty

During the pandemic and the series of lockdowns, Dixons Carphone donated £1 million to support disadvantaged pupils, parents and teachers as part of a long-term commitment to help end digital poverty in the UK.

Money was also used to equip 1,000 teachers and teaching assistants with the technology and other support they needed to deliver home schooling to 30,000 pupils during the Covid-19 crisis and beyond.

The consumer electronics brand is already helping thousands of elderly people to digitally connect through a partnership with the charity Age UK and is now offering the same support to tackle the digital divide in education.

The company was also one of three founding partners in the Digital Poverty Alliance, a group of organisations brought together by DAFA and the Institution of Engineering and Technology to tackle digital poverty in the UK.

With its scale, recycling and reuse operations, and 22,000 expert UK colleagues in shops Dixons is perfectly placed to have a significant impact.

The COVID lockdowns inspired collaborations that would have been unimaginable only a few weeks before.

When food did actually, start to 'run-out' and shop shelves were empty, an unlikely alliance of the leading grocery retailers coordinated the supply of staple products between them, to ensure that in any location products such as dried pasta were available in at least one of the shops.

The brands also worked to reduce the number of pasta shapes and bag sizes being produced to quicken up the factory and packaging processes, to ensure that shop replenishment was as quick and as efficient as possible.

The Z to A of retail disruption

MAKE YOURSELF ESSENTIAL ACTION PAGES

001

DO NOT FAIL YOUR CUSTOMER

Internal analysis & customer research

Take an honest step back and understand how you fail your customers. Find out by asking all members of the company from head office to shops, from product development to customer services. Run workshops with those who deal with customers face to face. Run customer focus groups.

Actions

- Prioritise the areas where you fail the most, and where you have the biggest opportunity to improve.
- Define the actions required to turn the biggest and most damaging failures into successes.
- Put those actions into place and follow through with continued analysis of improvements, impacts and benefits.
- Create a cycle of improving, analysing, and improving again.
- Stay close to your customer and continue to ask.

002

FOCUS YOUR CUSTOMER CONNECTION

Internal brainstorming

Don't try to be everything to everybody. Go back to your brand. Where should you be to be most appropriate to your customer on an emotional level? Fun and excitement or wellbeing and conscience? Consider where your brand perception is currently the strongest and weakest. Align the reality with the ideal.

Actions

- Identify the real touchpoints with your customer that effect the emotional relationship.
- Define the actions needed for each touchpoint to add in and build the appropriate emotional element
- Prioritise quick impact actions, but within a longer-term coordinated list of actions.
- Group action plans by emotional touchpoint impact and not by functions
- Make the changes to the touchpoints working across functions.

003

HELP YOUR CUSTOMER WHERE THEY MOST NEED IT

On the ground research, colleague feedback

Find out more about your customer, their lives and the problems in their lives. Find out about the things they care about the most, their families, their communities. Do they have children? Do they work? What do they like to do?

Actions

- Identify specific ways to help your customer, to make their daily lives better. To make them and those they love happy.
- Cost the actions against long term loyalty benefits
- Facilitate the actions financially and operationally with local funding, sponsorship, collaboration, donations...etc.
- Communicate and publicise by 'word of mouth' or social media. Never boast or glorify your actions.

Ultimate Retail Proposition
Diverse product & services

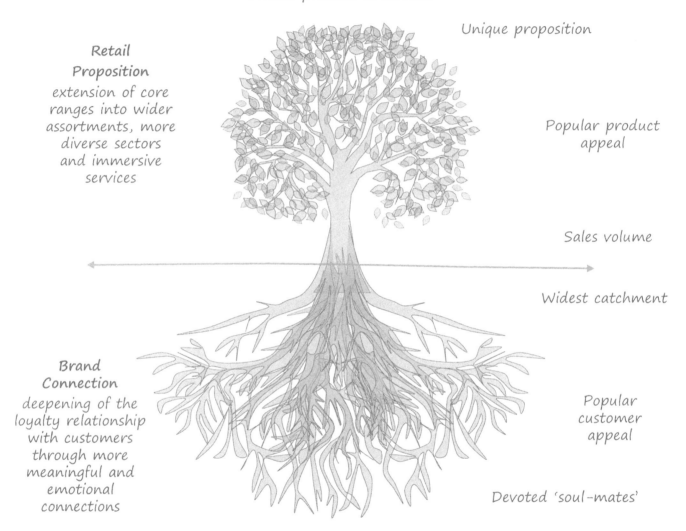

Unique proposition

Retail Proposition
extension of core ranges into wider assortments, more diverse sectors and immersive services

Popular product appeal

Sales volume

Widest catchment

Brand Connection
deepening of the loyalty relationship with customers through more meaningful and emotional connections

Popular customer appeal

Devoted 'soul-mates'

Ultimate Customer Connection
Strong synergy & loyalty

© 2021 vm-unleashed ltd.

Sketch 4   'Essential Relationships'

'Essential Relationships'

Building deeper relationships with the customer unlocks the commercial potential for retailers.

The deeper the connection the greater the opportunity.

One of the advantages of deep connections is that they help build opportunities to broaden assortments and related services. They open the potential to enter diverse product and service sectors and they provide the potential to deliver revenue generating loyalty subscription models with the most connected and engaged customers.

The 'downside' traditionally of the same deep connections is the inverse relationship between the depth of connection and the number of customers with whom you can have that relationship.

A more engaged relationship, a deeper connection, requires more synergy of values, ethical points of view and philosophies. The connection goes well beyond shopping. That synergy will only be found between a retailer and a select group within the population. The catchment is limited but the loyalty is strong.

Conversely a shallower less engaged relationship, focused on retail fundamentals only, is appropriate and comfortable for a wider section of society but will lack a binding loyalty with the retailer. In this scenario the retail fundamentals must be absolute best practice to ensure customers stay loyal to a single retailer when many competitors offer a similar relationship.

Therefore, retailers, like people, have a strategic choice. To be opinionated and to make strong friendships, but clear enemies. Or to agree with everyone, which will not create enemies but will not engender deep and lasting relationships either.

The middle ground is often more comfortable for retailers to deliver and for customers to engage with. However, it is a very crowded place precisely because it is comfortable.

In this middle ground, the focus of the relationship is on popular lifestyles, customer activities and aesthetic tastes. Best practice retail fundamentals are of course a pre-requisite, along with a clear if not contentious viewpoint on most things.

Levels of customer connection

None of the Basic, Advanced or Ultimate customer connection strategies are necessarily good or bad. They are just different. What they must be is appropriate.

The Basic Customer Connection is built around availability, value and functionality. The Advanced Customer Connection is based on customer lifestyle, customer activity and taste. The Ultimate Customer Connection evolves around customer well-being, customer conscience and philosophy.

In the basic connection retailers must ensure they do not fail the customer. They must have efficient supply chains with good stock availability and replenishment. Consistent and logical pricing must be matched with attractive and appropriate promotions. Shop environments, customer services and staff courtesy can never be anything other than excellent.

On top of these basics, advanced retailers can build a wealth of engagement through a vibrant and entertaining promotional calendar, they can introduce an endless sequence of attractive and distinctive products supported with additional services.

The ultimate icing that keeps the relationship sweet is made from the stories behind the stores. Stories about sustainability, heritage and origins, community engagement, employee welfare and colleague appreciation from the shop to factory floor.

1. **Basic Customer Connection:**
   a. Availability:
      - Distribution/supply chain/replenishment efficiency
   b. Value:
      - Price/promotional strategy/loyalty offers
   c. Functionality
      - Channel design and operations
      - Service efficiency

2. **Advanced Customer Connection:**
   a. Customer Lifestyle
      - Assortment structure planning/channel/ location strategy
      - Customer services, supplementary services
      - Traditional & digital marketing/loyalty bonuses
   b. Customer Activity
      - Events & promotions/sponsorships
      - Brand collaborations/influences/pop-up strategies
   c. Customer Taste
      - Product design/branded shop environments

3. **Ultimate Customer Connection:**
   a. Customer Wellbeing
      - Personal services/loyalty programmes/reward benefits
      - Cross-channel flexibility/efficiency/guarantees
   b. Customer Conscience
      - Community involvement/charities/reward partnerships
      - Social & product sustainability initiatives
   c. Customer Philosophy
      - Acceptable corporate ownership/responsibility
      - Compatible ethical viewpoints

Sketch 5   The 'Levels of Customer Connection.'

Primark: adding value to the price proposition

The reputation of Primark extends well beyond its current geographies. And whilst some of those 'pile it high, sell it cheap' perceptions are absolutely grounded in reality, for many customers visiting a store for the first time the experience they receive may well be quite different from the one they were expecting. Far more exciting and engaging.

Primark is a market leader. It is also a disruptor on a grand scale in so many ways. What it has done so successfully is to develop from simply a purveyor of everyday low-priced clothing, the lowest price clothing, to the number one physical retail destination for post-lockdown shoppers.

Primark is not new. It was born in 1969, in Ireland under the name Penneys. For many years it did just pride itself on its low prices. It was hugely efficient and offered availability and reliability in its assortment. The customer knew what they wanted, and Primark delivered. Well, the customer thought they knew what they wanted.

The brand proposition and perception grew initially around high fashion products, influenced by designer catwalks, produced and sold at prices which were incomparable to the 'real thing'. Through celebrity endorsement and accidental celebrity engagement with the products, the brand began to take off. It was cool to mix Primark with the most expensive brands.

However, the brand reached new heights when it began to evolve its basic physical shop relationship with customers into advanced connections, with a new emotional level of branding.

Its shops were transformed from dull destinations into state-of-the-art theatres of excitement. Anyone who has visited the converted bank in Gran Via in Madrid could not have been seduced by the 'wow' effect of entering the main gallery with its many floors stretching up to the domed ceiling.

The shop was alive with colour and atmosphere. Digital screens filled the space with action and music, whilst dynamic mannequin displays 'showed-off' the latest fashion styles. Product was visually displayed just like the most admired fashion boutiques whilst 'still' the lowest prices were communicated alongside product attributes and materials.

Primark had developed an emotional destination. The shop became a European fashion store of the year.

Primark has invested in best practice shop design, and in new visual merchandising capabilities and principles turning its lingerie and fashion departments into key destinations. The regimented displays of shiny black mannequins in the lingerie areas are an eye-catching feature, whilst POS graphics, combined with 'cheeky' packaging ideas steal the show.

Primark continues to be the lowest in price but has added ever more additional value for the customer. Its largest flagship store opened in Birmingham in 2019 and showed increasing assortment and service diversity, from dedicated Harry Potter shops, and impulse product marketplaces, to interactive beauty bars and services, and collaborations with Disney, such as dedicated kids departments and themed Mickey Mouse cafes. The shop even finds space for relaxation areas with soft furnishings, music, phone charging and free wi-fi.

Primark is still obsessed with low prices. It famously responded to increasing cotton prices and market speculation that its prices would need to increase, by celebrating its new assortment with 'prices lower than the previous year.' It has also evolved best practice shop replenishment standards, with strict rules on 'one basket' shop floor re-merchandising.

Primark has built on these operational fundamentals, which keep getting stronger, but has never stood still in its quest to add unmatched value to its low-priced assortment.

There are, of course, issues regarding the ethics and sustainability of mass-merchandising and its supply chains. However, as a commercial brand Primark's ability to never stand-still across many fronts, is to be admired.

The Z to A of retail disruption

1. Basic Customer Connections

There will continue to be a sizeable segment of any market where customers are simply looking for the correct retail fundamentals. Nothing more, nothing less.

The value sector contains some of the strongest retail propositions across all product sectors, and across all channels. Only one retailer in each can have the privilege of being the "cheapest" but there are other successful retailers who add important value to their low-price positioning through convenience, wide assortment, dynamic stock-turn, vibrant promotional activity and dynamic product drops.

Incidentally, when we speak of emotional connections never underestimate the excitement or satisfaction that can be generated in customers of all kinds through low prices and price reductions. Make every day for your customer, "their luckiest day!"

A basic customer connection is a 'satisfactory' position for both value driven customers and retailers. It requires less sophistication and investment from the retailer, who can rely on blanket messages. Importantly it demands less emotional investment from customers who are happy just to buy.

For existing retail businesses, the model is largely built around traditional retail skills sets which are established and already available and can be updated for modern markets. A good buying team, sourcing expertise combined with supply-chain efficiency and distribution will still go a long way to delivering a model that works well with a more basic customer relationship.

The danger of a limited relationship is that loyalty to the brand is weak, with reasons to buy such as generic assortments, convenience and price more easily copied or matched by competitors. In competitive markets there is also, always the risk of a promotional spiral to non-profitability as losing margin becomes the only tool to drive loyalty and sales volumes.

The shallow customer connection makes added-value assortment diversification and service extensions unlikely as they will not find traction with a transient customer base.

For market leaders the basic relationship is powerful and all consuming, however for competitors squeezed for custom the move to a more advanced relationship can give the potential to attract new customers. As all markets develop and all customers become sophisticated in their shopping habits and their selection of brands and retailers, it is increasingly the case that most operators sooner or later find the need to move beyond the basic customer relationship.

B&Q: online service marketplaces

DIY products are still generally sold from large warehouses as broad assortments, with a basic customer proposition and service offer. As a result, loyalty is not always strong.

B&Q is rolling out a new home improvement services marketplace through its NeedHelp App. It can now recommend skilled workers for kitchen installations, bathroom renovations, painting and flooring, related to its key product categories. The DIY retailer is reacting to the need to be more digital, and service orientated while leveraging its strong store assets. Online services marketplaces are key to the future loyalty.

Leroy Merlin: learning DIY

In the physical DIY space Leroy Merlin is launching new innovations including DIY classes and tool rental. Its customers in South Africa can book classes online, including "how to make a bench" and "how to fix a roof leak", for between £5 and £10. The retailer has also partnered with local small businesses to provide a tool rental service for big tools, such as circular saws or tile cutters, which may only be needed for one job.

The Z to A of retail disruption

Essential Topics of Connections:
- Availability:
  - Reliability
  - Convenience
- Value:
  - Price
  - Promotions
- Functionality:
  - Shop design
  - Digital channel design
  - Customer service
  - Delivery
  - Returns

Essential Retail Functions:
1. Assortment planning
2. Buying & merchandising
3. Product sourcing
4. Supply chain
5. Distribution/replenishment logistics
6. Wide distribution network
7. Shop design & build
8. Retail operations
9. Channel design & build

Basic Product Range

Basic Customer Connection

Viable retail propositions:
- Market leaders in volume markets online or offline
  - Basic connection with many customers
  - Best assortment, lowest price, most reliable
- Local convenience destination
  - Strong connection with local captive consumer
  - High frequency of visit

Retail opportunities and limitations:
- Comfortable position for value driven customers
- Relies on traditional and existing retail skills set
- Relatively inexpensive to initiate and manage customer communication
- Shallow customer connections makes assortment development and service extensions unlikely
- Limited loyalty motives other than possible convenience and price
- Dangers of price and promotions as only tool to drive loyalty and sales volumes

Sketch 6   The Basic Customer Connection

2. Advanced Customer Connections

Retail practitioners working at the advanced relationship level are many and varied. For some retailers it is a destination ambition, for others an interim stage to delivering the ultimate customer relationship. For all, it is a time of learning and evolution.

The advanced stage encompasses many different connection strategies. They combine everything from lifestyle to aesthetics, presented with the distinct brand "tone of voice" of each individual retailer.

Advanced Customer Connections represent the least acceptable level of development for a serious retail brand. Strategically it is a necessity to avoid being left-behind your middle market competitors or being challenged by ambitious mass marketers.

It is that comfortable place which should never just be too comfortable that you never want to progress and leave.

If successful in achieving customer traction and increased brand loyalty the enhanced relationship has the potential for significant commercial assortment diversification and supplementary services.

The processes required also involve significant personal data capture, possibly for the first time, which can be used to drive customer segmentation, promotions and personalisation.

Developing deeper relationships at this level, and at this point in the evolution of businesses must coincide with developments and new initiatives across other retail functions of the business.

'Engaging promises should never be operationally hollow!'

The investment required to move to an advanced relationship is within the budget of a variety of businesses.

- New brands & specialist retailers wanting to establish themselves both online or offline and to make initial connections with their target demographic.
- Mass-market retailers taking first steps to add value to their businesses with their first major customer insights
- High street brands seeking market advantage, evolving customer data analysis, with new services and diversification
- Mid-level digitally led Pureplay retailers with technology expertise but limited budgets seeking added-value relationships and data analysis. For pureplay retailers advanced relationships are an essential part of the D.N.A. of any digital channel business.

Developing a strong and focused customer relationship is simply part of the business of being a modern retailer. Advanced customer connections deliver what is required for many retailers to develop their brand commercially, whilst for the more ambitious developing the Advanced Customer relationship is part of an ongoing strategy to become market leaders.

Essential Topics of Connections:

- Availability
- Convenience
- Value
- Customer Lifestyle
- Customer Activity
- Customer Taste

Essential Retail Functions:

1. Branding & communication
2. Buying & merchandising
3. Category Management
4. Channel location & integration
5. Physical shop/channel experience design
6. Customer services
7. Cross-channel delivery, collection, returns
8. CRM & Retail intelligence
9. Marketing technologies
10. IT development

Wider Product Assortment & Services

Advanced Customer Connection

Viable retail propositions:

- New brands & specialist retailers wanting to establish online or offline
  - Initial connection with specific demographic
- Mass-market retailers creating added-value
  - First major customer insights
- High street brands seeking market advantage with services and diversification
  - Evolving customer data analysis
- Mid-level digitally led Pureplay retailers with technology expertise but limited budgets seeking added-value relationships and data

Retail opportunities and limitations:

- Brand added-value and distinction in competitive market
- Avoid being left-behind middle market competitors and being challenged by ambitious mass marketers
- Potential for assortment diversification and supplementary services
- Increased brand loyalty & customer data capture to drive customer segmentation and communication personalisation
- Ultimately deeper relationship must be built on genuine brand, assortment and service developments

Sketch 7   The Advanced Customer Connection

3. Ultimate Customer Connections

Ultimate relationships are becoming the new essential!

There are a growing number of retailers from non-traditional retail origins whose brands are vision and lifestyle inspired, rather than buying & sourcing led.

They are seeking to build deep meaningful relationships with customers communicating their individual propositions, their philosophies, ethical and sustainability credentials and their unique product attributes.

At the same time, successful and forward-thinking high street brands diversifying and supplementing their assortments and services, are also seeking deeper personal relationships with the customer to add-value, brand differentiation and to cement their patronage and loyalty. They will already be at an advanced stage of customer connection, with many things to say.

Pureplay brands will continue to invest heavily to develop further their customer relationships and protect existing customer sales, building value through repeat custom and off-setting the expense of finding new customers. They will already be in advanced customer connection models which they will strive to continuously improve and evolve.

Focused brands are diving deeper into the minds and attitudes of their shoppers. Deep-pocketed marketplaces led by the likes of Amazon and Zalando will invest further, as only they can do, in personalised marketing and customer interfaces. They will create deep personal buying relationships with a vast and diverse array of individuals.

They are breaking the precedent that mass market retailers cannot form deep relationships. They are achieving this by adopting sophisticated personalisation softwares to instigate individual conversations on appropriate product categories and brands. They create the illusion of being specialist retailers.

Ultimate relationship retailers are becoming polarized between specialists & 'personalisers.'

At one extreme, there will be genuine specialists. Unique brands who will drive high brand loyalty through distinct brand personalities. Developing assortment diversification and partnerships, with the potential to sell in specific physical locations, as well as international niche markets.

At the other extreme, ambitious mass-merchandisers will evolve ever-more sophisticated personalisation tools to deliver their unique and tailored communications.

In due course, competitor proliferation will gradually bring many mid-market retailers to the deep relationship table, where customers have an appetite to be involved more intimately with the retailers they buy from.

A major prize for any retailer that successfully develops such deep connections is the rich customer data analytics made possible, allowing ever more accurate personalisation and intimacy with customers.

The virtuous cycle to ever more intimate customer relationships beckons for the best in class, with the door open to ever more ambitious and commercially fruitful proposition developments.

Essential Topics of Connections:

- Customer Lifestyle
- Customer Activity
- Customer Taste
- Customer Wellbeing
- Customer Conscience
- Customer Philosophy

Essential Retail Functions:

1. Branding & communication
2. Product design/styling/materials
3. Shop/channel experience
4. Customer service
5. Specific location planning
6. Channel integration
7. Marketing technologies
8. IT development
9. Customer data analysis
10. Sustainable sourcing
11. Ethical business strategies

Ultimate Retail Proposition

Viable retail propositions:

- Distinct brands & specialist category/lifestyle retailers online or offline
  - Deep connection with specific demographic
  - Distinct, differentiated product, design, styling
- High level designer brands
  - Added-value relationships
- Premium high street brands seeking market advantage with services and diversification
- Sophisticated digitally led retailers with technology expertise and "big-pockets" seeking high added-value through personalised deep relationships

© 2021 vm-unleashed ltd.

Sketch 8   The Ultimate Customer Connection

Ultimate Customer Connection

Retail opportunities and limitations:

- High brand loyalty from deep customer connection
- High take up of assortment diversification and supplementary services amongst loyal customers
- Potential for large online/ international niche markets
- Enhanced customer data analysis
- Limited local catchments to fully engage
- Risk from any brand "lapse of concentration"
- Risk from economic situations effecting customer income, job security etc.

Aldi: developing 'click & collect' & deliveries

Aldi continues to perform exceptionally, gaining market share by consistently offering its customers the basics of price and convenience. Additional digital and delivery initiatives during lockdown have strengthened these credentials within its core customer base, many of whom were home shielding and self isolating, whilst attracting customers who are more service driven.

It has invested heavily in its ecommerce initiatives to grab market share from its grocery rivals at a time when an increasing number of shoppers are buying online.

Aldi also doubled the size of its trial of on-demand grocery deliveries with Deliveroo. Customers within a six-kilometre radius of the 42 participating stores are now able to choose from around 400 essential Aldi grocery items for delivery in as little as 30 minutes.

Aldi continues to evolve from a basic to an advanced customer relationship.

Waitrose: nurturing customer wellbeing

Waitrose is the grocery arm of the John Lewis Partnership. It commands both high prices and customer loyalty through an advanced relationship which spans community and product wellbeing.

They have fully supported the UK government's Healthy Start Vouchers, a scheme which strives to support healthy eating for those with the most needs. The vouchers are issued to pregnant women and low-income families with children under the age of four and can be spent on healthy foods, including fresh, frozen, and tinned fruit and vegetables.

Waitrose commitment saw it topping up the value of the Government's Healthy Start Vouchers by an additional £1.50.

Meanwhile the retailer unveiled plans for a new beef production facility at its Leckford Estate to enable it to deliver more red meat straight from its own farm under the best possible environmental and animal welfare conditions. The move will also free up land to help it produce more flour and oil for customers and create opportunities to trial a range of regenerative agriculture practices. Waitrose has farmed on the Leckford Estate for over 90 years. Crops grown, picked and packed from the farm include mushrooms, apples, pears, cider, sparkling wine, apple juice and flour.

Homebase: lifestyle collaborations

After a period of returning to DIY basics, retailer Homebase has made decisive moves to tempt the more aesthetically minded homeowner by partnering with House Beautiful, Country Living and Good Housekeeping magazines to create a new range of household and lifestyle licensed products.

Homebase hopes the initiative will allow customers to be inspired by what they see in the magazines and translate the inspiration into real-life purchases. They will also be launching kitchen ranges under Country Living and House Beautiful.

Nor is the world of influencers restricted to young fashion brands. Homebase has also linked up with Dick Strawbridge and his wife Angel, stars of TV programme 'Escape to the Chateau,' the true-life story of a couple renovating a French stately home. As well as a variety of content across channels, tips and advice, the couple will also be putting their names to an assortment of products.

Whilst Homebase is firming up its experiential and inspirational credentials, it is also employing the services of the Hut Group to deliver an end-to-end customer experience, from digital interfaces to supply chain logistics and customer delivery.

Homebase continues its journey to developing the ultimate customer relationships.

The Z to A of retail disruption

004

DEFINE THE MOST APPROPRIATE CUSTOMER RELATIONSHIP

Market analysis & customer research

Revisit and reaffirm your customer proposition. What are you offering the customer? What do you want to offer them?

What does the customer like about you? What does the customer want from you? What is the limit of what the customer wants from you?

Assess the level of connection that your competitors have with the customer How much should their relationship be dictating your strategy? Is your opportunity to make your current relationship stronger, or to evolve it into a deeper connection? How feasible, practical and cost-effective is it for you to deliver each deeper level?

Actions

- Define clearly and unanimously which level of connection is appropriate for your business - basic, advanced or ultimate?
- Define your strategic objective to either 'stick or twist' with your current level of connection
- Set out an action plan with timetables and key milestones to improve your current relationship, or to evolve to the next level
- Set out a ROI model for the business improvements required
  - Assortment structure & services expansion
  - Price point & promotional investments
  - Brand building, product design and marketing
  - Social media and selling platforms
  - Selling environments and colleague investment
  - Organisational and ethical principles
  - CRM capability and subscription services/products
- Beginning building the employee team for the future

005

ENSURE YOUR BASICS JUST KEEP GETTING BETTER

Internal analysis & customer feedback

You will fail at every level if your retail basics are below customer expectations.

Develop internal feedback processes and create customer feedback channels. Analyse what is the minimum acceptable level of proposition you can deliver to the customer to retain their loyalty. Assess what is required, and what can then move that minimum requirement to market leadership levels.

Actions

- Improve basic customer touchpoints by improving the integrated functions thar deliver each one of them.
- Improve essential functions to market leadership levels
  - Assortment planning
  - Buying & merchandising, product sourcing
  - Supply chain/Distribution/replenishment logistics
  - Channel design & build
  - Shop design & build
  - Customer focused services
  - Retail operations

The Virtuous Cycle of Customer Personalisation

'Deeper relationships are essential for retailers to be able to develop and diversify their assortments and services. New and attractive propositions are essential for a deeper relationship.'

The virtuous cycle between retail proposition evolution and relationship building is a series of cyclical steps from basic, advanced, and to ultimate customer connections.

Central to the benefits for retailers is the progressive building of trust and intimacy with the customer.

> The relationship should build from 'loyalty to the retailer' to 'reliance on the retailer.'

This is a significant series of steps that transform a relationship from where the retailer pays the customer with price promotions in a basic relationship , through a financially neutral advanced relationship, to the ultimate retailer connection where the customer pays the retailer via a subscription club, to be part of, and receive, the retailer's loyalty benefits.

It is the proposition and relationship combination that allows a retailer to transcend a traditional transactional model to a service benefit model.

The relationship between the limits of the proposition and the boundaries of the relationship is tangible. The economic relationship is transformed. It is turned on its head.

Commercial Symbiosis between customer and retailer is achieved. Communication is transformed to intimacy.

Evolving commercial symbiosis

A proposition of core product and services can only justify the blanket messaging of price and promotional messages.

A cyclical process can slowly introduce both assortment and service developments, running hand in hand. In turn the closer relationship allows for more segmentation and customization of customer communications. Customers who feel better about their retailer are more open to email and other CRM initiatives, which in turn facilitates the accuracy and depth of conversation.

As assortments and services diversify on the back of loyalty subscription services customer connections can gain even more traction. This personalization can lead to individual communication and retailer proactivity.

Personalisation – the customer relationship roadmap

Once upon a time, retailers communicated their brand position, values and philosophy to the world, and the people of the world decided whether it was for them or not.

Retail intelligence then enabled businesses to analyse their customers with tools such as market research and focus groups. It meant that retailers could segment their customers into like-minded groups and then customise communications by group.

Personalisation technologies gave retailers the ability to analyse individual customer's buying patterns, browsing histories, product attribute responses and associated shopping behaviour data to communicate pro-actively and respond to shopping journeys based on historical preferences.

Advanced personalisation technologies can now amalgamate data from customer's social media platforms, their activities, responses, opinions, relationships, to formulate detailed profiles, and to anticipate future buying missions, and calculate probable favourable product selections.

> *The evolution of personalisation is the history, past, present, and future of customer connections and relationships.*

Just as further technological and analytical advancements are simply a matter of time, then so is the adoption of personalisation by conceivably, every single retailer. The potential opportunities and benefits to develop deep relationships are so great that businesses are already finding themselves on the same irresistible journey.

However, it must be emphasized that whilst the 'ultimate' ambition for engagement may well be in the strategic 'minds' of retailer brands, the 'ultimate' level of engagement and the degree of personalisation will actually be in the 'hands' of the customer, or even the regulator in the role of protector.

The retailer is the customer's supplier of goods, not their life-long school friend. Many people still make that distinction.

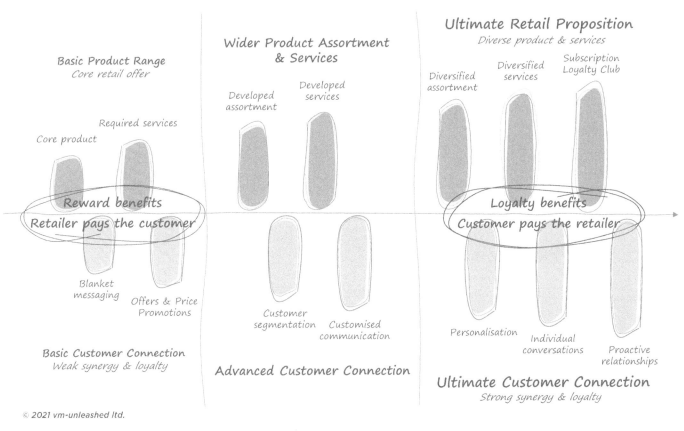

© 2021 vm-unleashed ltd.

Sketch 9   The Virtuous Journey of Proposition and Connection

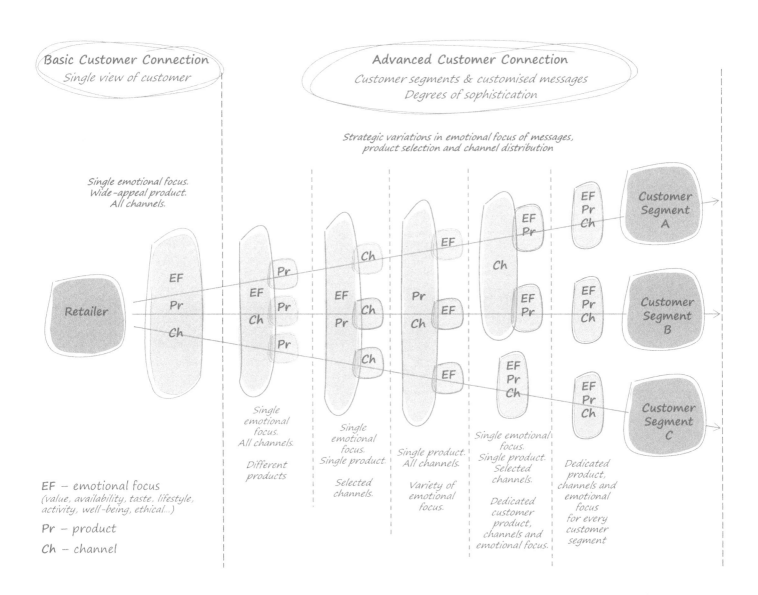

Basic Customer Connection
Single view of customer

Advanced Customer Connection
Customer segments & customised messages
Degrees of sophistication

Strategic variations in emotional focus of messages,
product selection and channel distribution

Single emotional focus.
Wide-appeal product.
All channels.

Retailer

EF
Pr
Ch

EF
Ch

Pr
Pr
Pr

EF
Pr
Ch

Ch

EF
Pr
Ch

Pr
Ch
EF

EF

EF
Pr

Ch

EF
Pr

EF
Pr
Ch

EF
Pr
Ch

Customer
Segment
A

EF
Pr
Ch

Customer
Segment
B

EF
Pr
Ch

EF
Pr
Ch

Customer
Segment
C

Single
emotional
focus.
All channels.

Different
products

Single
emotional
focus.
Single product.

Selected
channels.

Single product.
All channels.

Variety of
emotional
focus.

Single emotional
focus.
Single product.
Selected
channels.

Dedicated
customer
product,
channels and
emotional focus.

Dedicated
product,
channels and
emotional
focus
for every
customer
segment

EF – emotional focus
(value, availability, taste, lifestyle,
activity, well-being, ethical...)
Pr – product
Ch – channel

Sketch 10 Personalisation: The Customer Relationship Roadmap

Ultimate Customer Connection
Personalisation of customer & individual messages
Full sophistication

Communicating pro-actively and responding to shopping journeys based on historical preferences

Anticipating future buying missions, and calculating probable favourable product selections

The Road to Personalisation

The road to personalization begins with the potential to work flexibly with the product, the channel and the emotional focus of the message. These are the tools to focus on customer groups and their preferred touchpoints.

In the basic model every customer has access to all messages, about all products across all channels. Blanket bombing will ensure some customers take up of generic promotions, but there may be severe collateral damage to some of your customer relationships.

Advanced communication begins with segmentation of the customer into groups, where each has potentially similar product taste, similar preference of emotional message type and uses the same channels.

Communication can then customize messages by product, channel or emotional focus. Arriving at the point where the ever-smaller segments receive dedicated content.

The ever-smaller segments ultimately achieve the granularity of individual customers, where product, channel and specifically the emotional message can be personalized and rewarded individually.

006

BE A SINGLE BRAND FOR MANY CUSTOMERS, OR A DIVERSE BRAND FOR INDIVIDUAL CUSTOMERS

Internal brainstorming

Personalization is becoming common amongst leading retailers. Customers expect it. How do you want to approach this as a business? Do you want to communicate a single powerful brand message in a consistent way to all customers? Do you want to customize and personalize messages for your customers?

What is correct for your brand? What is correct for your customers? What is precious and common to everyone?

Actions

- Define your strategy for personalization
  - A single message
  - Customisation by customer segment
  - Personalisation of individuals
- Deliver that strategy consistently across channels
  - One shop, one assortment, one message
  - Shop clusters, graded assortment, focused messages
  - Responsive customer interfaces, personalized product grouping, personalized communication
- Integrate internal functions appropriately across marketing, buying, physical and digital interface design and build appropriate processes. For one-end, or several.

007

DEVELOP DATA CAPABILITY

Industry benchmarking & best-fit collaboration

If your relationship is developing beyond the basics you need to act in 3 ways regarding customer data. How to get data? How to analyse data? How to use data?

Are you going to develop your own in-house capability, collaborate with external specialists, or outsource? How will you collaborate? What existing internal teams and skill-sets do you have? Is your internal IT team capable enough to deliver and support your strategy? What additional internal and external skills do you require?

What and who is out there? Research external products and partners. Benchmark competitors. Integrate your decisions.

Actions

- Define the data you want
  - Define the touchpoints and technologies to extract that customer data?
  - Choose your partners, teams & skill-sets
  - Define what you want to achieve with your customer data
- Define the processes, technologies you require
  - Define the skills you require to process and analyse the data. Assess your internal resources, identify skills gaps and hire or outsource.
  - Ensure integration of new technologies with internal IT systems.
- Define how to deliver the data output.
  - Create precise channels of data distribution
  - Define technologies/training/deliverables to output the data insights directly to customers and across customer touchpoints. Invest in partnerships.

008

PLAN WHAT YOU ARE GOING TO SAY TO YOUR CUSTOMER

Internal analysis & competitor benchmarking

What and how you communicate to your customers is a complex thing. If you're stepping up from a basic promotional relationship, then finding your 'voice' literally has to be one of the most important things. This may already be clear to you.

We'll talk about the vision, values and proposition of a retailer later. That should help. But you will certainly need to have a clear 'tone of voice' and the people in your business to nurture and protect it. Verbal communication is as important as graphic identity so across the board your 'tone of voice' needs to be razor sharp and consistent. You will need a staged process of brainstorming, brand consolidation and formal guidelines.

In terms of customer communication, benchmarking competitors across their channels of communication can be invaluable. You need to look at what they are talking about from product to non-product, business, colleagues, customers or any wider topics. You need to assess the communication tools they use.

Is their communication conversational, informational, editorial, competitions, reviews, endorsements and so on? What media do they use? Text, photos, illustration and content. What channels, including both physical and digital do they use the most, and for what message types?

This analysis must be done over time to see the frequency of each parameter of communication as well as how they address seasonal retail events. Build up an appropriate strategy from what you learn. Something that works with your proposition, your values and your assortment, and something on which you can hang your brand personality.

Actions

- Revisit your brand identity. It's simply good practice to do so on a regular basis. Make sure it is water-tight and still appropriate to your brand strategy. Ensure that it includes guidance on 'tone of voice.'
- If 'tone of voice' is not in your brand guidelines, for both physical and digital communications then update them now.
- Set up a best practice competitor benchmarking project.
- Have a dedicated impartial team to monitor and analyse the communication delivery strategy of the best in class relevant to your business.
- Understand everything:
  - Message focus
  - Communication type
  - Role of product, colleagues, news...
  - Communication tools...competitions, quizzes...
  - Media channels
  - Role of influences and endorsements
- Understand communication strategies over time, related to retail and marketing calendars and seasonal events.
- Develop your own communications calendar
- Specify:
  - Timings
  - Message focus
  - Communication types
  - Media channels
- Ensure your dedicated marketing team are fully operational and integrated across the business to collect and coordinate content evolution and message development
- Invest in delivery technology and analysis
- Monitor the impact of your communication strategy, analyse and learn. Constantly adapt within your wider strategy.

Retail Relationships are not just Technology

In the digital-first world, it is easy to get lost in the truly incredible capabilities and applications of technology. It is easy to think that technology holds the answers to everything.

It certainly holds the answer to the future efficiency of many retail functions, but it is a misconception that it can single-handedly transform customer relationships.

Digital marketing will continue to grow in importance and application in communicating promotions, events, product suggestions, and wider brand messages. It is also of course behind the rich sources of customer data, as well as helping to continuously evolve the quality and engagement of customer interfaces and touchpoints. But it is not everything.

There is no better personal shopping experience than the one which occurs between two people in a shop.

Physical & technological customers journeys run in parallel from simple acknowledgement to intimate relationships. Shop staff can be helped by traditional physical training and digital support to improve the ways that they can interact with the customer transforming them from ambivalent visitors to loyal patrons.

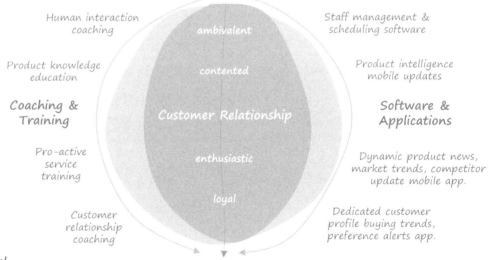

Traditional buyer/seller retailer
Basic adoption of technologies and personnel training

Human interaction coaching

Staff management & scheduling software

Product knowledge education

Product intelligence mobile updates

Coaching & Training

Software & Applications

ambivalent

contented

Customer Relationship

enthusiastic

loyal

Pro-active service training

Dynamic product news, market trends, competitor update mobile app.

Customer relationship coaching

Dedicated customer profile buying trends, preference alerts app.

Modern evolved retailer
Advanced & integrated evolution of people & technology

© 2021 vm-unleashed ltd.

Sketch 11 Digital & Physical training and support for physical shop staff

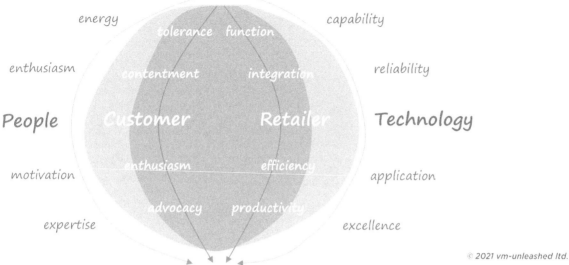

Traditional buyer/seller retailer
Basic adoption of technologies and personnel training

energy

capability

tolerance   function

enthusiasm

reliability

contentment   integration

People   **Customer**   **Retailer**   Technology

motivation

enthusiasm   efficiency

application

advocacy   productivity

expertise

excellence

Modern evolved retailer
Advanced & integrated evolution of people & technology

© 2021 vm-unleashed ltd.

Sketch 12 The Common Journey
of People, Customer,
Retailer & technology

Regular shop workers and regular customers often develop relationships and friendships. Inadvertently, shop managers build up mental databases of their customers, their likes and dislikes, sensitivity to price, brand preferences, and even their personal lives and life events.

Physical shops are a rich source of customer data. Even if we choose not to call it that. And physical shops are also still the main place where retailers meet their customers, get to know them, and build relationships.

The shop route and the technology route to developing customer relationships should be perfectly complementary and coordinated. As technology advances, the training of shop colleagues in interpersonal skills should evolve using the knowledge gathered from across every channel.

The potential for retailers to prosper will be through the balance of technology and people. Not a battle for supremacy. But an equal and coordinated collaboration of the best of both worlds.

There is good technology and bad technology and there are good people and bad people. There are efficient technologies and efficient people. And above all, there is game-changing technology and there have always been game-changing people.

We need the best, most efficient and most relevant technologies and people in our retail organisations, and we need them to evolve and develop side by side. In this way, the balance of technology and people, and a respect for each, will guarantee game-changing technology and game-changing people at every step of a retailer's journey.

People and technologies both need training and time to learn. Despite its reputation the impact of technology is not usually instant. Technology needs to test and modify its capability to be appropriate to meet its objectives. There then needs to be a period of bedding down to improve the reliability of the system. From here we see its applications really paying dividends, blossoming to a point of excellence.

People evolve in a similar way, beginning with energy and enthusiasm, they need to be managed, directed and motivated whilst acquiring the expertise to make them into real assets.

The initial beneficiary of a coordinated approach to people and technology will be the customer. They will be more satisfied, more content, more enthusiastic and more loyal, becoming advocates of the brand.

The ultimate beneficiary will be the retail business itself through increases in efficiency and productivity, leading to higher sales and profit. The ultimate goal for any businesses is increased productivity. This can only happen in today's retail world with the correct balance, of the correct people and the correct technology.

Customer Connection & Quality of Delivery

Ultimately the strength of a customer relationship will be defined by the quality of its delivery across every touchpoint and its interaction with the customer.

Brands which pitch their reputation on quality have no excuses when their own high levels fall below their customers' expectations. Customer connection cannot fail.

Brands which are built of reliability have nowhere to go when they fail to meet the most fundamental efficiencies. They must have the highest operational reliability. Trust cannot fail.

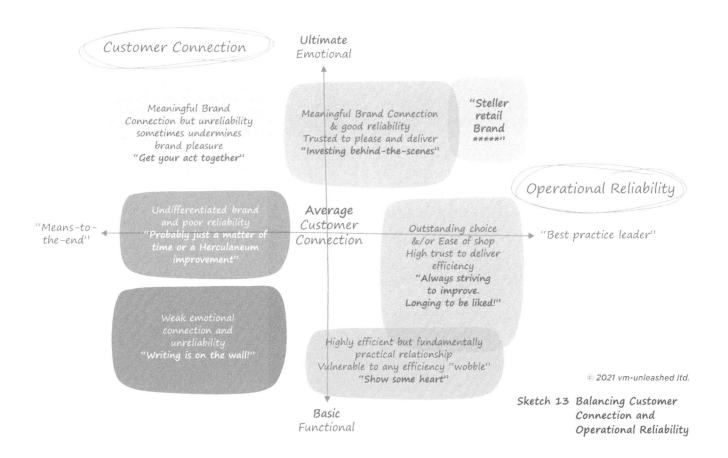

© 2021 vm-unleashed ltd.

Sketch 13 Balancing Customer Connection and Operational Reliability

009

PLEASE, ALWAYS CONSIDER TECHNOLOGY AND PEOPLE TOGETHER

Internal strategy

I've seen many business cultures across the spectrum, trying to balance people and technology, from the digital luddites to the emotionally ignorant technophiles. Getting the balance correct is so difficult, but so essential.

The simple fact is that the only 2 essentials you cannot do without are technology and people. And whilst essentials should probably be viewed as equal, in my opinion people have to come first. Simply because people, uniquely and solely are at the beginning and end of the retail process. People are the recipients of the application of technology.

Too much technology will upset people. Too little technology will upset people.

Too much technology can result is losing your 'heart.' This can result in a dispirited and disengaged workforce, and customer. All retailers need to 'show some heart.' Too little technology can result in losing efficiency and organisation. This equally results in dispirited and disengaged employees and customers. The repercussions are different. The result is the same. You get the balance wrong and you will upset everyone.

Technology may not always behave how we want it to. But it doesn't get upset, it doesn't complain, it isn't over-sensitive. Balance the needs and concerns of Retail People & Technology People and the balance of technology and people will be perfect.

Considerations & Actions

- There are, of course, many o...
  of new technology needs to b...
  are many occasions when the...
  be actioned.
- From my experience and obse...
  I would advise on the following ...erations and actions.
- The channel(s) you sell through are irrelevant to how you balance people and technology within the business itself. The internal balance and reasoning are identical.
- Ensure the reasons to act are always to achieve a happier, more engaged, loyal and productive customer, colleague and employee. This generates cash and profit.
- Actions should always include technology and HR stakeholders, whether driven by technology or HR needs and requirements.
- Have a single overview, a single ownership for all things technological. Integrate technology people across everything they do.
- Have a single overview, a single ownership for all things people. Integrate people people across everything they do.
- When introducing or integrating technology with retail people, recognize that different people need different methodologies for them to understand and embrace the technology
- When relating retail needs and processes to technology people, recognize that technology people need different communication methodologies for them to understand retail
- Always educate and integrate from the very top to the bottom of both retail people and technology people chains for any new initiative.

...y & Demand: ...vering what is ...ssential

Retailers have not always had to try so hard to be essential. The equation which dictates this is the balance of Supply & Demand. Here are some fundamental economics.

In emerging markets, where growing populations and incomes coincide, the demand can be greater than the available supply. Retailers who simply supply what is in demand become essential. These markets are a rare thing. These markets do not last for long.

Demand driven markets attract every retailer and supplier who can feasibly make profit considering the operational logistics required. The surge in supply shifts the balance. The supply is greater than the demand.

The customer has the luxury of supplier choice. They can select the retailers they want to buy from. They can give their money to businesses they like and respect, and not to those they do not. Retailers must work hard to be noticed, even harder to be profitable, and harder still to be "essential."

What the Supply & Demand balance teaches us in any specific market is simply – "How good do we need to be, to be essential?"

The Retail Evolution Curve

It is essential to analyse and identify where your markets are on the 'retail evolution curve.' As illustrated in Sketch 14. Those markets could be international, regional or local. The answers will inform some important questions and alert you to what you need to deliver to be successful in those markets.

You need to know – "What functionality and integration is required to be on top of the retail evolution curve?" "What levels of expertise and delivery are needed to stay ahead of the competition?" "What degree of emotional sophistication is essential to satisfy the customer?" "What level of Essential relationship is a must?"

Excellent retailers have always made retailing easier in any market in any times. Poor retailers seem to make retailing difficult anywhere. However, what was once important to define your level of profit is now essential to decide your fate!

The majority of markets in the world today are 'Saturated Markets'. This retailer saturation is being further driven by the proliferation of digital retail channels, specifically mobile, as well as easier, more dynamic ways to open physical retail space. Access to markets for many new businesses is faster, more flexible and less expensive than ever.

This contrasts with historical "Virgin Markets" where significant capitol and resources were required to build physical shop empires and recruit armies of central office and shop colleagues. The Retail Evolution Curve illustrates how markets change from 'Virgin' through 'Evolving' to 'Saturated Markets.'

It is now easier than ever to be a retailer, but more difficult than ever to be an essential one!

Innovation always leads

Each historical step of the Retail Evolution Curve is driven by a need to improve and maintain a competitive advantage as supply constantly increases in relation to demand.

At every step, the innovators always lead, some established competitors adopt, and new retailers appear already embracing the new retail functions of that evolutionary step.

At every step, the laggards fall by the wayside.

At every step, retail practices improve, and the customer experience is transformed. At every step, the pace of change increases.

At every step, more new retailers appear than at any previous step. At every step, more traditional retailers disappear than at any step before.

The rotation and evolution of retail formats and specific retailers, is as fast now as it has ever been.

The commercial lifecycle for brands is becoming less, and the duration to make profit is getting shorter.

Being 'essential' is about being essential for now. Not yesterday or tomorrow. A heritage, a history, a legacy are no longer necessarily an advantage in terms of brand, or indeed operations, and in many ways can be a hindrance and an obstacle to commerciality.

Life and Longevity

The exclusive club of the 'essential retailers' requires and gives no guarantees of longevity, just a chance to ride the wave of commercial success for as long as your strategy defines, or for as long as the customer values you.

Strategies at the birth of historical retail empires never really included a longevity, or duration clause. The assumption was that you would be around forever, or at least a personal lifetime.

Today's strategies for new retail businesses will of course plan for as long a lifetimes as possible, however the proposition should be realistic about the probable, and ideal durations. Many brands will shine brighter for the fact that they will shine for shorter. Some brands will last longer but never reach those dazzling heights.

Exceptional businesses will shine brightly many times if they have a strategy and the mechanics to keep re-igniting and re-inventing themselves. These are the truly 'exceptional' brands. They live to evolve, to enrich and to expand.

It is strategically valid to plan for a short and a bright existence. Entrepreneurs themselves see no fulfilment in creating jobs for life, for themselves. They move on to the next brand initiative. These leaders operate in the disruptive market, and they are happy for the consequences. They believe in their visionary ability to reinvent themselves.

To evolve, to enrich and to expand are the ways to keep businesses, in business, for the longer term. Truly gifted retail merchants from the age of learning can do this, because they have always seen the need and the necessity to learn, adapt and change.

Retail Function evolution:

20. Integrity & Circular economics
19. Flexible, people first organisations
18. Digitally led strategy, fluid-channels
17. Digital & fulfilment partnerships
16. Sustainable sourcing, recycling
15. Social selling, influences, DTC
14. IT, Big data, data analytics
13. Loyalty Subscription memberships

12. Mobile, Social media marketing
11. Fledgling multi-channel development
10. CRM & retail intelligence
9. Visual merchandising & events
8. Category management
7. Sourcing, supply chain expansion
6. Retail operations & technology

5. Customer service
4. Shop design, branding, advertising
3. Assortment supply expansion
2. Space expansion
1. Initial product sourcing

Land of the "Deal-Makers"

'Virgin Market'

The Retail Evolution Curve

The curve outlines the characteristics of the three ages of retail market evolution:

Sketch 14 The Retail Evolution Curve.

The Age of Discovery

- Demand led 'Virgin markets' with limited competition
- Developing retail functions, product & places
- Rapid growth of physical shop empires
- 1st Age of Exploitation – satisfying the market

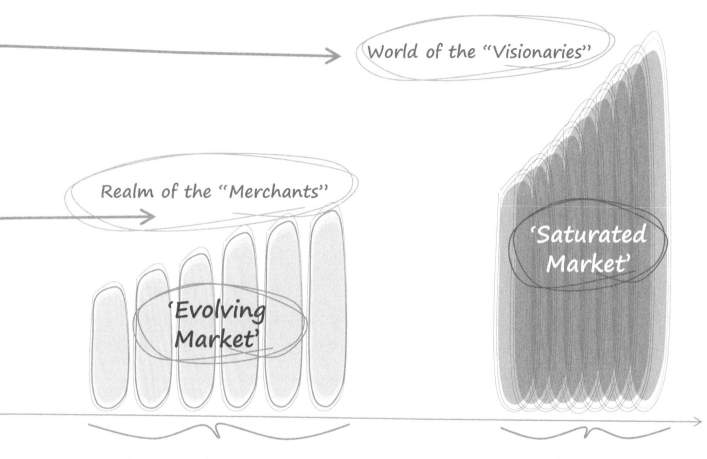

World of the "Visionaries"

Realm of the "Merchants"

'Evolving Market'

'Saturated Market'

The Age of Learning

- Supply & Demand Balance, 'Emerging markets' with growing competitor sophistication
- Understanding customers, products & the retail experience
- Fledgling growth of e-commerce & multi-channel
- 2nd Age of Exploitation – globalizing the supply chain

The Age of Disruption

- 'Saturated market' densities and proliferation of competitors
- Identifying & seizing disruptive opportunities
- Fluid & dynamic retail channels
- 3rd Age of Exploitation – the appetite for change

These true 'retail merchants' are behind some of the existing businesses that continue to thrive and grow through every market situation.

It is more difficult for the 'Deal Breakers' born into retail in virgin markets, who learned to exploit demand and resources as the route to profit. As both these avenues for growth become rarer by each passing retail year, the lights of exploitative businesses grow weaker. For a growing number, the lights have finally been extinguished.

The new exploitation is a symbiotic one. It is an exploitation of the customers' appetite for change and excitement, and in turn the customers' exploitation of the retailers' capacity to reinvent, to surprise and delight. It is the Ultimate Customer Relationship.

Without this ability to reinvent and surprise, established retailers are simply clinging on. And 'clinging –on' is no strategy at all, for longevity, for today or for anytime at all.

The Customer Delivery Mandate

In today's 'saturated markets' existing and new retailers must demonstrate 'best practice' across an increasingly wide variety of retail functions to deliver what the customer now perceives as essential to them.

A wide scope and high quality of delivery is now a mandate directly from the customer.

The specific retail functions required will depend on the brand positioning, product sector and channel strategy. But for most retail businesses 'best practice' is required across a number of common retail functions and strategic areas.

Many of these functions such as buying & merchandising hail from the earliest days of mass market retailing and have evolved and developed through every age. It is fair to say that every original retail function born in the age of discovery, went through significant transformations during the Age of Learning.

Functions from the Age of Learning

- Buying & merchandising
- Assortment structure planning
- Product sourcing & origination
- Physical location strategy
- Supply chain integration
- Distribution and replenishment
- Channel planning & allocation
- Shop grading & clustering
- Digital & Physical shop design
- HR & colleague training
- Customer service & services
- Visual merchandising
- Marketing, calendars & events
- HR & Organisational structure
- Retail operations

Functions from the Age of Disruption

- Fluid channel integration
- Mobile and social commerce
- Market research & intelligence
- Social media & digital marketing
- CRM, loyalty & membership clubs
- IT infrastructure
- Data analytics
- Digital & fulfilment partnering
- Circular economics
- Ethical management

Every function and exponent that evolved in the Age of Learning is still developing as every month goes by in the Age of Disruption. Priorities are changing, some functions are all but disappearing, or being revolutionized and renamed.

These are being married together with completely new but important functions born mainly from the opportunities of technology in both the front and back-end of business.

Inconceivable disciplines only a decade ago, are now in the hands of newly formed departments. Old dogs are learning new tricks or under the control of a new guard of retailers.

Significantly, the route to delivering 'best practice' is very different depending on whether you are a new brand, or an existing well-established one.

> New retailers have the advantage of being born into today's markets. They are also the customers of today and they will 'skill-pick' from traditional retail expertise.

New retailers will adopt instantly the principles of the Age of Disruption. They will be driven by a dynamic vision, be digitally led in thought and actions.

New retailers will selectively 'skill-pick' from the old.

New retailers rapidly develop their individual 'best practice' across new retail functions, becoming leading edge in technological, data, media and social applications.

New retailers need to quickly adopt the relevant principles from 'The Age of Learning' through collaboration with existing retailers and injections of expertise. They do not have the luxury of time to evolve this expertise internally and will adopt their 'skills-picking' strategy. Product assortment and buying & merchandising expertise will be the more important functions to be 'skill-picked.'

New retailers will avoid adopting outdated traditional methodologies, super-ceded by new processes more suitable for 'saturated markets.'

Slow and inflexible globalised supply chains with poor sustainability and non-transparency will be discarded for a flexible, local supply chain and fluid channel distribution.

Physical shop portfolios will be conceived differently from traditional location strategies. Physical shops will be flexible and dynamic in commercial strategy, size, longevity, customer service, assortment, and their role within fluid channels.

Traditional skills in customer service, shop design and visual merchandising will be incorporated appropriately within the new shop strategy, supported by technology.

New retailers will embrace physical communities and the value of people as colleagues and as customers. They will learn that technology is not the be-all and end-all. Its potential only truly realized when it is combined with people.

Learnings from 'The Age of Discovery' in 'Virgin markets' will be an irrelevant legacy of the retail industry. For new retailers there is no sentimentality, no legacy or history.

Against this they will engender a strong business integrity and ethical values for the new world, adopting circular economy philosophies. For new retailers there is just the future.

Hotel Chocolat –
vertically integrated irresistibility

Whether you are classed as a 'new' or an 'old' retailer, does not just depend on the time when you were founded. It is more of a philosophy, a culture than a time stamp. It is a reason why not to judge a busines by the plaque above the door. Innovation and disruption have always occurred.

Founded in 1987 Hotel Chocolat, the British chocolatier and cocoa grower, might not be the newest kid on the retail block but it never fails to reinvent itself, disrupt the way of doing chocolate retailing, and the way it delights its customers. Its consistency through the ideas and directions of travel is its singularity of vision. To own chocolate in a way that has never been seen before.

I can remember walking into one of their first boutiques. It was an experience well ahead of its time. The shops were like luxury beauty boutiques, the chocolate was packaged and displayed like works of art, oil paintings in chocolate, and a lady with a silver tray tempted you with samples. You did feel as though you had wandered into the foyer of an exclusive boutique hotel, but it always felt as you belonged there.

Hotel Chocolat, first and foremost is a chocolate innovator. The brand invented the now much-copied slabs of chocolate with their murals in shades of brown, and white, adorned with candies and fruits.

On another wall were the pick 'n' mix selector packs with their now familiar multi-offer promotion. This dynamic incarnation of everything that is delicious and popular in chocolate is a living wall of fame. It tells the history of chocolate preferences since 1987 and is more popular than ever.

It is a testament to the incredible ideas that Hotel Chocolat brought to the market, that these innovations seem everyday now, adopted by other retailers. But this was disruption of the highest order. These little packets of 6 identical treats were a license to experiment and enjoy. Tastes and design came and went, favourites still exist from the beginning, whilst seasonal drops make their exciting entry, and then fade to memory.

Beyond the chocolate, the many fans of Hotel Chocolat have been able to join its membership taster clubs and receive monthly samples of new products. It has around 100,000 members and has trialed over 1,500 different recipes.

A highlight of COVID lockdowns was to receive chocolate discovery packs, and chocolate evenings in a box. What better way to pass the hours. The business also runs classes in several of its cafes where customers can learn how to make and style their own chocolate creations and host parties for their friends and families.

The company early on evolved a vertically integrated structure from the growing of its own cocoa beans to the manufacture of the assortment. In 2006, the company acquired the Rabot Estate in Saint Lucia, and is, to date, the only company in the UK to own its own cocoa plantation. Over a hundred new jobs have been created since the estate's opening, and with prices guaranteed to be 30–40% above the world market price of cocoa, as well as being paid within a week of selling their crops, local farmers are provided with a secure income.

Hotel Chocolate continues to innovate its assortment, and the ways for its customers to enjoy chocolate against a business ethic of sustainability and ethical workers rights and rewards. Its core values of quality, innovation and an unswerving customer focus make it the only hotel worth staying in.

If you're in London then book a chocolate making party at the Monmouth Street shop and cafe. The basement is a theatre of fun, the staff are so delightful. An informative and inspiring brand experience.

The Z to A of retail disruption

Made.com –
fabricating a new approach to furniture

In contrast to Hotel Chocolat, Made.com was founded much more recently in 2010, as an online retail enterprise. All the same, it exhibits the same entrepreneurial culture, a desire to innovate, and an appetite to disrupt the traditional way of doing things in its own sector.

Imagine a furniture concept that throws out the baggage of the traditional ways and re-invents the whole process from the perspective of the customer and the designer, and you can imagine Made.com. Its disruptive thinking encompasses every aspect of furniture design, production and sales.

Let's take the design side of things. Made.com is a conduit for designers, both new and established, who complement the Made.com aesthetic profile, the brand's take and philosophy on what we should all fill our homes with. It has collaborated with a number of designers including Nina Campbell, Philip Colbert, Ilaria Marelli, Genevieve Bennett, John Stefanidis and Alison Cork. It is a celebration of good taste.

The philosophy is taken to its extreme with the 'Made Talent Lab' where potential designers meet crowdfunding investors and final customers in a process that rewards talent, foresight and the love of an idea. New designers pitch their product, with design drawings and prototypes to the Made.com public. The public votes and invests in the products they like.

Their investment will be financial if the product proves popular enough to make it to market. If support is sufficient, the customer receives a limited edition piece of furniture or interior design, the product of their taste and commitment.

Made.com customers also have their moment in the sunshine. 'Made Unboxed' is a clever thing that indulges those proud of their home-made places and helps customers to see their potential purchase in the full glory of a real-life setting.

The way it works is that existing customers create profiles and post images of their purchases. But not in cameo isolation but in splendid context, with buyers showing how they brought together their Made.com furniture with additional interior design touches and decoration. The idea is a source of inspiration for potential buyers, stimulation and re-assurance to purchase, whilst the platform also propels the proud 'posters' into the role of design gurus. This is self-perpetuating, self-fulfilling marketing of the most stylish kind.

Nor is the practical process of product selection ignored in this new way of buying. The cunning 'Sofasizer' is another work of genius. It is a single click and drag tool that instantly reduces the sofa assortment by size and dimension to fit your available nook or cranny. It then modifies the search by colour and price and presents the perfect possibilities with videos, reviews and, of course our Unboxed heroes.

The sensible inclusion of a search by delivery time filter pacifies the most impatient. It cleverly defines the customer journey and experience for either those that are willing to browse, enjoy and wait for a unique piece of design, from those who need something for visitors to sit on by the weekend.

A breath of fresh air in a stale and sedentary sector, Made.com is combining a passion for style and an acumen for business for the benefit of both furniture designers and homeowners alike.

That's putting on the style.

Apart from everything Made is a true omni-retailer. Visit the website, browse a while, explore and you will quickly get the magic of the brand. Visit any physical showroom. I recommend Charing X Road. Browse a while, engage with the colleagues and you will equally get the magic of the brand. Shop online, receive at home, experience the brand everywhere.

The Z to A of retail disruption

Existing retailers have the dis-advantage of being born into a different age of retail. They need to 'forget' and 'un-learn' many principles & practices from the Age of Learning itself.

Traditional retailers must maximise their relevant existing expertise whilst collaborating with new and disruptive partners.

They must re-learn and adapt quickly. They must become digitally led, firstly by introducing a new mind-set at the highest levels of the organisation. Existing retailers need to 'forget' and 'un-learn.'

Existing retailers need to invest in and collaborate with new suppliers and digitally led partners to compete in automating the supply chain, product distribution and delivery, digital marketing, social communication, digital channel functionality and channel fluidity.

They should consolidate their strengths in product design and development, with more diverse design influences, becoming more dynamic and flexible in planning and supply chains.

They need to nurture their expertise in people, evolving new best practice in HR, team building and training to meet the needs of a more flexible, diverse, responsible and multi-tasking workforce.

Leveraging traditional strengths, physical retailers should build on their considerable presence in physical customer communities generating loyalty across all multi-channel touchpoints.

They must flex and re-invent existing relationships with landlords, and leverage influence with councils and government, to create a fair, profitable model for physical retail stakeholders, and competitive advantage in the physical channel.

Existing retailers must re-invent their traditional location planning by adopting flexible commercial strategies, shop sizes & longevity rent planning, customer service & assortment propositions, and the role of shops within fluid channels.

Existing retailers should discard the perceived benefits of a long history for the real attributes of a new visionary business.

Existing retailers must adopt a 'years young' mentality instead of a "years old" preoccupation.

The 3 stages of exploitation

The Retail Evolution Curve identifies '3 stages of exploitation.'

Of course, the best of retailers always take advantage of favourable market conditions. They work hard, they evolve, and they take profit. It is important to the business ethos that shareholders, colleagues, suppliers, customers and the environment all benefit from their gain.

The worst of retailers, of course, do the opposite. Unfortunately, they exploit the situation and take the profit. They exploit the customer, their workers, their suppliers and their resources. They take the profit.

The window for exploitation is narrowing. Resources are becoming finite, suppliers are becoming protected, colleagues are becoming empowered, and customers are becoming aware and engaged. Everything is becoming transparent.

Progress is sometimes frustratingly slow, but new and existing 'essential retailers' will need to widen their perspective from market profiteering to playing a role in the world beyond retail.

This is the beginning of the age of integrity in retailing. It has been on the horizon for a while. The COVID era, and the soul-searching it encouraged, has accelerated its arrival.

History teaches us at least one thing that remains true through the ages to this day - the importance of staying ahead. In this Age of Disruption, in this post-COVID world, just as before the innovators will take the lead and gain a market advantage.

Existing retailers, whether 150 years old, 50 years old or 50 days old have the same choice. To lead, adapt themselves, or simply crash and burn.

A week in retail is a long time, and there is never such a thing as an 'existing new retailer.' The mantle of newness is quickly shed even for the most disruptive and inventive of businesses. We must all be on our guard to stay ahead on the Retail Evolution Curve.

History also teaches us another thing. Where it was once possible for individual businesses to be driven by extraordinary figureheads, the pioneer deal-breakers and the enlightened merchants, it is no longer possible to move forwards effectively without taking our colleagues, our suppliers, and our customers with us on every next step of that journey.

Extraordinary retail leaders are still amongst us, but they are extraordinary enough to take their council and advice from the colleagues and customers around them.

Sports Direct: the 'changing of the guard'

There is possibly not another retailer that exemplifies better the changing times that are molding the industry than Sports Direct. It has been built into a retail powerhouse by the energy and leadership of one man. Mike Ashley began with one shop and built a 'pile it high, sell it cheap' empire.

Sports Direct has earned its fortune in a time where consumers have shifted to wearing sports brands for leisure. Mike Ashley has been the archetypal 'deal-breaker' working, albeit uncomfortably at times, with the top sports names, whilst acquiring a raft of secondary and heritage labels.

Notoriously, working from his command team module, he has also acquired and absorbed ruthlessly both competitors in the sports retail market such as JJB Sports, whilst moving into more diverse acquisitions such as House of Fraser. His 'bullish' and outspoken approach has ruffled many feathers, alienated as many customers as it has acquired. However, it cannot be denied that Mike Ashley has been a 'stellar' retail performer and a figurehead of the 'virgin' and 'evolving' athleisure market.

The shop concept has also evolved. The brand has taken a triple market approach based on the same consumer trends, but for different end-uses. Sports Direct satisfies the commodity sports customer, USC the leisure brand shopper, whilst Flannels, another acquisition, has evolved into a fashion occasion proposition. Superstores which present together the three concepts have indeed lit up many retail parks across Europe.

But perhaps the greatest achievement of Mike Ashley is his recent realization that the 'disruptive' market we have now entered, is beyond his natural skills-set, contrary to his retail inclinations, or even beyond his ability to learn and adapt. His recent announcement that he is now handing over the reins of the business to his future son-in-law and a cohort of younger, tech-savvy, disruptive retail executives shows perhaps a humility that was not expected, or simply illustrates a commercially smart strategy to extend the financial success of 'his' business.

Either way, intelligent and successful retail leaders know when to buy, when to stick, and when to shuffle the pack, leaving the playing table, even if they own the casino. It is all part of being a commercially astute retailer, in any market situation.

The Z to A of retail disruption

Next: the 'bellwether' for disruption

The expression 'bellwether' is an unusual one. It has been adopted by the retail industry for businesses that represent leadership, stability and are indicators for the impact of market changes. It can be a bit of an albatross around the neck, as previous unofficial incumbents such as Marks & Spencer and John Lewis might testify. Next currently wears the mantle and its looks unlikely to relinquish it for the foreseeable future.

Next opened its first shop in 1982, which seems a lifetime ago. A lifetime when 'disruption' was as unused in retail parlance as 'bellwether' is today. However, it has always been a disruptor, and its innovation has always come through its leadership from the entrepreneurial founder, George Davis, to today's leader Simon Wolfson, the pragmatist and visionary guiding the brand to new peaks of stability and success even through COVID.

Its ability to evolve to this day is laid testament by its current leadership into online marketplaces, multi-brand propositions and collaborations with brands like Amazon to drive footfall in its shops through Click & Collect.

Much of Next's innovation has come through its channel management, even in the days before the internet. The brand initially evolved on the back of a very successful mail order catalogue. Innovative and disruptive as ever, it evolved the first 'free' paper catalogue available directly to individual customers, in a world where catalogue operations and sales were still generally carried out through agents.

Next was always very smart with its design and branding. The initial 'Next Directory' became a collectors' item. In fact, the whole series is very much a best practice record of mail order trends and designs. Next also developed physical shop concepts for every occasion with facias for jewellery, flowers, home and its 'X' facia that led the way in shop design experiences. It worked with interior design pioneers such as Din Associates.

Against this innovation Next developed unrivalled buying & merchandising capability, populating its mid-market ranges with commercial assortments with the minimum of risk. Its process became the model for many others. Its short sharp SALES period of sometimes a single day to remove the relatively small amounts of excess stock is the envy of the industry.

I have personally taken clients around many Next shops to look at the assortments and discuss the product design process. The overwhelming response to a Next assortment is that there is very little if anything to discourage a sale, other than your taste. They are what they are, and they are very good at it.

Next digital channels have replaced the paper catalogue as industry leaders. Its next day delivery offer competes with the most efficient, its click & collect and returns to shops have brought synergy across channels and maintained physical footfall through the online process. Its RFID technology is seamless across channels.

Next has moved smoothly to a business that now makes more money from digital. It has acquired collected and collaborated with competitor and compatible brands to create what would once have been an unimaginable multi-brand marketplace concept. On shops it has given physical space to brands such as Waterstones, Paperchase, Hema, Laura Ashley & Homebase to create lifestyle assortments. It has also acquired Victoria's Secret in the UK.

Never one to miss an opportunity delivered by circumstances, Next was the first to move and take-on some of the retail space vacated by the demise of department store Debenhams. They have become the home to its new Beauty & Home Concept. Of course, the move into beauty is a strategic and calculated omni-initiative. The access to wider beauty brands the physical shop offers, will be magnified many time through its online sales.

Most strikingly it has built an online services platform for other brands, Total Platform clients pay Next to operate their brand's website and online fulfilment, including elements such as website systems, warehousing, distribution networks and returns handling. In this area it has propelled itself in terms of a facilitator to the levels of Amazon, Ocado and The Hut Group.

Next is a story of how disruption changes its focus and points of impact. In its origins, in its pre-middle market, its design ideas

The Z to A of retail disruption

and branding were 'cool' and desirable. A surprise there for your now grown-up kids! They were then cool and disruptive in their buying and merchandising, even if it amounted to casual shirts and shorts. Now they are disruptive across digital channels and services.

There are many ways to be disruptive. And you don't have to be 'cool' doing it, unless you consider commercial success 'cool.'

Amazon: a 'classic' disruptor

Believe it or not Amazon is not new. It was founded in 1994 when even I was still frequenting the 'cool bars' and trendy nightclubs of life. Contrary to popular belief it is not responsible for destroying retail, it has simply re-invented it. Although simply probably understates the obvious truth.

Amazon has not just re-invented retail once, but many times over because retail is always changing. There are always leaders, always laggards and always those who fail. Amazon could have failed at any stage, as new enterprises joined the market learning from both Amazon's successes and from its mistakes. But it never has because it has worked hard, innovated hard and fought hard to be where it is today.

And whether you like it or not, buy from it or not, there are billions of customers out there who now see it as their go-to retailer, music channel, entertainment portal...keep counting the benefits and attractions.

Amazon is guided by 4 big principles which it lives and breathes:

1. Customer obsession (rather than competition focus)
2. Passion for invention
3. Commitment to operational excellence
4. Long-term thinking

It is successful today, because it doesn't spend today looking at today's figures but at tomorrows potential and tomorrow's figures. It is never complacent.

There are books out there just about Amazon. I recommend them. You can buy them from Amazon. However, if you want to see how disruption works, sometimes for the better, sometimes for the worst, then take a look at this list of Amazon firsts.

Many of these innovations are now so common, so widespread across industries that we forget that Amazon did them first.

- Customer reviews
- 1-click shopping
- Personalised recommendations
- Prime – subscription for content and services
- Fulfilment by Amazon
- AWS – Amazon Web Services providing on-demand cloud computing platforms and APIs to individuals, companies, and governments
- Fire Tablets
- Fire TV
- Kindle, direct publishing,
- Amazon Echo
- Alexa

And, with or without Jeff Bezos at the helm they continue to forge ahead with their 4 key principles. Even into the physical world of retail.

The Amazon Go or Fresh shop with its walk-in and walk-out payment technology may not become a destination concept worldwide but elements of its strategy, technology and operations will be adapted by convenience store owners everywhere. Watch learn and adopt. It's all there.

We cannot all be Amazon with its scale and investment in newness, but we can all learn the principles for staying on top of the Retail Evolution Curve. Leading from the front.

By continually innovating and disrupting Amazon has grown to a business where its Prime membership has now apparently increased to more than 100 million subscribers, paying an average $99 per year. That's over $10 billion income before we even buy anything. Now that's disruptive retailing

The Z to A of retail disruption

010

PLAN FOR THE END OF YOUR BUSINESS

Strategic planning & market insights

Now is a better time than most to consider and plan for the end of your business. An end that will be strategic rather than cataclysmic. Whether a new retail brand or traditional business define what you want from the brand, how you will achieve it, and how long you think you should carry on, how long the customer will allow you to carry on.

Actions

- Research the insights, projections and developments for your retail sector and markets
- Draw the Retail Evolution Curve ahead of you.
- Define your strategic longevity, and the periodic stages and initiatives that will get you there.
    - Product and service proposition
    - Channels, touchpoints & collaborations
    - Organisation, processes & skills
- Plan your progression and your disruption
    - Disrupting yourselves
    - Disrupting your market
    - Disrupting other markets

011

GET WHAT YOU NEED FROM OLD RETAILERS

Strategic planning & investment

Decide what you need to succeed from traditional retailing best practice, processes, skills, experience, infrastructure.

Actions

- Re-affirm what your business needs to be doing in its projected evolution
- Define what is missing to make the plan happen
    - Vision, capability, organization, experience
    - People, skills, teams
    - Technology
    - Infrastructure
    - Channels
- Define how to get what is missing
    - New or additional leadership
    - Developing or hiring in internal skills and teams
    - Collaborating on skills, functions, facilitators
    - Mergers & acquisitions
    - Invest in infrastructure
    - Funding & capital
- Define a timed action plan
    - Milestones and markers for actions
    - Contingency & risk

012

GET WHAT YOU NEED FROM NEW COLLABORATORS

Strategic planning & investment

Decide what you need to succeed from new retailers, brands, partners, collaborators, individuals, leaders, disruptors.

The 'Personal Destination Retailer'

In this new era, what does the essential retailer look like as it attempts to develop customer relationships and to become profitable once more in our ever more saturated markets?

The 'essential retailer' is not restricted to any specific origination, sector, category, scale of business, number of shops or geography of markets. Nor is it limited to being a physical retailer, pureplay, mobile, social or any combination of these channels.

It is defined by its philosophy to develop and embrace its customer community. Whether it reaches that community through its physical shops, via a mobile, computer or other medium it is obsessively driven by a customer connection that is local, it is personal, and it means something important to every single customer.

Sometimes these essential retailers look like small independent shops on a high street, with the same friendly face always welcoming you from behind the same old counter. Sometimes they appear as websites, with enormous invisible infra-structure behind them, constantly changing to delight us and attract our attention.

Some of these retailers exist already, but not as many as they would like to think. But in the aftermath of the retail shockwaves of the COVID lockdowns they will grow in number and are set to become the prevailing presence as they develop their own 'ultimate customer relationships.'

These essential retailers satisfy the functional needs and the emotional desires of their customers. The experience is personal, individual, and immediate. They are what I call 'Personal Destination Retailers.'

Personal is emotional

Personal destination retailers generate a close connection by being local and immediate to the customer, in every possible sense and context.

Physically, they are part of the customer's community, their neighbourhood, their town and their space. The way that they act and integrate with the physical space and the people in it makes them local, even if their origins and scale of business are from another place.

Their behaviour makes them personal. They are familiar and comfortable in the customer's locality.

They may be selling fishing rods from a 10sqm hut, or next year's fashion from 500sqm of light and music, but they belong in the customers locality. They are present, in person.

Digitally, they are equally adept at creating personal spaces and local places. Their sites and media channels generate a personal world which is for each customer. It is a community drawn from celebrities, influencers, friends and like-minded strangers, filled with content, music, and rich media selected for each customer.

The customer may be discussing and buying plant seeds with expert farmers or parachuting into enemy territory in their latest game purchase, but in every scenario, they belong with the retailer. In this virtual locality, the customer is made to feel like the local, familiar and comfortable with their surroundings.

Destination is functional

Essential retailers must 'not fail' the basic needs of their customers. Beyond functionality, the total experience must be equally appropriate and reliable.

In terms of availability, efficiency, convenience, operations, services and price, the customer must always be sure that the retailer will be there for them. Gaining the trust of the customer is the number one objective for a Personal Destination Retailer.

The scenario may be a physical environment, where a wide variety of options is being explained in depth by a trained colleague. It may be a high-tech digital environment where the customer is immersed in the brand and inspired to make a self-purchase. Either way, the retailer must not fail.

The full assortment must be available to see and touch, the colleague must not forget their lines when explaining the product options, the digital screens are all working, the payment machines always available. Everything works. Everything is efficient. This is my destination.

Filling in the missing pieces

To be a personal destination, the retailer must present a functional and emotional experience that will not fail the customer.

The challenge for many existing retailers is to 'fill in the missing pieces.' To ensure that they are both personal and destination. Far too often, retailers fall disappointingly into the stereotype of what we expect. Customers with a choice of retailer generally fall only once into that clichéd trap.

The local independent, run most often by a friendly 'local' with excellent service rapport, must evolve from being the opportunist of other people's destination footfall, trying in vain to please the customer with his amateurish operations, availability and outdated practices.

The multiple fashion chain must back up its central retail expertise with a personal and caring customer service proposition. It must pay as much attention to the world around its shops and the local economics of its customers, as it does to the analysis of its sales data and its own profit economics.

Personal Destination retailers always deliver the ultimate customer relationship and shopping experience.

The 'shopping experience' myth

The shopping experience is not the 'Saviour' of the high street

'Shock. Horror.' Popular myth tells us that the 'saviour' of the physical shop is the 'shopping experience.' Not true.

By this, we are talking about an exciting interactive engagement with a physical shop, physical product, physical sales assistants and with our physical friends. It is a totally social experience.

Of course, this is correct when considering physical shops. It makes physical shopping a powerful emotive experience, bringing pleasure and excitement to millions of customers. It is unique from digital shopping.

However, this is not the only deep and meaningful experience that a customer can have with a retailer. It is not the only emotional experience.

Emotional connections can be realised as much through the digital shopping experience as the physical. Emotional connections can be delivered with the same social intensity of friends online, as much as they can be offline.

Exciting emotional shopping experiences are certainly essential for physical shops to survive. However, they won't guarantee survival, not for any retailer.

The misconception comes from a certain nostalgia, but also from assuming all people feel emotions in the same way. It is a trap for any physical shopping enthusiast not to fall into. A lot of people do not like shopping trips. It's a fact. In reality, they never did. But they had no option, before now that is.

Personal Destination Shopping Experiences

For every type of experience that a customer requires from a retailer, whether that is full of adrenaline excitement, or simply facilitates a functional buying process, both physical and digital channels can provide this.

Both functionally and emotionally, online and offline mirror each other. No better, no worse. They are simply more relevant to customers who prefer physical shopping, customers who prefer digital shopping, and for those customers who like both and who swap between channels and touchpoints when one is more convenient, enjoyable or relevant than the other.

© 2021 vm-unleashed ltd.

Sketch 15 Personal Destination Shopping Experiences

In the physical world a variety of shopping formats supply the customer with emotional engagement from the wow impact of flagship showcases, the urgency and informality of pop-up shops, to the community engagement of local neighbourhood shops.

A less personal experience may come from a multi-brand wholesaler whilst micro-distribution shops and fulfilment dark stores will satisfy the functional needs of physical shoppers wanting to order, collect and return.

On the digital side, most interfaces offer the practicality of ordering, whilst delivering a range of immersive and functional shopping experiences that mirror physical shops.

Streaming rich media content allows one-touch shopping in a highly immersive environment, with product placement converting into product purchases. Social media and editorial feeds also allow for single-touch buying. Any combination of apps and messaging streams stimulate and facilitate links directly to e-commerce via mobiles and desktops.

E-commerce and traditional websites themselves offer a range of experiences from DTC brands with rich media sites through to the traditional product catalogue marketplaces.

Shopping for Fun

If we consider shopping for fun. In physical shopping trips, purchases are often the bi-products of the primary objective, which is having a good day out. The day itself with friends, music and bright lights is the stimulation for buying.

If we consider watching a rich media channel for fun. If we consider watching something that is a hobby, a pastime or a passion such as music, or sports, celebrities or superheroes, then we are often in an equally exciting emotional place as well.

Dropp TV: immersive digital music shopping

DroppTV is the World's first shoppable streaming video platform. It represents a growing wave of providers who are now offering direct sales from streaming video content.

The first phase of droppTV's consumer rollout was dedicated to music videos. It allowed musicians to broadcast music videos with pop up shopping functionality that used AI to recognise clothing in the video, sell it to viewers and then allowed the artists to earn commission.

For the first time fans watched music videos and bought what they saw in real-time with the click of a button. The platform's debut video, 'Stop Panickin' from New York City artist Kid Daytona featured products from COOGI and minority-owned footwear brand Jaclar.

The DroppTV platform is powered by the company's proprietary artificial intelligence, machine learning and computer vision algorithm, which recognizes products in video content and tags them in real-time, allowing for frictionless, one-click in-content purchasing.

DroppTV has identified music videos as the perfect entry point for streaming retail, with their unique connections to culture, art, music and fashion. They were the obvious choice for the first large-scale application of the technology.

However, the technology opens the way for direct shopping from popular TV shows, films, specialist hobby and pastime celebrities, TV shopping channels and the prospect of a move from influencer marketing to influencer selling. As a DTC channel it offers potential for brands, and for entertainers with a small but attractive product initiative to by-pass traditional retailers and sell direct to their followers and fans.

Many thanks to Dropp TV for their excellent press releases.

The Z to A of retail disruption

John Lewis: virtual personal shopping

When you have an unrivalled reputation for customer service, your omnichannel business is market leading, and you have commercialized the 'click & collect' concept then it makes sense to bring these elements together.

Department store group John Lewis has done just that with its latest initiative. The launch of a virtual personal shopping service using Zoom.

In the physical world John Lewis had increasingly been focusing on providing high quality in-store experiences. This culminated in its London Westfield shop which was reduced in size, in terms of assortment, but was rich in experience. The shops contained experience desks and concierge services to direct customers to the correct experience.

There was a fashion space, as part of the upscaled fitting rooms, dedicate rooms and weekly calendars of workshops and demonstrations, technology interactive experiences and food demonstration areas. The retailer has been seeking to replicate this expertise with virtual services including home interiors and personal styling advice, and virtual classes such as wine tasting and skincare.

The Zoom service enables customers to be shown around departments on video by an in-store adviser. They can book a free 30-minute appointment, supplying details about what they are looking for. On the call they are then shown products selected by a personal shopping adviser and have an opportunity to ask questions and see other products. Items can be sent to customers' homes or click and collect arranged.

The initiative is designed to win back trade and utilise stores in an omni-channel world. And as the brand reduces the number of physical shops that it has, such services are essential to remind virtual customers of John Lewis' impartial expertise and advice, and to make it available to customers who can no longer access a physical shop.

Alibaba & Ted Baker: livestreaming shopping

Livestreaming has become a huge phenomenon in China, with apparently 9% of all ecommerce sales in the country estimated to have come via the channel last year in 2020. Many expect that the trend of combining shopping with entertainment will become a rapidly growing retail channel worldwide.

The key is entertainment, where livestreaming is made into an unmissable event. Its stimulation and format is allied to celebrity and lifestyle TV, rather than traditional shopping channels.

During Alibaba-owned Tmall's Singles' Day livestream, a swathe of celebrities took part and heavy discounts were awarded throughout the broadcast. The Singles' Day livestream reputedly raked in 498.2bn yuan (£55.1bn) across an 11-day period, with 800 million consumers participating and live performances from Katy Perry and many Asian pop stars.

Whilst western excursions into the concept are in their early stages the potential for lifestyle brands is becoming a reality. Ted Baker has unveiled a livestream shopping experience aiming to bridge the gap between physical and digital touchpoints.

Initial streams are modest in comparison to Alibaba, as brands measure both the market appetite, and the format and promotional combinations that hit the right trigger for their customers. It is reported that Ted Bakers first event, attracted 2,500 viewers across Europe. It ran for around 15 minutes and featured a pre-recorded session from DJ and influencer duo Jordan and Loanne Collyer, who showcased a handful of items from Ted Baker's spring collection. Shoppers could click through to product pages and add items to their baskets while the "live" stream continued to play in the corner of the screen. 'Tea-breaks' allowed the hosts to answer pre-recorded questions.

I have no doubt that since I wrote this page, since it was published and distributed, many new initiatives will have occurred in the world of livestream shopping. Watch this dynamic, entertaining, engaging and lucrative space, as they say.

The Z to A of retail disruption

We watch our sporting heroes and buy the shoes, we watch the latest single and download it instantly, we learn how to make greetings cards and we buy what we need to make them in the moment.

Rich-media shopping has arrived and for those immersed in it, it equals and surpasses the emotions of a physical shopping trip. It is being adopted not only by digital enthusiasts but also by those who enjoy a fun day out in physical shops.

They are two sides of the same coin. They are two sides of the same customer, and they must be the two sides of the essential retailer, the personal destination retailer.

Retailers not channels win and lose

Retail in the COVID lockdown may have been perceived as a battle of channels. Practically at least, with most physical shops closed for weeks on end, it was a gift of sorts to online and mobile retailers.

However, retail never was a battle of channels. It was just a continuation of the war between retail businesses. The battle goes on to be 'essential retailers' not 'essential channels.'

Destination Stores are anchored in physical locations. Personal Destination Shops are located wherever the customer is!

From 'Retail location planning' to 'Customer location planning'

'Channel' is already becoming an obsolete word. Customers and retailers are connecting via an array of 'Shopping touchpoints.'

These 'shopping touchpoints' will continue to be a fusion of traditional and new shop formats and customer 'lifestyle locations,' across digital and physical worlds.

Retailers themselves will not be the ones to decide which channels to offer the customer. It will be the customer who dictates where and when, and how, they wish to connect with their 'essential retailers.'

'Retail location planning' a standard discipline of physical retailers to define the best places to locate physical shops will be supplemented and overtaken by the new discipline of 'Customer location planning.'

'Customer Location planning' will be the study of the distribution of retail touchpoints to maximise the transient movements and location patterns of the customer.

The shift in retailer mentality & functions must move from one of planting static physical shops to one of planning flexible mobile interfaces.

Retailers must move from waiting for the customer to enter their shop, to exploiting places to enter the customer's life. It is the shift from destination shop, to 'personal destination shop.' It is a subtle but profoundly significant change.

Finding the customer

Being 'personal' or 'destination' are just abstract keywords unless they are based on the reality of the customers you wish to sell to. For that you must embrace and respond to the paradigm shifts involved in finding and being with them.

Offline, Online & Everything in-between

Knowing your customer is important to your marketing and communication. It is also critical to simply finding where they are, both digitally and physically.

The haystack is very big and diverse for your needles. You need to know if the customer is socially active online? They could be on a digital platform. You need to know if they are interested in sustainability? They could be on a campaign site.

If they are more active in the physical world you need to know where they are. They could be at a leisure or entertainment venue, or standing in a field, in a country pub. The retailer needs to be there too.

Even in the physical world of the traditional shopper, we need to know their preferred type of shop, we need to use community shops to go to them, pop-up shops to follow them, and maybe as a last resort, even built amazing flagship shops to attract them to us.

Everything that is part of the customer's life is a potential place to interact and to sell.

Personalised data should be used as much as possible to identify both the physical and digital places where your customers are.

They may frequent traditional physical shops, and shopping locations from megacentres to local town centres.

They may frequent traditional e-commerce sites on their PCs and laptops or more immersive mobile interfaces

But they could also be anywhere from influencer sites, to standing by vending machines, in rental shops or concert venues.

© 2021 vm-unleashed ltd.

Sketch 16 Offline, Online & Everything in-between

Timberland: 'addressing' the local community

Timberland continues to build a community around its brand. That community is based on its heritage of quality and reliability, but increasingly on its more recent initiatives on the environment, and the sustainability behind its products.

Walk into one of its new concept shops and you will soon appreciate that community is the key thing here. Both the wider brand community, as seen in all the environmental statements and product displays around the shop, and the local community through event spaces, workshops and information boards.

A sign of its intent is immediate in the layout of its shops. The customer journey directly from the entrance introduces the local community collaborations, in a space that is focused on the communication and the 'hosting' of its numerous community events.

Product displays are prominent of course, and eye-catching in the combination of product presentations and environmental settings, but product plays the role of destination in the middle and to the rear of the shops. In these shops the purchase is still the goal, but increasingly the bi-product of brand stimulation and the Timberland passion that comes before it.

Timberland colleagues have always been essential to the shop proposition with their technical expertise and brand enthusiasm. Nothing has changed in terms of priorities, but the role of colleagues has evolved projecting them as ambassadors of the wider brand message, and as integral parts of the customer communities.

Ideally, the managers and staff in the shops are local and a pre-requisite at the very least for the role is to be involved in the community.

The events and activities delivered by the shop teams range from 'how to upcycle your waste into new products' to 'starting up a window box garden for flowers and vegetables.' You can get a picture of the wider brand message, and Timberland continues to walk the walk in its ongoing connection with the locations around their shops. Previous initiatives have seen shop teams volunteer to tidy and renovate local footpaths, to build new boardwalks and complete walking routes.

In a previous incarnation of the shop design local pathways and environmental projects filled one highly visible wall in the shop. The walls linked the world's Timberland shops via footpaths. In a new location a tourist would do well to visit the Timberland flagship shop and follow the footpath maps on the wall. The NY map for one led to a roof-level environment boardwalk along the Meatpacking District. Way to go.

The full picture of community can also be seen on the Timberland websites and across its social media platforms. Apparently, every full-time employee gets 40 hours of paid time to volunteer in their communities. By 2020 that amounted to more than 1.5 million hours worldwide. The statistics are impressive. There have altogether been 11,000 community service events around the world, with 80% of Timberland employees participating in everything from land reclamation to building social housing.

Timberland also collaborates in programmes such as Generation T, where T stands for Trades. They sponsor workshop events bringing young people together with local trade businesses to try new skills and work towards employment. Some of the trades find it hard to find skilled workers or train new ones whilst the youngsters have trouble finding work. Its another example or building practical communities on top of the emotional connections that Timberland is well known for.

The brand also continues to partner with Pittsburgh-based social enterprise Thread who provide upcycled materials such as plastic bottles to use in footwear. Fabric created from plastic bottles collected from the streets, canals and neighbourhoods of Haiti and Honduras is traced and tracked at every step of its journey, from bottle collection to fabric creation to the delivery of the fabric, to the manufacturer of Timberland footwear.

The Z to A of retail disruption

Rapha: active in cycling communities

Rapha was started in 2004. It has a reputation for making some of the best cycling clothing that you will ever see on a bike.

However, it has always been more than riding gear and has progressively engendered an 'inclusive' community around cycling, whether that be high performance professional racing, local clubs, or the world of the keen enthusiast.

The brand came to many peoples' notice as the clothing supplier to Team Sky from 2012 to 2016, where successive triumphs in the Tour de France pushed the brand exposure to new levels. Always a force for good in the sport, and after publishing a two-year study on the state of cycling, titled the Rapha Roadmap, the brand returned to the men's WorldTour with EF Education First Pro Cycling in 2019.

Rapha sells direct to customers across digital platforms and has also continued to invest in its physical estate. It has grown its family of 21 physical shops or 'cycle clubhouses' across Europe, Asia and the US. Whilst you can buy kit and get expert advice in any of the clubs, it is the community around them which is key to their success and popularity. It has always been a strength of the Rapha philosophy to view ROI in these physical spaces as being much more 'brand holistic' that just the sales and profit from merchandise.

I can testify personally to the excellent croissants in the café, and the coffee blend which is also available to buy for home making, even if I don't qualify from a cycling proficiency perspective. It is the cafes and the chat within them that are the key to the physical rapport and customer camaraderie. The clubhouses are all in cool locations, in interesting buildings, and packed with good company, advice and cycling stories.

Online and socially, 'The Rapha Cycling Club' was founded in 2015. Its aim was to bring cyclists together, and today there are apparently already more than 17,000 members worldwide.

Rapha takes cycling, and the Cycling club to the cyclist wherever and whenever the customer wants its practical and emotional support and presence.

An active social network is key to the community, and the app is key to that. It features hundreds of rides, routes and group chats every week, keeping a global network of more than 13,000 like-minded, passionate cyclists and ride leaders connected.

The cycling club's aim always is to bring its community together, physically wherever possible in meeting places, and of course to cycle. The Rapha Clubhouses and a network of approved partner cycling cafés around the world offer bike hire and 50% off coffee to members. The casual tourist can pick up a bite and have a ride around Regent Street, whenever they choose.

Organised year-round riding events and experiences are open to everyone, broadening the community profile. From some of the world's most famous sportives to hosted weekends away with curated routes, great food and evening socials. 'Escapes' are smaller-scale events that are run locally by Rapha staff members and local Ride Leaders exclusively for Rapha Cycling Club members. These are day, overnight or weekend events attended by a small group of RCC riders hungry for adventure.

Meanwhile The Rapha Foundation provides funding to not-for-profit organisations, with the mission of building a better future for the sport by inspiring, empowering and supporting the next generation of racers.

Rapha has truly created a cycling community at every level.

So having visited the Timberland flagship shop in any major city then head off to the nearest Rapha Clubhouse for a convivial cup of coffee and some alternative opinions on how to spend your afternoon. Whether its a Timberland Trek or a Rapha cycling route you will undoubtedly be engaging favourably with a best practice 'Local Destination Retailer.

The Z to A of retail disruption

013

DEFINE YOUR COMMUNITY

Customer research

If you're intending to be a personal destination retailer, which you must, then you need to firstly know what community you are wanting to connect with. You need to know as much about your customer community as possible. What makes them your 'type of customer?' What makes them 'your customer?'

Actions

- Research your customer across all channels.
- Do not focus or differentiate by channels or locations.
- Define what makes your customer distinct in terms of the way they think. What are their viewpoints, their passions and philosophies.
- Define what are the elements of your brand proposition that attracts them to you.

014

BRING YOUR COMMUNITY TO LIFE

Customer insights & brainstorming

In both the physical and digital worlds of your customer community you need to create and deliver an integrated and coordinated 'community location' for them with common emotional attractions, experiences and group engagement.

Actions

- Define what physical and digital environment your community wants.
- Define what interaction they want with you, and they want with each other.
- Deliver the structures, tools and contents that will create the community environment.
- Deliver an integrated solution across channels.
- Plan a 'community calendar' of events and activities.

015

DEVELOP COMMUNITY TRUST

Customer insights & brainstorming

In both the physical and digital worlds of your customer community you need to build trust. Trust with individuals and trust as a group with you.

You need to define what 'trust' means to your customers.

Actions

- Define what physical and digital environments, services and customer touchpoints build trust.
- Deliver excellent 'trust building' solutions and processes to support them.
- Build community communication and interaction channels to build and share trust experiences.

016

BUILD YOUR COMMUNITY

Strategic action planning, coordinated operational activities

Today, you need to go to your customers, wherever they are.

You need to re-create the same coordinated community environment wherever your customer goes, and to facilitate the community 'spirit' wherever they all are.

Actions

- Define the physical and digital places where the 'community environment' needs to be.
- Build the physical community structure, physical places
  - Physical shops
  - Physical hubs
  - Pop-up hubs
  - Third party environments
  - Venues
  - Mobile physical hubs
  - Customer 'home hub' elements
    - Accessories
    - Music
    - Digital tools
    - Clothing
    - Smells
    - Environment
- Build the digital community structure, digital places
  - Apps
  - Social media
  - Chats & community hubs
  - Video interaction
  - Emails
  - Blogs
  - Webinars
  - Podcasts
- Plan and deliver integrated physical/digital community events
  - Media and news events
  - Community activities
  - Leisure & social
  - Product promotion & selling

From 'Economies of Scale' to 'Scale of Economies!'

The principle behind making money from 'economies of scale' is to produce high volumes of products, which reduces the individual unit cost. The more you make and the more you sell the greater the margin and the greater the profit.

'Economies of scale' profit is made in the buying process.

The principle behind making money from 'scale of economies' is to generate the highest demand for your products in the local economy surrounding your shop, or the potential local economy around your digital touchpoints, by creating added-value within those communities, through creating a positive relationship with the customer base of those economies.

'Scale of economies' profit is made in the selling process.

The more collaboration of actions and 'generosity of spirit' you give to the local economy, the stronger the relationship and the higher the demand for your product, and the more people will be willing to pay for your product. Profit is made from the selling process. Cash is generated locally at the selling point, and not just achieved remotely in the buying process.

Too much stuff

The unbelievable quantities of merchandise being created by the volume model is becoming too much for even this materialistic world of voracious consumers. Desperate dynamics of product rotation and marketing campaigns have attempted to prop up a system that increasingly cannot sell enough product volumes at any margin to make a retail profit.

Too much stuff for customers

Too much stuff to keep, to wear, to dispose of. Too much stuff for consumers who have become increasingly aware of the damage to the planet caused by the production and the disposal of their possessions.

Too many stories of modern slavery and worker exploitation in the quest for lower costs. Too much plastic in the sea and too much wildlife and environments suffering.

After COVID more customers than ever have seriously questioned the volume of goods they consume and resolved to buy less. The renewed awareness of what is important in their lives does not, for many, include the same volume of possessions.

The Supply & Demand model is shifting dramatically to a substantial over supply situation. The re-balance has already seen the demise of a considerable number of retailers focused on the volume model.

It is true, that some market leaders, the best practice of the retail juggernauts, will survive and flourish. They have built large retail empires not only on volume but on excellent assortments, powerful emotive branding and competitive but realistic pricing. They have built deep supplier and customer relationships on the back of value, availability and convenience.

Consumption

Waste

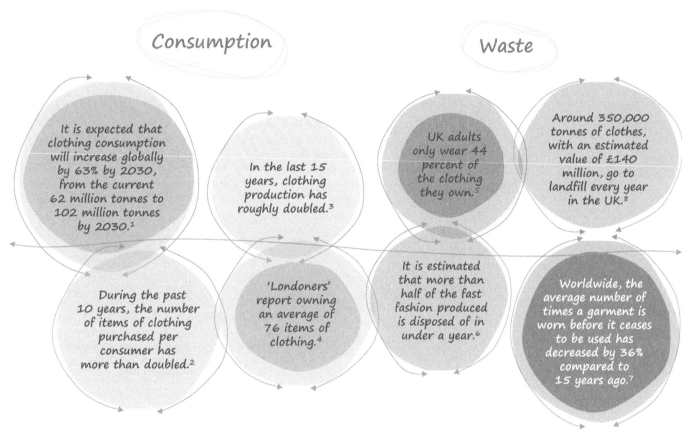

It is expected that clothing consumption will increase globally by 63% by 2030, from the current 62 million tonnes to 102 million tonnes by 2030.[1]

In the last 15 years, clothing production has roughly doubled.[3]

UK adults only wear 44 percent of the clothing they own.[5]

Around 350,000 tonnes of clothes, with an estimated value of £140 million, go to landfill every year in the UK.[8]

During the past 10 years, the number of items of clothing purchased per consumer has more than doubled.[2]

'Londoners' report owning an average of 76 items of clothing.[4]

It is estimated that more than half of the fast fashion produced is disposed of in under a year.[6]

Worldwide, the average number of times a garment is worn before it ceases to be used has decreased by 36% compared to 15 years ago.[7]

1,2. *Global Fashion Agenda and Boston Consulting Group, Pulse of the fashion industry* (2017)

3, 6, 7. Ellen MacArthur Foundation, A new textiles economy: Redesigning fashion's future (2017)

4. *TRAID, Recycling Clothes, London (2018), p.15*

5, 8. *WRAP, 'Valuing our clothes: the evidence base'* (2012)

Sketch 17: Product consumption & waste

> *Retailing: noun –*
> *'the business of selling goods*
> *directly to consumers'*

The success of the rest depends on adopting an 'Economies of Scale' mind-set to complement and ultimately replace the current 'Scale of Economies' mentality.

Irrespective of however important 'Economies of Scale' are to your business model, all retailers must re-focus on the 'Scale of Economies.'

> *The strategic shift is moving*
> *away from one that is*
> *solely focused on 'making a*
> *profit from buying' to one of*
> *'making a profit from selling!'*

The physical retail business priority is evolving from just the places where retailers buy, to the places where retailers sell. This brings us back to our Personal Destination Shop. Back to the true art of retailing itself.

"Scale of Economies." A Return to Selling!

We can no longer view our shops anonymously, treating them as spreadsheet numbers. Valuing them only as product disposal machines. Taking them for granted as revenue generators selling anonymous stuff to anonymous people.

It is essential to understand the potential 'Scale of Economy' of your shop, to work to establish your shop as part of that community, create local connections and manage your 'Personal Destination Shop' for the community it serves and sells to.

Retailers must learn again to cherish each shop as a precious opportunity to generate sales. They need to understand its qualitative assets as well as its quantitative value. A need to understand locations, customers, and the colleagues who run each one of them.

Shop portfolios must be built on quality and not quantity, where quality is not just defined by the potential to sell, but the potential to build lasting and fruitful relationships with the location and the local customer community.

The potential for commercial viability should be gauged on whether the community and populations around the shop are significant enough and appropriate enough, for the retail brand to build the desired relationships to generate the required footfall. Is there the opportunity to convert this community of individuals into regular customers, engage with them as loyal patrons and convert everything into a healthy revenue and profit?

This is the potential 'Scale of Economy' that 'Personal Destination Shops' were built for.

Locations for 'Local People'

The process of location selection must have more input from 'local people' who know the area, including regional managers and adjacent shop managers.

More visits and research must be carried out. Competitor analysis should not only be based on the number that exist, not even just on the quality of their shops, but their wider propositions, how well each one is engaged with the location, the communities and the customer base.

'Opportunities to be local' can be found and made everywhere. Collaborations with local clubs and societies, council and trader groups, local supplier cooperatives, local environment schemes, popular local activities and sporting teams, sponsorships and endorsement, local events, activities and historical landmarks, charities and good causes. The politics, the mood and the philanthropy of the town. The community.

The familiarity of your colleagues with the local customer base, and the personal relationships they can develop with them will be an important asset to maximising the 'scale of economy' potential of the shop. Depending on the service proposition and required job roles, retail businesses need to find the balance between retail expertise and experience, and social and inter-personal communication skills.

What is important in terms of 'Retail Scale' is being redefined.

The move of business priorities to the 'places where they sell' rather than 'the places where they buy' creates new and more realistic opportunities for selling. Here the relationships can be equal, open, mutually beneficial, mutually reliant, and secure.

The local supply support network

When the COVID chips were down, startling collaborations, partnerships and flexibility flourished. Many of these initiatives will continue. The re-awakening of the local world of flexible and reliable supplier and support networks. Re-born and re-imagined to take up the strain.

The local initiatives of national retailers went further. Retailers prioritised the payment of smaller local suppliers, recognising their cash-flow dynamics. They linked up with local and national delivery companies to supply customers by van, bike and e-bikes. Retailers met customers on the side of roads and in the middle of fields.

Retail competitors worked together. The complexity of product sizes and range varieties were simplified, focusing on what customers needed to significantly speed-up supply chains and improve replenishment. Competitors even collaborated on 'pooling' essential product ranges to ensure that between them appropriate supplies were available to local areas.

Retailers have hopefully re-opened their eyes to the importance and value of local supply support networks to deliver local 'personal destination shops.'

Expect to see the growth of both 'local destination retailers' and 'local destination suppliers,' and a dynamic and exciting middle-ground as the boundaries between them dissolve.

Making, supplying, selling and delivering will blur into a single proposition offered by 'Personal Destination Businesses.'

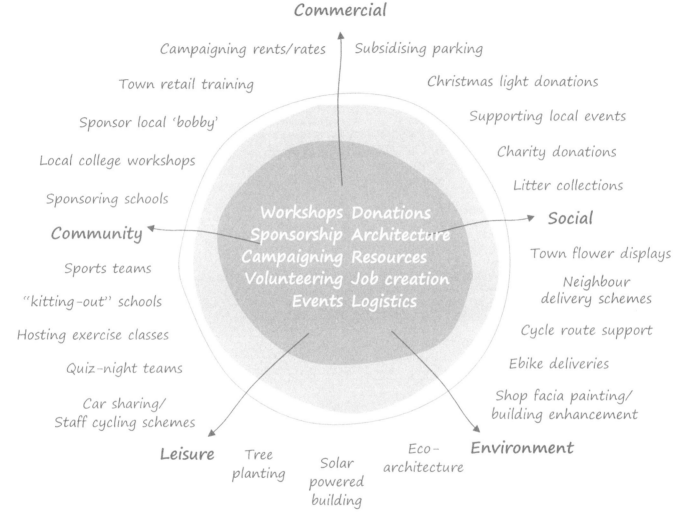

Commercial

Campaigning rents/rates

Subsidising parking

Town retail training

Christmas light donations

Sponsor local 'bobby'

Supporting local events

Local college workshops

Charity donations

Sponsoring schools

Litter collections

Community

Social

Workshops Donations
Sponsorship Architecture
Campaigning Resources
Volunteering Job creation
Events Logistics

Sports teams

Town flower displays

"kitting-out" schools

Neighbour delivery schemes

Hosting exercise classes

Cycle route support

Quiz-night teams

Ebike deliveries

Car sharing/
Staff cycling schemes

Shop facia painting/
building enhancement

Leisure

Tree planting

Solar powered building

Eco-architecture

Environment

Sketch 18 'Personal Destination Businesses' A Return to Communities

Personal destination businesses

Personal destination businesses will encapsulate the local community economy, participating and stimulating in its vibrancy and commercial success.

Their involvement will be across five major areas...

- Commercial
- Social
- Environment
- Leisure
- Community

The focus will depend on the specific values and vision of any brand but there is plenty of opportunity for any retailer, supplier, and business to be local.

Already retailers are activating on a commercial level, creating apprenticeships and training for local people, as well as contributing to parking and environmental initiatives to drive new footfall.

Community and social involvement probably has the most direct impact on the potential customer base. Personal interaction outside the shop will likely lead to commercial interaction within the shop.

Retailers can involve themselves in local schools and colleges with a philanthropic perspective. They can also involve themselves with a variety of leisure activities from local pub teams to collaborations with gyms and sports centres.

Social initiatives can bring life to a town through permanently effecting the fabric and wellbeing of a location, adding sparkle at Christmas and colour in Springtime.

The personal destination business impacts locally, whatever and wherever its origins might be.

Co-op: a 'small business charter' supporting local suppliers

The Co-operative movement has a long heritage of community and collaboration. Its philosophy of shared ownership created many retail businesses, all working and partnering with a wide array of small suppliers, entrepreneurial shopkeepers and millions of loyal customers who also bought into the ethics of the co-operative, as well as its diverse assortments.

True to this collaborative ethos and heritage, the Co-op has recently launched a new small business charter, in a commitment to double the number of smaller local producers that supply to its stores. The retailer hopes to be working ultimately with up to of 1,200 small suppliers.

The key aims set out in the small business charter are to build sustainable long-term relationships with local suppliers and produce growers, and to deliver practical advice and support for small businesses to create and deliver better market access.

Of greatest importance, is that the Co-op is not 'seeking exclusivity' with its suppliers. This has historically been an existential problem related to the terms so often demanded by large retail chains. Exclusivity arrangements have notoriously created barriers to growth for small firms, closing off other income opportunities, and stopping suppliers selling directly to the customer.

From family-owned micro-breweries to local vegetable suppliers, small businesses are the heart of the Co-op. They are also at the heart of the UK economy, with small and medium food and drink manufacturers generating more than £22bn a year and employing over 127,000 people.

The co-operative has had a remarkable renaissance. It has regenerated its organisation and managed to direct its diverse stakeholder ownership, whilst remarkably the market and customer sentiment has turned backwards towards businesses with a more local perspective and a community involvement.

The Z to A of retail disruption

Morrisons: local business partnerships

Morrisons is one of the Big 4 grocers in the UK marketplace. Probably more than most it stays close to its origins as a family business working with other family run suppliers.

In its physical shops it remains one of few that is still committed to investing in its 'fresh food market' proposition, with service counters for meat, fish, dairy, delicatessens and bakery products. Morrisons has built its shops around these vibrant areas. Walk into any of them, including its new Market Kitchen concept for more urban locations, and you can literally taste the collaboration, the sourcing and local production.

Morrisons's sourcing team echoes the same principles in its supplier collaborations. The retailer has just acquired Falfish, a family-owned seafood wholesaler based in Cornwall, that has worked with the grocer for 16 years. This will guarantee that 80% of Morrisons' fish and shellfish will come from wholly owned operations.

The deal will also remarkably see Morrisons acquire a 30ft trawler, the Jacqui A, which Morrisons says will make it the first British supermarket to own a fishing boat. I suspect they are correct in their assumption.

In reality, the acquisition of a business like Falfish is a great fit for Morrisons. Not only is Falfish a reputable British company supplying high quality fish and shellfish, but the two businesses also share a commitment to sustainability and for local sourcing.

Fishing has been the subject of some recent high-profile documentaries on sea pollution and fish stocks exploitation so this collaboration on protecting fish resources and reducing fish waste is a timely one.

From a Morrisons perspective the acquisition also further strengthens their position as Britain's biggest food maker. The deal is also beneficial to Falfish's Cornish operations and the wider community. It represents investment, access to many new opportunities, and at the very least offers security for employees and their families in an industry under pressure from many directions.

As Britain's biggest food maker, Morrisons also continues to deliver on its promise to be the first supermarket to be completely supplied by net zero carbon British farms. It has already started working with many of its existing meat and produce farmers to create carbon neutral models that can then be applied across the whole range of its suppliers.

The programme includes the rearing of different and more diverse animal breeds, using low food-mile feedstuffs, building renewable energy and low emission farm housing, reducing fuel and fertiliser use, planting more grassland, clover and trees, restoring peatland, improving soil health and the widespread re-seeding of hedgerows.

Climate change represents not just one of the biggest challenges of the generation for the wider world, but particularly for the food industry, with its responsibility to supply fresh produce to its customer, and as a key contributor to greenhouse gas emissions.

One visible incarnation of Morrisons' commitments that the customer will have picked up on in shops is the introduction of the its 'Wonky' fruit, vegetables and salad products. The retailer is selling products that would historically have been rejected for sale because of size and shape 'non-conformity.' It is a commitment to reduce food waste on purely aesthetic grounds.

Morrison's success has not gone unnoticed by potential courters. It is now the focus of several takeover bids from private equity businesses. It is a startling sign of our new times that there is a huge public outcry regarding fears that a takeover will destroy Morrisons' commitment to local suppliers and the environment. The range of interested parties from customers and suppliers to the government itself lays testament to how much the values Morrisons has exhibited during the COVID lockdowns are enbedded in our new sentiments towards retailers. Private equity is having to justify and explain its intentions to the world like never before. Surely not a bad thing for retailers, suppliers, customers and the local communities they represent.

The Z to A of retail disruption

eBay: supporting local enterprises

You don't necessarily need to be a physical retailer to be local to communities. In fact, not being 'tied' to specific locations allows online brands to apply some strategic thinking to the ways that they interact nationally, regionally and locally with their vendors and their customers. Locality is as much about mindset as it is about physical location and adjacency.

> *Locality is as much about mindset as it is about physical location and adjacency.*

A network of collaborators at every level is the key to success. From central government and national organisations, through to local authorities and down to community groups. Even the largest and 'remotest' of retail brands have opportunities to become 'local destination retailers' if they invest in the right partners.

eBay has launched a multi-million-pound programme to create jobs and opportunities in parts of the UK that have been hardest hit by the coronavirus pandemic. The e-tailer is planning to create a dedicated 'eBay for Change' hub on its UK website, allowing shoppers to easily find small businesses that reinvest their profits back into their communities, either in Britain or overseas.

It is a substantial shift in focus from the enormous range of buying opportunities that eBay represents, where the final selection is usually based on lowest price, or a price driven bidding process, to one that segments the alternatives not just by location but by the contributions of vendors to that location.

In many ways it is a return to some of the original values of eBay, in being a platform for individuals to sell-on their unwanted products, where locality was an advantage to delivery and collection, and one of the key messages was sustainability, namely the recycling, the re-use of possessions.

In addition to its 'eBay for Change' programme, the pureplay business has also partnered with UnLtd, a firm that offers support to social entrepreneurs to help them develop their businesses.

eBay and UnLtd will establish a dedicated social enterprise ecommerce start-up programme for early-stage social entrepreneurs across the UK. It aims to work with at least 100 social entrepreneurs in the first year of the partnership, offering training, coaching and financial support to help them grow their businesses and positively impact their communities.

eBay explains its position as wanting to be a part of building a fairer and ultimately more sustainable economy. It is a recognition that customers are becoming increasingly aware of the impact of where they choose to spend their money, whether it's supporting small businesses or charities. 'eBay for Change', will give customers the satisfaction that the proceeds from their purchase will support communities.

eBay has more recently launched a new finance initiative to help small businesses bounce back after the coronavirus crisis. They will provide 300,000 sellers on its UK platform with new access to financing through a partnership with YouLend.

The Capital for eBay Business Sellers (CEBS) initiative will offer loans ranging from £500 to £1m, which will be repaid directly from the sales the company makes through eBay's platform.

Apparently hundreds of eBay sellers have already signed up to receive funding through CEBS and the etailer plans to unveil two further financing partners in the coming months to expand the proposition.

The Z to A of retail disruption

017

BUILD SHOP PROFILES

Location research & analysis

You will all have profiles of your shops, and your channel touch-points, to a greater or lesser extent. These can range from precise numerical data to 'local here-say.'

Shop and touchpoint profiles need to include both data and informed opinion, and everything in between. The profiles need to be both commercially data driven, and qualitatively broad on customer demographics, to form a report that specifies the reality and the potential of the communities and individuals that generate those figures.

Actions

- Define and set-up the 'remote' knowledge input channels
  - Commercial data
  - Location data
  - Demographic profiles
  - Shopping trends & patterns
  - Competitor presence and analysis
  - Location and market trends
- Define and set-up 'local' input channels - Shop team input
  - Strength, depth and 'heart' of communities
  - Retail role and opportunities in the community
  - Competitor community engagements
  - Customer personalities and lifestyles
  - Shopping preferences & sales opportunities
- Plan regular inputs and updates from shop managers and teams

018

PLAN ACTIVITIES FOR COMMUNITY SHOPS

Internal brainstorming

Every shop, or touchpoint, should have a plan to maximise its opportunities within its community of potential customers.

There will be several 'templates' for community development, linked to a shop grading and clustering process. Shop managers, teams and regional managers will be required to add and evolve the specific actions for each shop and location.

Actions

- Develop several community action plan 'templates' for existing shop grades/clusters.
- Create the input channel for shop teams to input specific initiatives, collaborations and partnerships for individual shops
- Develop specific activities plans for individual shops
- Support plans with budgets and resource planning
- Manage activities at local, regional levels
- Monitor practicalities and effectiveness of actions
- Analyse ROI of actions- sales, footfall, frequency, loyalty schemes, reviews, feedback, shopping patterns, basket size and contents, social media response, local brand coverage and awareness
- Set-up a shop grading and clustering strategy based on the level and direction of local community potential and activities

'Authenticity' is the new brand differentiator

Best practice leaders set new standards at every step of the Retail Evolution Curve which gives them the competitive edge. Competitors duplicate and improve.

They duplicate through combinations of benchmarking and analysis. Whole industries have emerged that do nothing but benchmark and replicate assortments, price architectures, promotions. Even more creative and aesthetic elements can be copied. Shop design and visual merchandising are relatively easy to replicate. "Build me a shop with the 'kit of parts' of my major competitor. I want to copy the fixtures in shop X! I need the mannequin displays of retailer "Z!" Visual elements can all be photographed, analysed, and recreated.

What about the elusive physical retail experience, apparently, the final step of best practice competitor advantage? Sadly, this too can be replicated by implementing the usual checklist of product demonstrations, tastings and giveaways, interactive digital screens and Instagram moments, enthusiastic staff and even the introduction of a coffee bar, lounge area and barber's chair.

Find yourself blindfolded in the middle of a shop. Take off the blindfold. Know where you are? Probably not. All this replication and duplication can get you up to the next operational level. But is that good enough anymore?

So where, in the saturated and disruptive world, is the next best practice competitive advantage? In a world of ever more reduced demand and intense competition, how can the survivors edge ahead, and forge a decisive lead?

Following decades of brand artifice, fabricated consumerism, and synthetic sentiments, old fashioned honesty and integrity will light a path through the commercial gloom and consumer weariness.

In all things that retail businesses do now, they must be genuine. Absolutely authentic.

There is nowhere to hide. Your shops and staff are 'face to face' with the customer. Your social media feedback and reviews are there for the world to see.

Retailers need to be genuinely there for the people in their lives. There for their colleagues and their customers, for their suppliers and yes, even their shareholders. Retailers must apologise honestly when they fail, and they must make generous amends to keep their relationships alive.

> To be an essential retailer it is important to be yourself. To be genuinely invested in creating a better retail world and yes, making some well-earned profit.

If that doesn't sound like you then maybe retail is not your industry. Or perhaps, it is your industry, but it's just not your time anymore.

The Road to Authenticity

The journey begins with the basics. Appreciating and facilitating the coming together of the customer and the product.

Retailers must be clear on their customer relationship strategy. They should implement brand communication which is either Basic, Advanced or the Ultimate relationship delivering retail fundamentals, lifestyle engagement or ethical empathy. The strategy must become real in the form of the Personal Destination Retailer, embracing customer communities across both physical and digital channels.

The road to becoming personal and a destination must involve the integration and collaboration of people and technology.

Retailers must build intimacy, inspiration and integrity across a wide range of touchpoints, where each touchpoint is understood and managed for its customers. It is the commercial scale of the local economies that will define success not the scale of economy from mass production and volume retailing.

Commercial success will come from a fundamental 'return to selling' and not a kneejerk 'return to buying,' in businesses where the many traditional and disruptive functions will be turned towards the customer, and not the buyers.

Basic Customer Connection
Single customer view

Advanced Customer Connection
Customised messages

Ultimate Customer Connection
Personalisation of messages

Coaching & Training
Human interaction Coaching

Product knowledge Education

Pro-active service training

Customer relationship coaching

1.
Essential connections: Functional & emotional

Essential Retailer

2.
The Virtuous Cycle of Deeper Customer Relationships

Personal Destination Retailer

3.
The Collaboration of People & Technology

Personal & Emotional

Destination & Functional

Basic Product Range
Core retail offer

Wider Product Assortment & Services

Ultimate Retail Proposition
Diverse product & services

Software & Applications

Staff management & scheduling

Product intelligence

Dynamic product news/trends updates

Dedicated customer alerts

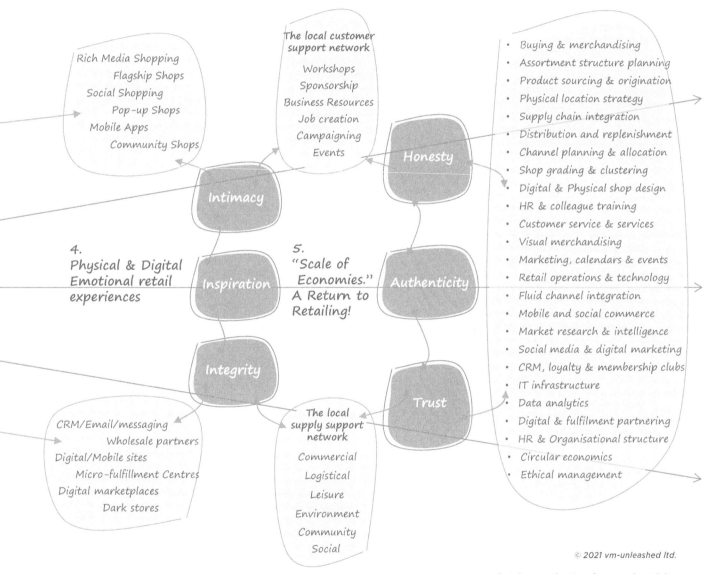

Rich Media Shopping
Flagship Shops
Social Shopping
Pop-up Shops
Mobile Apps
Community Shops

The local customer
support network

Workshops
Sponsorship
Business Resources
Job creation
Campaigning
Events

• Buying & merchandising
• Assortment structure planning
• Product sourcing & origination
• Physical location strategy
• Supply chain integration
• Distribution and replenishment
• Channel planning & allocation
• Shop grading & clustering
• Digital & Physical shop design
• HR & colleague training
• Customer service & services
• Visual merchandising
• Marketing, calendars & events
• Retail operations & technology
• Fluid channel integration
• Mobile and social commerce
• Market research & intelligence
• Social media & digital marketing
• CRM, loyalty & membership clubs
• IT infrastructure
• Data analytics
• Digital & fulfilment partnering
• HR & Organisational structure
• Circular economics
• Ethical management

Intimacy

Honesty

4.
Physical & Digital
Emotional retail
experiences

Inspiration

5.
"Scale of
Economies."
A Return to
Retailing!

Authenticity

Integrity

Trust

CRM/Email/messaging
Wholesale partners
Digital/Mobile sites
Micro-fulfillment Centres
Digital marketplaces
Dark stores

The local
supply support
network

Commercial
Logistical
Leisure
Environment
Community
Social

Sketch 19 The Road to Authenticity

Brick Lane Bikes: the genuine article

Brick Lane Bikes is a small workshop in London's Shoreditch. Unassuming on the outside, it hides a story of one man's passion to build a bike, which culminated in him creating a retail phenomenon.

Brick Lane Bikes began as the dream of a former London street courier. The aim was to create the first all-track bike shop in the UK. The little east London shop quickly grew to be Europe's fixed and vintage destination, stocked full of a dazzling variety of track components from vintage classics to the funky and new.

As requests grew for quality yet stylish bicycle components, the in-house brand 'BLB' was launched. The initiative perfectly reflects the brand's celebration of individuality and is passionate to supply the demand for bespoke bicycle parts and frames. Soon after BLB, Bigmama distribution was created to quench the thirst for unique & stylish components to all shops, small and large throughout Europe and beyond.

The hub of this empire is still in Brick Lane, in the streets of east London. The store exterior is plastered with stickers left by admirers from across the globe whilst the interior bursts open with a myriad of bike frames, parts and tools. This is a genuine working environment. This is still a business that thrives on its initial passion for street cycling and continues to draw inspiration from its many loyal customers, their bike stories and their own individual cycling passions.

Brick Lane Bikes hosts a popular and busy fully fitted workshop, a hive of activity bustling with experienced professional mechanics. As with all local businesses, or international destinations, no booking required, just pop in, feel the passion.

Brick Lane Bikes exemplifies the opportunity for local specialists to remain local and grounded , yet become 'international niche destinations.' In effect 'Personal Destination Shops' to the world via digital retailing and product distribution.

Lyle & Scott: great yarns, the untold riches of a humble past

The last decade has shown us that brands need to connect very strongly on an emotional level with their customers in order to survive and flourish. Brands are re-born with a fanfare of future expectations, but equally valid and valuable are the stories behind the brand evolution and history. Brand authenticity.

It almost seems that the humbler and more authentic the struggles of distant decades were, the more battered and bruised the identity has become, then the more value and connection the customer feels for the brand.

Lyle & Scott is no fabrication. It was founded in 1874 in the Scottish town of Hawick. The brand still draws from a 125-year-old archive that includes designs by Christian Dior and Michael Kors. Its golf range appeared in 1967 and was quickly worn by top golfers such as Tony Jacklin, Gary Player and Greg Norman.

The rejuvenation of the brand can be traced back to 2003 with the launch of the 'Vintage' collection with its 'Golden Eagle' logo. It was taken up by a host of youth TV presenters and indie bands including the Arctic Monkeys, Kasabian & Pete Doherty. Lyle and Scott has also featured in urban culture films such as The Firm and Green Street. Cristiano Ronaldo has also been seen wearing the famous gold eagle logo.

Undoubtedly the quality of the storytelling is as important as the facts themselves. The art and skills of modern authorship and branding becoming in turn part of the rich tapestry of the brand where fact and fabrication are woven in unison to pull at the customer heartstrings. The weaving of a great yarn...Lyle & Scott, fashion brand of choice to the smart young man.

Sadly the brand's flagship shop on Carnaby street has closed. It design and its personality embraced both its history and its future. Let's hope for a new physical destination soon.

The Z to A of retail disruption

Changing retail for the better

There are four scenarios where retailers "change for the better."

1. It is simply in their DNA.
2. They respond proactively by asking customers and staff how they should change.
3. They respond reactively when falling customer loyalty, sales and profits force them to change.
4. They only change when legislation makes them.

It is true that some customers don't care, or cannot afford to care, whether retailers have changed from their exploitative ways.

But where choice can be afforded, it will be the growing number of retailers who have been born with the new retail DNA, and those proactively trying to change their ways, that will be taking more and more customers with them on this exciting new step on the retail evolution curve.

Either way, it is best to be honest with the customer about who you are and what your values are. Even when your actions and motives are not always what they could be, then at least honesty can be commended.

Let customers be the judge of that.

To be essential, retailers need to be authentic, and genuine and honest. Are you ready for the next step in the journey to becoming an "essential retailer?"

Do you have the 'agile organization' and the 'astute strategies' that can make it work for you?

Oxfam & M&S: independent audits

Conditions in the retail supply chain are increasingly under the spotlight. A study by Oxfam independently commissioned by Marks & Spencer, found a raft of concerns among workers in some of the retailer's supply chains in the UK and India.

The work was undertaken at the request of M&S to improve understanding of the issues. Oxfam's research showed a disconnect between the information that M&S managers receive based largely on third-party ethical audits, and what workers report as their actual experiences. M&S is proactively working towards ensuring their stringent standards are applied in the reality of every supplier and the reporting mechanisms.

Boohoo: 'agenda for change'

Online fashion success story, Boohoo has been embroiled in controversy about supplier factory conditions. As a result, the brand has set out its 'Agenda for Change', aimed at ensuring full ethical compliance across its supply chain.

Subsequently, Boohoo has published its full UK supplier list, and helped its suppliers to remove the need for sub-contracting. Each UK-based supplier on the list has also been audited at least twice, with any non-compliant supplier removed.

In addition, a purchasing app is under-development so that Boohoo's buyers will have full visibility of suppliers' capacity restraints, whilst it is also set to open a model factory in 2021, run on 100% renewable energy, and showcasing supply chain best practices to local businesses.

Boohoo has also agreed that its board will now connect 15% of its bonus scheme to implementing its 'Agenda for Change.'

As always, the customer will be the final judge.

The Z to A of retail disruption

019

PLAN TO 'BE HONEST'

Soul searching & customer researching

None of us are perfect but hopefully we are trying to move in the right direction. Being honest is a good starting point.

Customers of all types of retailer respect and now demand honesty. That honesty could relate to pricing, the quality and attributes of the product, or the sustainability and ethics behind the product.

It 'boils' down to two questions. How honest does your customer want you to be? How honest do you want to be?

It's a bit of a 'chicken and egg' thing. But whether you see the chicken first, or you see the egg first, well that probably says a lot about how honest you want to be.

It's your choice. Brands will live or die by it.

Actions

- Define what level of honesty your customer demands of you
  - Absolute transparency
  - Old fashioned honesty
  - Not important
- Define what areas your customers want honesty
  - Everything
  - Ethical stances
  - Sustainability generally
  - Product sourcing
  - Suppliers & growers
  - Workers conditions
  - Product information
  - Prices
  - Complaints
- Define your attributes that its good to be honest about
- Define your attributes that its not good to be honest about
- Develop an action plan to improve what its not good to be honest about
  - Situation & reality
  - Market leading objectives
  - Milestones
  - Benefits & welfare
  - Progress
- Develop an 'honesty' communication calendar
  - Best practice stories
  - Improvement stories
  - Define your story tellers
    - Customers
    - Colleagues
    - Experts
  - Define channel strategy
- Monitor, measure feedback & go again!
- Always go beyond the levels of honesty that your customers require and expect.

"The madness of retail will be perceived only by those who find no meaning in it. Whilst the essential retailers will be those that embrace the sense of it."

2. Evolve into...
Agile Organisations

The New Landscape for Retail Business Communities

In the 'life & times of the essential retailer' we discussed the consumer world and the customers that now await every retailer in our saturated markets. We looked at how retailers need to connect both functionally and emotionally with customers, to deliver a proposition that is both personal & local, whilst having the integrity to be a worthwhile destination.

This new world has some profound implications in terms of how retail businesses are organised and structured. The evolution of the retail vision, and the formation of the retail organisation around it, are fundamental to being an essential retailer.

However, before delving into each function, it is important to consider how they all should fit into the wider business model. To see how the parts of our business need to work seamlessly together to deliver best practice retail, relevant for today's customer.

If we were retail tourists, planning a 'grand tour' of a best practice retail organization, then the itinerary we would plan today would be very different from the schedule we would have travelled even ten years ago.

In those relatively recent but otherwise distant times, the journey would have been straightforward in every sense. We would have followed a linear route that visited all the important retail departments, all the 'tour highlights and must-sees' in order, and independent of each other. We would have followed a path through the business functions that replicated the journey of the product, from buying to selling.

Tour No. 1. The familiar landscape of the citadels of retail power

The familiar 'Ivory Towers' of traditional retail businesses reflect the 'Age of Discovery' in the history of retail evolution. This was the time of demand led markets and limited competition.

> *Product was king.*
> *Buyers were the kingmakers.*

Naturally enough, the organisational structure and processes of many retailers are still built around the familiar product functions - buying, sourcing, merchandising and space allocation. Until recently, the drivers of profit related directly to how much product you could put into every square metre of your shops, and the initial and realised margins you could buy and sell your products for. To a greater or lesser extent, all other functions were there to support.

Shop formatting and design functions created spaces for product, visual merchandising made products look good, customer service assisted in the sale of products, whilst marketing and promotions teams stimulated the frequency of purchases and the amounts of products sold on each visit.

Store operations ensured the availability of product, and the availability of the staff to sell the product, whilst sales & commercial teams made decisions on price and promotions, on replenishment and re-distribution, to maximise the sales of every product across the assortment, in every shop.

Tour No. 1.
The Familiar Landscape of the Citadels of Retail Power
A one-way ticket from buying to selling

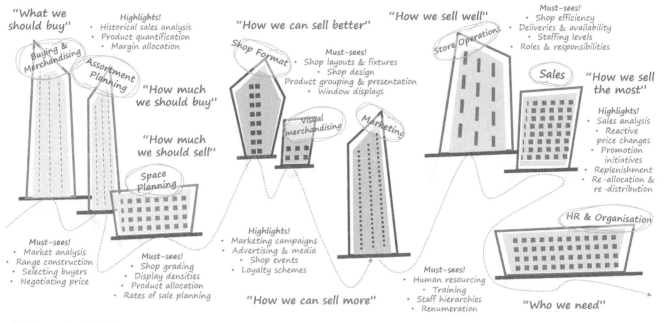

"What we should buy"

Highlights!
• Historical sales analysis
• Product quantification
• Margin allocation

Buying & Merchandising

Assortment Planning

"How much we should buy"

"How much we should sell"

Space Planning

Shop Format

"How we can sell better"

Must-sees!
• Shop layouts & fixtures
• Shop design
Product grouping & presentation
• Window displays

Visual Merchandising

Marketing

"How we sell well"

Store Operations

Must-sees!
• Shop efficiency
• Deliveries & availability
• Staffing levels
• Roles & responsibilities

Sales

"How we sell the most"

Highlights!
• Sales analysis
• Reactive price changes
• Promotion initiatives
• Replenishment
• Re-allocation & re-distribution

HR & Organisation

Must-sees!
• Market analysis
• Range construction
• Selecting buyers
• Negotiating price

Must-sees!
• Shop grading
• Display densities
• Product allocation
• Rates of sale planning

Highlights!
• Marketing campaigns
• Advertising & media
• Shop events
• Loyalty schemes

"How we can sell more"

Must-sees!
• Human resourcing
• Training
• Staff hierarchies
• Renumeration

"Who we need"

© 2021 vm-unleashed ltd.

Sketch 20 The Familiar Landscape of the Citadels of Retail Power

The priority of the 'retailer mentality' follows the buying process. "What we should buy." "How much we should buy." "How much we should sell." "How we can sell better." "How we can sell more." "How we sell well." "How we sell the most." and "Who we need...to sell."

This is a sales focused, supply chain-based model, where the functions of sourcing and buying are supported by volume shop grading, volume operations and sales analysis.

The highlights and must sees of the tour are concentrated on sales and performance analysis which are historical and internal. Merchandisers are essential for tourists to meet on the tour as

they talk about quantitative analysis, range construction, initial margins, allocation and price. The sourcing team and the buyers as negotiators are also 'must-sees' to understand the processes and principles behind the business.

The tour would see a 'lightening quick dash' through marketing and visual merchandising, to allow plenty of time for more meetings with the sales and operational teams. To learn about volume selling.

The tour is rigid and 'set-in-stone' but expect delays as the timing of the buying and selling teams can be unpredictable at times.

Human resources, as a function, was largely seen as a support to the buying and sales functions. And in due course, the IT department has become the same, empowering the functional needs of buying and selling, often without an overall technology strategy, never-mind the vision of a digital-first business.

The result has been organisational structures which have evolved naturally, or 'more often than not' unnaturally, around the core buying functions.

Any initial or original vision or passion that existed, can easily be diluted or lost in a series of un-coordinated product-led developments to drive sales and profit. However, there has generally been no vision for the future of the business other than performance growth, and more of the same.

Certainly, the customer was not central to the vision, except in terms of body numbers. The proposition for them became confused over time as ad-hoc additions took the shopping experience in contradictory directions, and usually onto a lower trajectory of experiences and shopping enjoyment.

The organisations themselves started to feel the strain, particularly when the positive effects of growth began to wear thin. The coordination of teams, the efficiency of processes, the allocation of resources started to become unwieldy and un-manageable.

Employees, like customers were not at the centre of the vision. They too became confused, frustrated, and de-motivated. This is not how you build a vibrant and engaged workforce. This is not how you design and assemble an essential retailer fit for today's markets.

This type of retailer was a buying & selling machine. It was the product of retail engineering. Engineering of the highest order, but engineering nonetheless.

Tour No. 2. The New land of retail business communities

Today, the landscape around these retail citadels has changed dramatically. The 'ivory towers' are less prominent and recognisable as the revered places built by the original buying powerhouses of the retail industry.

Our journey, and indeed the path of the product, is no longer just linear. We need to see the end of the selling process as it feeds into the beginning of the buying process. We need to hear the opinion of the customer that defines the buying decisions.

The shining citadel is now the 'vision' of the brand at the centre of the organisation, permeating into every function of the process. It is strong and unyielding, yet continually refreshed by the flows of customer analysis, market research and product appraisal that surround its foundations.

The influence of the vision drives the buying and selling processes. The results of their labours wash-up at the feet of the encircling customer. And so, the cycle continues afresh.

This is a transformed experience for the retail tourist, immersed in this new landscape. Some functions have merged into single entities, through alliances and organic growth. Others have diminished in importance, fallen into disrepair, or disappeared completely.

Entirely new functions have been built out of the empty landscape connected by super-highways and dynamic infrastructure to the centres of activity around them. And some places have been re-named, re-branded, or simply given 'place-making' treatments to make them suitable for today's retail dictionary.

The route maps, the buildings, the people, and the lifestyles of modern retail are changing with the times, responding to the saturated markets, stimulated by the new retail visionaries.

Tour No. 2.
The New Land of Retail Business Communities
An immersive and interactive exploration

"Where we sell"

Must see!
- Local shop clusters
- Community engaged shops
- Colleague ambassadors
- Head office integration

Local Retail Communities

"Who we are"

Vision & Strategy

Product research

Market analysis

CRM Customer insights

Marketing

Highlights!
- Corporate vision
- Central research
- Customer focused inputs
- Marketing outputs

"What our proposition is"

Buying & Merchandising

Must see!
- Strategic assortments
- Customer focused deliveries
- Complementary services
- Emotive experiences

Buying & Merchandising

Buying & Merchandising

Digital Management

Physical Operations

"Where our technology is at"

Digitally-led strategy, support and delivery

HR & People Dev't

Channel Allocation & Distribution

Highlights!
- Digitally-led strategies
- Coordinated solutions
- Integrated supply chains
- Hi-tech collaborations

"Where our product is"

Highlights!
- Flexible supply chains
- RFID product location technology
- Centrally pooled inventory
- Integrated channel allocation, home delivery, C&C and returns

Must see!
- A visionary workforce
- Collaborative processes
- Informed & empowered colleagues

"Who our people are"

Sketch 21 The New Land of Retail Business Communities

The new tour of retail landscapes is exceptionally well organised.

It must be as the route is not linear, and never quite the same. The itinerary is constantly and subtly changing and improving as the guides take constant feedback, they listen, and they modify. The guides and the exhibits change for the customer. This tour experience is all for the customer. The route has flexibility to allow for the preferences of the tourists.

Immediately there is more life around the tour with many employees constantly moving between the functions. The whole campus is designed to allow for easy and perpetual collaboration. The people are friendly and always ask how things are.

The highest tower of the retail vision is resplendent. From here there is an unparalleled view of the business. The tower houses every possible source of enlightenment for the development of the vision, the product proposition, the range of services, the evolution of channels and customer touchpoints.

The doors are always open to employees from every corner of the new business communities. Its influence spreads down through the buying and merchandising processes, and to the physical and digital infrastructures. The selling community and the customer are always in view.

Expect many questions from the buyers to fuel their constant curiosity about the needs and wishes of the customer. There is always time for customer visits and interaction.

Inditex: a very stylish revolution

At the beginning of my retail career. Not quite when retail dinosaurs ruled the earth, but certainly when they walked with a swagger in their step, I was told to go and visit a new format in downtown Madrid. It was called Zara.

Sadly, on my arrival it was half empty, in the throws of removing the old stock, still awaiting the new. Such missed assortment opportunities would certainly not be tolerated today. The shop was small compared to today's expansive flagships, about 150sqm in size, and it was 'made' from brown wood. In its first conceptual adventure, it was literally a wardrobe for fashion, dark and heavy, not our familiar white box.

My journey in retail has been synchronized with that of Zara and the Inditex group. I feel fortunate for that and humbled to have followed the rise of a brand that has quietly and stylishly, but utterly, revolutionized the way of working in fashion. A business that has inspired or forced so many other retailers to change their buying and merchandising principles, processes and operations.

It has been my pleasure to work with many ex-Inditex employees across Europe and the world. They always add expertise, professionalism, urgency and vibrancy to any business.

I would also go as far as to say that they bring a contentment, a piece of mind, a confidence in their skills and their purpose. They have an assurance that they have learnt principles and processes from the very best. Essentially, they have become the very best and most sought-after employees in the marketplace through the organization and processes that nurtured them.

From the beginning Inditex has been customer focused and has built its business and success around the customer.

It is certainly no coincidence for me that Amancio Ortega, founder of Inditex, on leaving school at the age of 14 found his first job as a shop hand for a local shirtmaker called Gala. This business still sits on the same corner in downtown A Coruña. Ortega learned to make clothes by hand.

What in effect he undoubtedly learned was to talk, to listen, to learn, respect and make clothes for his customer. He was at the sharp end, 'for better or for worse' and experienced the immediate and genuine reaction of the customer.

The design processes in Zara are both mythical and legendary. Rooms filled with stylists and designers finding stimulation amongst heaps of fabrics and garments, scattered across the floors between their squatting intensely focused frames. The process is undoubtedly inspirational however it is precisely supported by every kind of intelligence on the customer and the market that is available. Inspiration without a good commercial business case is cast aside amongst the other remnants.

What Inditex also has is fluid access to the shop managers and teams across their estates. The business is a daily flow of feedback and recommendations arriving in to the creative and commercial buying hubs. With new products arriving in shops twice per week, and a creative period as short as three weeks the flow of communication is continuous. Decisions are made quickly and production instantaneous.

This is what revolutionized the retail landscape those 35 years ago. A business was formed that understood the importance of putting the customer at the heart of every decision and reacting quickly to please them, again, again and again. Inditex built its organizational structure, its processes and its buying and selling dynamics around the citadel of the customer.

Inditex, through Zara, didn't kill off the dinosaurs, but they certainly made them work harder for an easy retail meal.

The Z to A of retail disruption

The Customer Focused Retail Proposition

The customer used to buy products. Then they bought brands. Today, it is the proposition that the customer buys, and it is what they buy into.

The proposition is the 'complete package' that the customer experiences with a retailer. It is a combination of products and services, and is delivered as a physical retail shop, a pureplay digital site or any combination of channels, touchpoints and media. It is more emotional that just a product. But more functional than just a brand image.

A good retail proposition is built and managed in 5 stages:

1. The Vision

This is the combination of a powerful brand concept & commercial strategy with clear value delivery parameters. This is defined at the origins of the business and encapsulates how the business will make profit from a customer focused perspective, allied to the pragmatism of commercial buying.

2. The Assortment

Assortment categories, sub-categories and ranges are defined by the vision of the business, the brand concept and the commercial strategy. The buying & merchandising teams are always aligned to the vision of the business. Ultimately the assortment may be very limited and focused or spread across many categories and ranges, but the values of the business are always adhered to.

© 2021 vm-unleashed ltd.

Sketch 22 The Retail Proposition

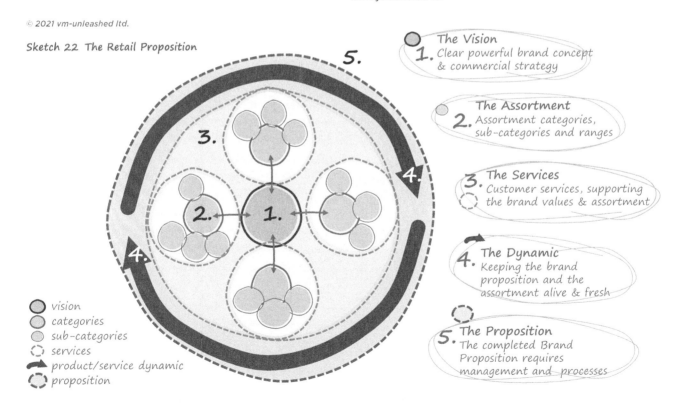

The Vision
1. Clear powerful brand concept & commercial strategy

The Assortment
2. Assortment categories, sub-categories and ranges

The Services
3. Customer services, supporting the brand values & assortment

The Dynamic
4. Keeping the brand proposition and the assortment alive & fresh

The Proposition
5. The completed Brand Proposition requires management and processes

Legend:
- vision
- categories
- sub-categories
- services
- product/service dynamic
- proposition

3. The Services

More than ever, customer services supporting the brand values and the assortment, are essential to a people focused business operating in a saturated market.

They will include front-end marketing services and back-end operational services, personalisation, ordering, collection, delivery and after sales.

4. The Dynamic

Keeping the brand proposition and the assortment alive is an imperative in the dynamic world of the customer. The proposition dynamic keeps the perception of the brand, assortment and services fresh, relevant and customer focused.

The reality of the business dynamic lays in the assortment and services development teams but the communication to the customer makes it real for them with vibrant marketing campaigns, events and promotions.

5. The Proposition

The completed Brand Proposition requires constant attention and management. It requires a team with the right skills, expertise and passion for the vision through all its customer focused activities. It requires an appropriate organisational structure, and functional buying and operational processes to enable the team to deliver the reality of the vision.

Simple & Ugly propositions

The proposition is important for everyone involved in a retail business. It helps them to understand the fundamental parameters that they can work within. It clearly defines the boundaries of what they can produce.

> The beauty of a new business is that the vision is everything. The horror of old businesses is that everything is the vision.

The worst thing that can happen to a proposition is for it to lose its clarity. Its clarity within the business, and ultimately its clarity to the customer.

By moving outside the boundaries of appropriate products, taste, principles and values the customer becomes confused. The same confusion effects a workforce in a similar way, particularly when it effects the culture, the type of employees, external collaborations, and how the business values and rewards its employees. The proposition must be clear and consistent inside the business as much as outside.

Best practice businesses keep their shape, they keep their balance and their proportions. They keep the beauty of a simple proposition, no matter how large they become.

Ugly businesses lose all these things. They become unattractive to customers and colleagues. A proposition which has grown with no central vision or boundaries grows, only for growth's sake.

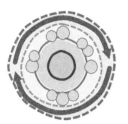

A retail business can be successfully built from a vision whilst remaining focused on a single hero product range and sub-ranges.

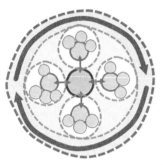

A retail business can grow and diversify its assortment and services into different categories, but still keep its balance and focus with a strong vision at the heart.

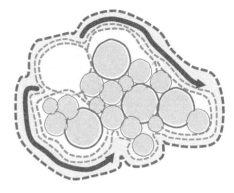

A proposition which has grown with no central vision or boundaries grows, for growth's sake.

It lacks clarity and becomes confusing for customers and employees.

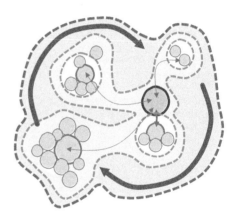

A retailer that has a clear original vision and brand boundaries grows misshapen if it evolves unbalanced and uncoordinated assortments and services away from the core values.

○ vision
○ categories
○ sub-categories
◌ services
➤ product/service dynamic
◌ proposition

Sketch 23 Simple & Ugly Retail Propositions

What is retail growth?

The subject of the retail proposition brings into focus once again the concept of 'growth.' What does growth mean for you as a retailer? As part of your proposition, you need to have a definite objective of what growth represents for you, the vision, assortment and services.

Your attitude to growth will define your retail strategy, and everything beyond that, from your price position, sourcing & cost approach, channel and shop location strategy, service levels, staff investments, and your organisational balance. Your growth will affect dramatically your proposition, for better or for worse.

Your approach to growth might be focused on driving your immediate profits. Alternatively, it may be more aligned to business growth for a sustainable period of profit. How much profit you want to generate in the short-term and over the lifetime of the business is what will define the size, shape, balance and beauty of your proposition. It is your choice.

One thing is for sure. To generate profit growth of any kind does require a deeper commitment than was once the case. Sustainable business growth requires a commitment to growth across all functions and areas that create the deeper relationships between you and your suppliers, your employees and to the customer.

> *You are investing in growth to make your business as essential as possible, to as many different parties as possible.*

If we consider the concept of the product proposition and our ambitions for a basic, advanced or ultimate customer relationship then our strategy must be focused and coordinated across our objectives.

Growing the Basic Customer Relationship 'proposition'

We need to grow services and reliability. We will probably want to grow the size of the assortment, but not necessarily. Growing our competency at delivering our assortment in line with our key values is what is most important.

In the Basic Customer Relationship, we need to grow the availability of products, minimise empty shelves, grow relationships with suppliers for add-value, more reliability and consistency.

We need to grow our operational expertise to ensure the experience the customer has is always efficient. We must grow the loyalty of our customers.

Growing the Advanced Customer Relationship 'proposition'

We need to grow services and the dynamics of our assortment, but not necessarily the size of the assortment.

In the Advanced Customer Relationship, we need to grow more into the lives of our customers. We need to grow our understanding of the customer, to develop more meaningful services and appropriate products for their lifestyle. We need to be more locally involved with our customers growing our influence in their communities.

As a business we need to develop our own personality, our 'tone of voice' and our opinion on things that also matter to our customers.

We need to develop more of the things our customers like such as the type of rewards they want, the brand collaborations and the sponsorship with other companies and events they want. To grow the loyalty of our customers, we need to grow the beauty of our proposition, literally.

Growing the Ultimate Customer Relationship

We need to grow our values. We need to grow our assortment in terms of added-value and variety, but again, not necessarily its size.

In the Ultimate Customer Relationship, we really need to understand more about what our customers think and believe about issues beyond retail.

We need to grow our own viewpoints, ethical policies and conscience, and we need to take actions to support them. More charity collaborations, more supplier monitoring, and a better way of appreciating and caring for colleagues' wellbeing.

We need to be sustainable in every way, growing the number of products that are recyclable, designing our shops to be energy efficient, and growing relationships with sustainable partners.

Practically we need to dig further into our customer data, grow our understanding, grow the quality of our communications and grow our numbers. We grow the loyalty of our customers.

We need to grow the depth of our loyalty. We need to grow the beauty of our proposition, not just skin deep but below the skin.

Your Retail Proposition, with a vision and a commercial strategy at its heart, built on assortments and services, driven by dynamic and appealing communication, is what will generate the beauty. The beauty that is loyalty, and which is based on trust. Trust of investors, from employees and colleagues, and most essential, the trust of customers.

Apple: a business designed on simplicity

The best advice I ever received in Design College? Keep things as simple as possible.

The temptation always when seeking beauty through design is to add more 'beautiful' elements to it. In fact, the way to design beauty is to be brave enough to remove as much as you dare to reveal the absolute beauty of simplicity.

I'm sure that Apple needs no more of an introduction than that.

Personally, I would say that Apple has as close to a perfect proposition as you are ever going to get. The brand values are written through everything that the customer ever experiences with them, from hardware to software, colleagues to shops.

Those values were of course originally written through the DNA of its founder Steve Jobs. He was the living incarnation of the precision and simplicity of the brand. And he found his soulmate in the form of Jony Ive, who interpreted the beauty of the brand into the simplicity of the product design.

So much for beautiful beginnings. So much for a simple proposition, but what about growth?

Growth has not tainted the Apple brand or stretched the proposition into unfamiliar shapes. Firstly, because the values have not been ignored, and secondly because the assortment has grown slowly and organically. In fact, it can be argued that the brand values only strengthen as every faithful addition to the product portfolio takes its first bow.

We can see how everything comes together as one physical expression when we visit one of their flagship shops. It is easy to take them for granted now, even after such a relatively short period of time, but we should not forget the adoration and admiration that greeted 'another Apple revolution in retail' when they unveiled the glass cube at the top of fifth avenue.

What an entrance, in every sense, to a new world of retail. Retail spaces were re-invented at a stroke. The brand DNA of Apple built into the fabric of the shops.

We see simplistic environmental design reflecting the design of the products themselves. We see the evolution of the large table as a display and practical presentation solution, just like the product interface. Incidentally, for those that don't remember shops before Apple, the product went on the walls, accessories hidden on the floor. There were no tables. The use of the large floor table revolutionized retail design thinking for many businesses. Apple re-purposed the table in the retail environment.

We see the conformity, reliability and expertise in the shop colleagues, participating in organised presentations, personal demonstrations and casual conversations. Always available, working calmly under pressure, just like their products. We see a high volume of expert colleagues. We see customers immediately served, no waiting, no impatience.

And what we see are huge communal spaces, packed full of bustling people, whilst remaining comparatively empty of product. We see customers at peace in the simplicity, within the cavernous reassuring space that is Apple.

The success of its proposition should be measured in the densities of the shops. The product option per square metre density is one of the lowest in the world, only beaten by car showrooms, and luxury ones at that. Its customer density per square metre is one of the highest. Decidedly higher than any car showroom.

Apple's proposition is huge, its assortment is small. Both are simple, beautiful and desirable. A price worth paying.

Shops busting full of bustling admirers lay testament to that.

The Z to A of retail disruption

Pets at Home: 'a retailer that is for life.'

It could be argued that the true test of a retail proposition comes when everything doesn't quite go according to plan. Things rarely do. That's when relationships are made.

From the unexpected pitfalls of everyday life to the completely unpredictable scenarios of national lockdowns. When a retail business needs to adapt and move into new and challenging environments, then that is when the strength of a single proposition can be judged.

Pets at Home is a booming retailer. The largest 'pet shop' in the UK. It has continued to perform strongly during the lockdown period. Its ability to adapt and grow whilst retaining its proposition has been impressive. The success has not been built on increasing the assortment size, but though the addition of a range of services that support the physical foods, baskets, hutches, toys, rubber bones and the animals themselves, that make up the traditional pet-shop.

2020 saw the business reach a landmark point in its evolution. This was when the revenue from services grew larger than that made from physical products.

When a business moves into services in a big way, the strength and consistency of the proposition is put firmly in the hands of the people who run those services.

Pets at Home has always built its proposition on its people. You need to be nothing short of a pet fanatic to work in their shops. Loving animals is of course a pre-requisite but hiring people who care for their pets also brings with it an enormous amount of knowledge, experience and empathy that they can share with the customers.

The people at Pets at Home keep the proposition true.

The additional services have been built in a considered and balanced way, through 'Petplan' insurance, 'The Groom Room' pet care & grooming, Vets4Pets veterinary services, 'Tailster' dog walking, the 'Puppy & Kitten Club' and a VIP club offering discounts, an app community and a percentage of profits going to animals in need.

Pets at Home has also purchased veterinary telehealth provider The Vet Connection in a bid to broaden its online services. The acquisition of TVC also marks an important next step in the development of the digital capabilities of the brand, providing trusted advice and even more convenient pet care services outside the physical shop confines.

The potential integration of shop colleagues into the remote helpline is a win-win solution for customers, colleagues and joint venture partners, providing 24/7 access to trusted advice with increased flexibility around veterinary work-life balance.

Increased convenience and personalization of the proposition is also a priority for shops. Traditionally a big shed retailer, Pets at Home plans to roll out new small Pets at Home stores on local high streets and city centres. They will essentially still be a combination of services and retail but fine-tuned for each customer. Typically, there are more cat owners than dog owners in cities, shoppers purchase slightly smaller bag sizes because of their need to physically carry, and they usually buy more premium ranges.

Pets at Home has moved from a product to a service retailer. It has grown from a big shed physical retailer into the world of remote and distanced services, to customized spaces. It has acquired and integrated a number of independent service companies, embraced thousands of independent service providers, and through all these strategic and enforced changes it has kept its proposition focused on its original core values.

Now that is what you call a brand.

The Z to A of retail disruption

020

BALANCE YOUR PROPOSITION

Internal analysis & customer research

Time to take another honest look at your brand. We need to go back to the core values of the proposition. What do you stand for? What do you represent to the customer? Why do they need you?

It is then time to look at the assortment, the services and the dynamics of your proposition and to assess how well they align to your core objectives. To take decisive actions.

Actions

- Define and re-affirm your brand values.
- List the elements of your customer proposition
  - Physical assortments – categories, sub-categories, ranges, iconic products
  - Brand portfolio
  - Partners and collaborators
  - Colleagues
  - Customer service
  - Customer services
  - Events & promotions
- Analyse the 'brand fit,' commercial performance, customer feedback and ROI for each element
- Define an action plan for each element

021

REMOVE THE 'UGLY'

Strategy meetings

Propositions can develop in an imbalanced way for a variety of reasons. The most common is simply short-term, 'chasing the cash.' Short-term 'chasing the cash' can soon turn into out-of-control opportunistic buying.

For sustainable growth you need to return to your original values and deliver a proposition based on those elements that work commercially within your proposition.

Actions

- Define honestly which commercial elements of the proposition do not fit.
  - Assortment elements not appropriate
  - Brands that are not a good fit
  - Partners with different values
  - Colleagues & employees with different values
  - Services nobody uses
  - Events & promotions that are not appropriate
- Carry out an exit strategy for each
- Replace with a more appropriate alternative if the element itself is appropriate and commercially viable

022

ADD THE 'BEAUTY'

Qualitative & quantitative analysis, customer 'focus group' feedback

When you consider what's working for your proposition, and what isn't it is easy to fall into the trap of being only quantitative.

Analysis of performance data across the board can apparently tell you 'what to get rid-of!' - firmly out of the business. However, sometimes it's the qualitative part of the equation that is the reason why something doesn't belong in your proposition, and probably isn't selling.

We need to introduce here such qualitative elements as 'taste' and 'style.' Is it a case that the product or category is still valid to your proposition, and if only the taste & style were made more appropriate and closer to your brand values then this would make the product or category a viable and valuable part of the proposition?

For the sake of your proposition, the credibility of your qualitative analysis, , employ customer inputs in the shape of 'focus groups" and internal workshops. Remain at the higher level. This is not the place for a fully-blown assortment review process.

But ask such questions as.

- 'Whichever way we style this category, is it right for us as a brand?'
- 'If we think there is a role for this category, how should the general styling and taste be different?'
- What other elements will add beauty to our proposition, price positioning, functionality, reliability, product related services, customer service selling?

Actions

- Review in more depth existing elements of the proposition that could be appropriate if they were designed or delivered in a different way.
- Carry out customer 'focus groups" and internal workshops. Ask the question, 'how can we make this part of our vision?'
  - Product:
    - Functional attributes
    - Taste & style
    - Colour, shape, sizing
    - Brand selection
    - Price positioning
  - Partners and collaborators
    - Brand reputation
    - Tone of voice
    - Service capability
    - Reliability
  - Colleagues/customer service/events
    - Tone of voice
    - Service capability
    - Reliability
- Take decisive action to bring each element back behind the proposition
  - Re-educate, Re-train or replace people
    - Designers
    - Category managers
    - Buyers
    - Service personnel
    - Partner personnel
    - Marketing personnel
    - Creative agencies

023

GROW THE PROPOSITION

Strategic planning

Your proposition should never stop growing, it will stagnate.

But your proposition can grow in different ways. The most appropriate way for it to grow is linked to the level of relationship you want with your customer.

Just as your relationship grows from being , basic, to advanced and then to the ultimate, the proposition must grow at the same time and in the correct way at each stage.

If you are clear where you stand on the level of relationship you want with your customer, then just act.

Actions

The Basic Customer Relationship 'proposition'

- Grow the quality of the existing experience
- Develop action plans:
  - Reliability – operational expertise
  - Availability of products – sourcing, supplier relationships, distribution
  - Convenience – shop locations, densities, services
  - Range (if appropriate) – suppliers
- Apply appropriate levers for improvement, training, hiring, technology, systems, new partnerships

The Advanced Customer Relationship 'proposition'

- Grow the excitement of the existing experience
- Develop action plans:
  - Service – HR, external partners, operations
  - Dynamics – buying and sourcing, marketing
  - Personalisation – CRM, apps, messaging
  - Choice (if appropriate) – brand partners
- Apply appropriate levers for improvement, new internal skill sets, new external creative agencies & facilitators

The Ultimate Customer Relationship 'proposition'

- Grow the depth and meaning of the existing experience
- Develop action plans:
  - Values – sustainability, community, charities
  - Loyalty – loyalty programmes, rewards, subscription
  - Variety (if appropriate) – brand partners
  - Services – external partners, facilitators
- Apply appropriate levers for improvement, sustainable and ethical collaborators, charities, new internal skill sets, new external agencies & facilitators

The Organisational Structure

Having the correct proposition in place is so important because everything else within the business is then created and developed to deliver it - assortments, services, promotions, events. Organisational structures should be built around the functions required to deliver the proposition. As the proposition grows, then the organization and processes grow and evolve with it.

Traditional organisational structures which are not proposition led mean very little at best. They occur most often, almost by accident, as the result of buying & selling 'profit functions.'

Functions that drive lower costs and higher initial margin are often seen as more important than functions which add value to the product. The focus is on "What the product costs"

Similarly, functions on the selling side that control operational costs, or drive product volumes to fill stores are seen as being more important than those which add value to the shopping experience and maintain margins. The focus is on "What the customer gets."

The overall priority is "What can the product make for the business today" with little concern for the customer or indeed a majority of the work force and their opinions. That is until recently. We can no longer rely on the customer to just buy whatever we give them. We can no longer take for granted the loyalty of our colleagues and employees.

Structures and hierarchies, when they are personalized, can be even more damaging to a business. They are primarily built around known individuals, not generic roles. These structures, in effect, reflect the balance of power within a business. They highlight often the senior executives behind the initial investment, family or personal relationships, rather than merit or the benefit the individuals might bring to the ongoing and future performance of the business.

The organisational structures resulting from these scenarios are not just unbalanced in terms of structure, but also in the value, reward and the satisfaction of the workforce. An unbalanced hierarchy creates an unbalanced sentiment, with some departments and employees empowered and fulfilled, and others frustrated and demoralised.

The damage that a simple A4 organizational structure can do to a workforce should never be underestimated.

The bottom line is that retail businesses must reflect a balanced approach to profit growth, recognising that all the functions are important to achieving this goal. Balanced propositions, organisational structures, hierarchies, appreciations of worth, and rewards of effort will give the best chance of a balanced account sheet.

A balanced hierarchy leads to a single motivated workforce.

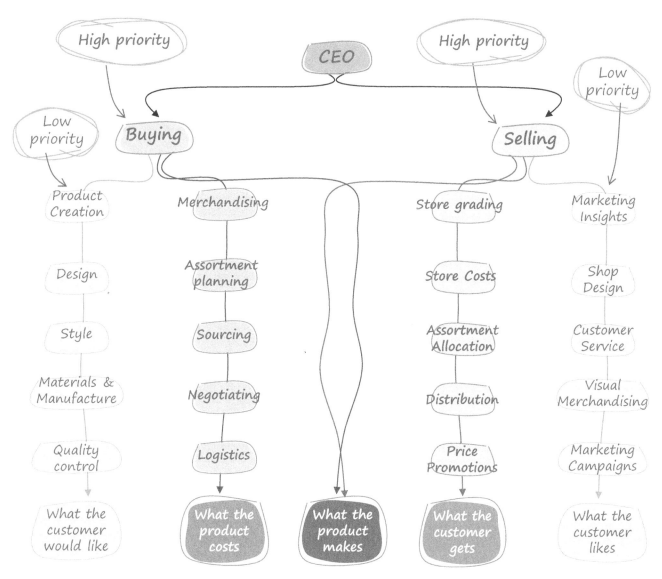

Sketch 24 The Imbalance of Traditional Organisational Structures

The Customer Focused Organisational structure

The customer focused organisational structure not only puts the customer at the heart of the business, but also the workforce. It is people focused from top to bottom. From left to right. From whichever direction you want to consider. In many ways, it is beyond hierarchies. The only dominant party is the customer.

The organisational structure illustrated in sketch 25 puts the customer at the centre of the selling process. The new wealth of customer and market data is used to guide the decision-making process throughout the business including the continual refreshment of the vision itself.

Departments are fully integrated because they are guided by the same customer intelligence inputs, and conclusions, and by the same principles and objectives.

- "Find out what the customer wants"
- "Create & deliver what the customer wants"
- "Plan and manage what the customer wants"
- "Deliver when and where the customer wants"

Those objectives bear little resemblance to those of the traditional buyer driven businesses.

If all goes according to plan, if the research is correct, and the processes efficient, the customer gets much more of what they want. Commercially a healthy profit exceeds the investment required for sustainable growth in the long term, as well as cashflow for short term initiatives and rewards.

Building those essential customer connections and relationships begins with an organisational structure with the correct customer focused functions, in terms of both research and delivery.

The customer focused organizational structure reflects the physical layout of the buildings in our hypothetical tour of the business landscape of the future. This is in fact more of a reality in today's business world, than just theory.

Many of the forward-thinking IT enterprises of Silicon Valley and beyond create a campus layout for their head offices in a similar way. Functions are logically housed in appropriate offices, which surround a central hub of intelligence. The buildings whilst undoubtedly distinct and architecturally eye catching carry no hierarchical stigma to them.

The CEO, brand director or MD will be submerged in this rich world of knowledge at the centre of the business, not gazing from afar. Large central atriums offer every conceivable place to meet and discuss, across functions, across hierarchies, sharing the same language and agendas.

It is one of retail's great ironies I think, that it has been the digital business leaders, with no foothold in the physical world of commerce, who have been the ones to stimulate the overdue physical re-landscaping of traditional retail organisations.

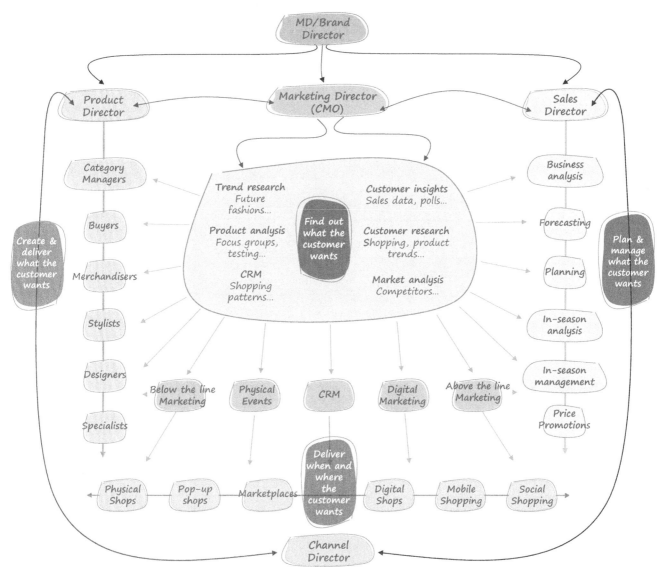

© 2021 vm-unleashed ltd.

Sketch 25 The Balance of Customer Focused Organisational Structures

Very: building work in progress

The difference between the same retailer's treatment of their retail shops and their physical head office can be remarkable. It only serves to re-enforce the segmentation within a business between those who buy and those who sell.

I have seen the extremes of both possible scenarios. Retailers with shop estates where high investment delivers an excellent customer experience, whilst head office executive are squeezed into mind-numbing open plan offices. Some of the biggest retailers.

Equally I have seen palatial head offices, whilst shop colleagues and customers suffer dirty and poorly maintained conditions.

Places where colleagues are expected to engage and empathize with their customers, whilst struggling to find enough backroom space even to stir a teabag in their corporate mug.

Head office campuses are the thing. Stimulated by silicon valley. Whilst the investment may not quite reach the levels of Google & co. head offices should at least reflect the culture of the business, the need for collaboration and integration of departments.

The Very Group is one of the leading online fashion retailers. Its head office needed to cater for the group's 2,100-strong head-office workforce when they returned after COVID lockdowns. It was not just refurbished, but re-thought, to create the optimum team working space.

Open plan and collaboration spaces are the magic combination to allow the required freedom to circulate, whilst offering private room for discussions. The group's 12,400 sq m head office Skyways House is a former aircraft hangar which certainly helps with the 'free-flowing' space side of things. It has indeed been redesigned into an open-plan environment with breakout and collaboration spaces for interactive group working.

Hot desking is another important consideration, not just to allow working across flexible teams but to facilitate the new flexible working practices and hybrid head office attendance.

Very is literally building its physical spaces around the customer, in the form of the retailer's customer care centre, called The Hub. This office is home to the 750 customer care colleagues. It features collaborative zones, hot desks, quiet pods, breakout spaces and training rooms of varying sizes and specifications. It truly is a leading-edge flexible contact centre for staff. The physical proposition built around the customer proposition.

It is essential that all new offices capture the topical necessities of the day from gender-neutral bathrooms and accessible kitchen spaces to sustainability initiatives. In the case of Very, all the existing furniture in place before the renovation has been recycled for the new fixtures and fittings.

Flexible working means that in essence a business like Very needs to consider every employee's home as part of the central offices, complete with technology hardware, infrastructure and communication tools.

In many instances it is meetings that involve both physical attendees around a table, and remote colleagues that represent the biggest problems. All meeting rooms now must be technologically enabled for such meetings ensuring that remote does not become 'out of sight, out of mind.'

The goal is to ensure that people are as productive as possible at home, and super-collaborative when they are in the office. Each experience needs to be as efficient as possible. The Very new office spaces will be about high-energy, high-impact creativity and collaboration, with a focus on improving the experience for both colleagues and customers.

Younger workforces will expect nothing less from the employers they chose to work for. For this generation, the enforced working from home has been difficult, but they will still expect to be able to choose that option as part of building a flexible lifestyle, balancing work and play.

Very hopes that by offering a better balance of work and home, increased flexibility, stimulating interaction and an amazing place to come together, that they can attract outstanding new people, and retain the ones they already have.

The Z to A of retail disruption

024

MAKE YOUR ORGIANISATIONAL STRUCTURE ANONYMOUS

Strategic soul-searching

It is so common in every size and scale of business for organizational structures to be twisted towards individuals, whether that is family or friend.

The main damage is not just to fairness and motivation, but quite often the command structures become illogical with those in command inappropriate to their role. Beware this.

Use the organizational structure to resource correctly, and as the skeleton to develop processes that link parts of it together.

Resist always the temptation to create hierarchies, and never consider people for roles, until the anonymous structure is completed

025

POPULATE YOUR ORGANISATION ON MERIT AND POTENTIAL

HR, resource and operational planning

It is the individuals and personalities that will make an organization 'buzz.' They will add energy and deliver results.

However, avoid the temptation to be seduced by personalities until the structures and team plans are drawn up and job description written.

'Pragmatism before personalities."

Actions

- List the elements of your proposition
  - Assortment, services, events...
- Define the functions of your business that are required to deliver the elements of your customer proposition.
- Define the functions required to keep the whole business operationally running.
- Define the retail intelligence functions
- Sketch the organizational structure
  - Group propositions first. Initially consider every proposition element as omnichannel.
  - Group the functions to deliver each element of the proposition. At this stage consider and separate channel requirements.
  - Group marketing inputs and marketing outputs
  - Place retail intelligence centrally accessible within the wider marketing function
- Apply (anonymous) senior roles to fit your structure
- Define 'team structure' across functions, not top to bottom
  - Create teams from the bottom up beginning with what needs to be done and delivered
  - Apply lean, precise and efficient management and senior roles
- Always consider and keep the business organisational structure, and the separate team structures apart
- Write job descriptions, candidate profiles, career paths and training programmes for every role in the business.
- Populate every role the most appropriate candidate
  - Read profiles & CVs anonymously
  - Be honest about your employees
  - Be generous to your employees
    ○ Judge potential and merit
    ○ Train and support

'Intelligent' Retail Intelligence

Retail Intelligence, in the form of research and analysis of markets, customers and competitors, has been around for a considerable time.

In pre-digital days it was a combination of extensive customer interviews, market research and sifting through sales and consumer data that gave valuable insights. As per now, these insights were used to develop the correct assortments, adjust price points, develop promotions and to evolve the customer experience and portfolio of services. And of course, to drive strategy.

The principles have not changed but the digital world has provided ever more sophisticated ways to gather data, making available an unprecedented richness of insights. The digital world is also presenting an ever-wider range of channels, platforms, and media where the new insights can be applied, to develop loyalty and drive performance.

The opportunity is to use these rich insights and immersive experiences to develop advanced customer connections. To use deep data to develop deep relationships. To use big data to turn big opportunities into realities.

To be an essential retailer, we need to develop these deep relationships. To make this possible we must place these Customer Intelligence Functions at the heart of the retail organisation.

Data opportunities have grown exponentially, but the same pitfalls remain. It is still the responsibility of those involved in the intelligence functions to find the game-changing insights within the data. It is in effect a larger task than ever.

> For every nugget of data gold identified and utilised there is a river of opportunities that flows away to the depths of the information oceans.

Finding Intelligence

It is the role of retail businesses to transform data analysts into retailers. To train them to spot the key findings, to turn those findings into palatable visualisations and to present them with context to the wider retail functions.

There has always been the temptation for analysts to produce data and insights for the sake of it. To focus on the "delivered" button.

There has also been the temptation for the directors and colleagues within buying and selling retail functions to file-away insight documents, overwhelmed with the task of deciphering and absorbing the information. To focus on the "received" button. Today, there is more risk than ever of drowning in data, whether as researchers or retailers.

The problem is the process not the possibilities. It is the responsibility of any business to make Customer Intelligence functions work for the good of everyone. It is essential that Customer Intelligence functions are not pushed to one side because they are too difficult, time-consuming or inconvenient to make data work for you.

People & Technology Together

There is a role for people and for technology in the gathering of customer intelligence at the heart of the retail business. It is important to integrate the strengths and benefits of each. Together they allow us to intelligently 'mine' our data.

De-personalisation: Consumer Mining

The most technological route is the analysis of consumer data. There is a wealth of big data here, but the risk of consumer mining is the de-personalization of the data and the remoteness of the process from the reality of day-to-day customer interactions.

There is also a potential 'vagueness' to findings in that the output is telling us 'what the general consumer groups will probably do.' This is predictive intelligence of the masses.

However, through combining elements of market analysis, customer insights, trend research, product analysis, and sales data at this level, retail intelligence can be very useful for picking trends which can be fed into high level business strategies and assortment directional work.

The word 'Consumer' itself is a depersonalization of our customers.

Personalisation: Customer Mining

Analysing personal customer data takes us a step closer to understanding our customer, rather than the consumer per se. The use of AI and algorithms now informs us in great detail 'what each customer has done, and what they might do, under the correct circumstances'.

We are discovering the customer and their behaviours on an individual level.

This level of analysis is still distanced in as much as the personal profile is developed from a series of quantitative analytics. Nonetheless these analytics are detailed and highly revealing of a retailer's interactions with each customer.

They represent the richest and most beneficial source of retail intelligence going forwards, from the perspective of customer groups and segments, as well as individual customers. This intelligence will allow us to predict behaviour, to pre-empt it, and to react to it in real time.

De-personalisation
Consumer Research

The consumer group
Traditional research channels
Trends & behaviour
Predicting behaviour

Remote
Observational

Market analysis
Competitor benchmarking...

Product analysis
Focus groups, testing...

Trend research

Customer insights
Sales data, polls...

Customer research
Shopping, product trends...

CRM
Shopping patterns...

Analysts & Consumers

What the consumer groups will probably do

Algorithms & Customers

customer purchase history

shopping journey behaviour

browsing patterns

product attribute responses

news responses

personal relationships

social media behaviour

social opinions

lifestyle activities

Personalisation
Customer Mining

The customer & the individual
Digital information gathering
Behaviour & personality
Reacting, anticipating & encouraging behaviour

Distanced
Interactive

What the customer has done and might do

Personal
Profile Making

The person
Empathy
Mood & spontaneity
Facilitating, inspiring & impacting behaviour

immediate
Intimate

advice

understanding

greetings

observations

Shop Colleagues & People

empathy

responses

conversations

suggestions

congratulations

sympathy

commiserations

What the person is doing and could do

Sketch 26 Customer Intelligence

Personal: People Profiling

A missing piece of customer intelligence is the harnessing of the shop teams, and the customer service teams across all channels and touchpoints, who engage directly with the customer.

Particularly in physical shops the engagement is immediate and intimate. Observant and empathetic colleagues can identify 'what customers actually do, and what they would do under different circumstances.' Their input can lead directly to actions for swift commercial improvements.

Such physical and direct encounters with customer behaviour can be precise and specific in making changes to the retail experience that will result in commercial improvements. Those changes could be to shop layouts, changes to fixtures, packaging and product grouping, re-allocation of service personnel, improvement to replenishment, the application of new graphics or the use of digital interfaces. To see is to know. And to know is to act!

Many retailers may wish to re-evaluate the role of their shop managers and teams in developing customer relationships and gathering intelligence. The de-personalisation of the customer to the 'role of consumer' is most of all a tragedy for the person who enters your shop, whatever you want to call them.

Uniquely, people mining can say what would have happened under different circumstances.

The Role of Shops in Customer Intelligence

One of the great tragedies over the recent decades of retail evolution has been the demise of the shop worker.

It is a tragedy for the people themselves. They have been under-valued and neglected. It is no less a tragedy for the wider retail business that their true worth has not been recognised and their potential to input and improve areas as diverse as the product assortment, to the shopping experience has not been realised.

Too many businesses have fallen into the trap of remaining in the mind-set of the age of discovery, with its virgin under-supplied markets. They have under invested in adding value, and put their faith in product stacked on shelves, shops as branded boxes, and forests of cardboard signage. They have dispensed with the experience of shop managers, the creativity of visual merchandisers, the expertise of product managers and the engagement of service specialists.

Retail executives have completely over-looked a unique and enviable resource of customer experience, knowledge, insights, and relationships. In a market where customer intelligence is more essential than ever, retailers have dispensed with the very people who know more about the customer than anyone. Who know about them in the most intimate way.

Whilst all facets of customer insights are to be embraced, customer data simply does not travel well. Its accuracy and clarity is diminished by distance. The further away from the subject, the customer, the analysis is carried out the less value it will be to everyone.

The Data Intelligence Department

Placing the customer at the centre of your business is the first step to becoming a data-centric business. However, as we know, simply having a data resource doesn't necessarily make it work for the business. The 'resource reassurance trap' is always an easy one to fall into. Having data gathering does not mean that we are automatically best practice and up-to-speed in how we use it.

The data department needs to be correctly structured, within itself and as part of the business. The common mistake with many support departments, and data is no exception, is that they pride themselves on their productivity, not so much their distribution, impact and ultimate benefit. The key is that the department needs to be both back-end and front-end focused.

It goes without saying that in the back-end there needs to be expertise and experience in all types of data collection from the consumer research to customer mining and to the involvement of retail channels in creating personal profiles. This all requires specialist expertise. However, specialists tend to know 'more and more about less and less.' They need to be managed. There expertise and output needs to be managed.

The fact is that data delivery needs to be front-end focused. We need to bring together what's on offer and what is required. A fully functioning data department needs specialists in retail functions that cross-over the divide into data collection expertise, or certainly awareness. These invaluable people can be based in the data department, or in the retail functions but their objective is to be active, dynamic and collaborative, constantly crossing the boundary between data specialism and retail specialism.

> *Don't get caught in the 'resource reassurance trap.'*

Above all this whirlwind of data activity, there must sit a Data Director, or Data Intelligence Office, depending on your business nomenclature. His role is to liaise at the highest level across the retail functions of the business.

In any forward-thinking retailer, his services and those of his team should be of the highest demand. His role is to coordinate demand and manage expectations. However, his role may initially be to build authority and awareness around his department's activities and potential benefits.

Often, to retail functions who are used to the physical thrust and energy of designing products, touching and feeling materials, journeying to distant factories, experiencing the noises and sounds of active retail environments, the thought of data sometimes feels as dry and lifeless as dust.

> *Data needs 'sexing-up' to get people to use it.*

Data needs its own marketing offensive so that it doesn't gain the same impassive and disengaged badge that so many IT departments have acquired. Rightly or not. It needs 'sexing-up.'

Data as a department, its visual identity, its physical environment, desk layouts, break-out areas, brainstorming oases, soft furnishings and brain stimulating ambient music all need to be considered to make this essential resource, seem essential.

All documents and outputs should be branded. And these should not just include the continuous updates and bespoke reports, but also podcasts, information quizzes, interactive exercises and engaging tools to firmly set it as an attractive, engaged ally in the modern retail business.

Product Director

Buying & Merchandising
Product design & styling,
category management,
assortment structuring,
sourcing & merchandising

Sales Director

Sales & Distribution
Supply, demand, channel
allocation, in-season
management,
replenishment

CMO

Marketing
CRM, personalisation,
above and below the
line marketing,
events & promotions

Data Intelligence
Front-end
Demand

Data Intelligence
Sales Specialist

Data Intelligence
Product Specialist

Data Intelligence
Marketing Specialist

Coordination
of source material
into demand-led
reports

DIO
Data Intelligence Officer

Head of
Consumer Research

Head of
Personal Profiling

Head of
Customer Mining

Data Intelligence
Back-end
Collection

Consumer Data Mining
• Market analysis competitors
• Trend research
• Product analysis,
focus groups, testing
• Customer research,
shopping, product trends
• Customer insights,
sales data, polls

Customer Data Mining
• Customer purchase histories,
browsing patterns
• Shopping journey behaviour
• Product attribute responses
• Lifestyle activities,
social behaviour
• Personal relationships,
social opinions

Personal Profiling
• Behavioural observations
• Social stimulations
• Product interactions
• Mood management
• Empathy responses

Sketch 27 The Data Intelligence Department Coordinating front-end demand with back-end collection

Burberry: data learning academy

Data skills have never been more critical to the future of retail.

Machine learning and advanced analytics have the potential to make the way we do business exponentially faster, stronger and better. Burberry is one brand that appreciates the importance of this and are putting in place initiatives to ensure it will be a best practice leader.

They are building data skills in-house and sending out a powerful message about their commitment to future ways of working. They are enhancing their business opportunities whilst making themselves an attractive proposition for the best potential data analysts in the industry and beyond.

Investing in data technology is one thing, however investing in the people to be able to work with it and apply it to retail situations is quite another.

Burberry is one the more advanced retail brands working with its young employee teams, training them in retail data capabilities and preparing them for a retail world where it will become an essential skill.

It has just announced that the first batch of employees have graduated from its in-house Data Academy. The two-year programme teaches cutting-edge data science techniques such as machine learning, data visualisation and coding whilst the students are still employed in their day jobs with Burberry.

The Data Academy is an innovative way of developing teams with business-critical data skills. For Burberry, running the programme has demonstrated the value that a data-driven approach brings across the IT department. Teams can now apply their expertise to key areas like data security and master data management.

WalMart & Tik Tok: data relationships

Walmart has always been about numbers, now it is about data. It has been the unassailable titan of traditional mass market retailing for many years famously generating turnovers more than the total GDP of some of the world's nations combined.

Today it is just as much a compelling force. But not just through selling mountains of merchandise, but by embracing the sophistications of the e-commerce revolution. It has exchanged blows with pureplay giants such as Amazon and is now battling against some of the mightiest digital businesses such as Oracle.

From retail warehouses, through digital marketplaces, to the world of subscription services, entertainment, content ownership and advertising, the retailer has prioritized customer data, insights and personalization as its assets and product streams for the new age. This has required a remarkable and agile transformation in its organizational structure, processes and functions, and its attitude to collaboration. The beast that once steamrollered everyone is now a smart accomplice for tech and data rich enterprises.

The strategic shift is summed up in its interest in Tik Tok. As I write this, Walmart is reported to be hoping to snap up the video-sharing social media network in a deal worth as much as $30bn. It is the ambition to do so, as much as the outcome of the current negotiations, that signals the strategic shift. Tik Tok's active user base in the US alone, is approaching 100 million per month in 2021. This opens-up new customer relationship opportunities and potential advertising revenue streams for Walmart, on top of its current retail and services.

Retailers such as Walmart like to be where the customer is. Whilst that still means retail parks, it is now also about being in the virtual world, taking it to customers, and collaborating with new entertainment enterprises such as Tik Tok.

The Z to A of retail disruption

Zalando: fashion & technology innovation

In an act of commercial flattery, Zalando was initially launched in 2008 to emulate the Amazon owned Zappos in the world of online footwear retailing. Now the mega European e-commerce company, based in Berlin, offers fashion and lifestyle products to customers in 17 European markets.

Zalando sees itself as both a fashion and a technology business and invests heavily in its technology infrastructure. The strategy is to make itself as essential and invaluable to the myriad of brands that sell on its platform, as it does a direct retailer to customers. As a third-party marketplace it has structured its organization and its resources around leading solutions across logistics, artificial intelligence and data analytics & personalization. This is the core of the proposition that it presents to brands

Zalando has three technology hubs in Germany and another three across Dublin, Lisbon and Helsinki. These labs work on ensuring the day-to-day reality of shopping with Zalando keeps pace with the retailer's ambitions to be the most advanced option for brands, ahead of competitors in the market.

The different labs focus on a variety of key specialisms of the data world. Apparently, in Ireland, R&D staff focus on deep data and engineering and are working on building real-time analytics around its fashion offering. In Portugal, employees are focused on developing the Fashion Store app, while in Finland the focus is on the personalization of the customer interfaces.

Zalando also runs a research-focused lab in Berlin, which brings together the worlds of customer analysis with new technologies and analytical processes. Scientists project how certain technologies will be used in the future and work towards making it a reality at the business.

Zalando identifies that the Berlin lab's work is currently centred around artificial intelligence. Researchers there are focused on machine learning 'natural language processing,' apparently a branch of AI through which computers can learn to understand and talk like people. And 'deep learning' – the next step of machine learning, which allows computers to act like a human brain and to analyse data as a human mind would.

These dual aims to have computers think like humans and then to communicate like humans potentially opens-up a new world of not just analysis, but meaningful analysis of customers, potentially at an individual level, and then the ability to communicate with those customers in the most relevant and personal way.

'Saying the right things, in the right way.'

Not surprisingly, Zalando reports that researchers are currently working on an AI-powered fashion adviser, which would act like a stylist by understanding product and trends and recommending them to the consumer.

It portends some interesting opportunities of course, but also some brand conundrums. The potential is there to speak in a human way, but what should that human way be? Should Zalando speak with one single voice to everyone, 'the voice of Zalando' or adopt a variety of voices and 'tones of voice' to speak to many customers in different ways? Advanced technology leads us back to a very human question.

Alongside Zalando Research, the business also runs an annual tech-focused Hack Week across the whole organisation and a quarterly 'Slingshot', where staff are asked to suggest ideas to transform the customer experience that can then be 'slingshotted' into existence through being awarded funding.

Both initiatives involve employees stepping away from their 'silos' to initiate ideas for the whole business. It would seem, Zalando is successfully harmonising people and technology.

I am indebted to Retail Week for an excellent insight into Zalando. Well worth a read – "Inside retail's global giants: Zalando" October 2018.

The Z to A of retail disruption

026

BECOME A DATA-CENTRIC ORGANISATION

Strategic planning

In action plan 007 Develop Data Capability, we talked about the 3 essentials considerations of data

- Define the data you want
  - Define how to extract that customer data?
  - Choose your partners, teams & skill-sets
- Define what you want to achieve with your customer data
  - Define the processes, technologies you require
  - Define the skills you require to process and analyse
- Define how to deliver the data output.
  - Create precise channels of data distribution

These ambitions cannot be left to stagnate in some peripheral office in a rarely visited part of the office or hidden within IT or marketing. It is now time to integrate that capability into your organizational structures and processes. To make yourselves Data-Centric & Digital-First.

There is a whole industry of IT and data implementers whose services you can call upon, however before you dive head-first into years of financial and logistical commitments you must clearly define what your objectives are.

Actions

- Ensure the CEO is a 'dataphile'
  - Evangelise data
  - Finance the data department
  - Re-name it: "Data intelligence' or 'Retail Intelligence'
- Appoint data to the board
  - DIO (Data Intelligence officer) or RIO (Retail Intelligence officer) at the highest table
  - IT director to answer to DIO/RIO amongst others
- Re-brand the department:
  - Make the dept look new and innovative
  - Locate the dept centrally within the building
  - Refurbish and 'technify' the area
  - Re-brand all documents/materials
- Create an appropriate DI team structure
  - Simple hierarchy to liaise horizontally with functional peers
  - DI specialists dedicated to functions
    - Product design
    - Assortment planning
    - CRM
    - Supply chain
    - Customer personalization
    - Marketing
  - Cross-functional collaboration & team fluidity
- Make DI experts into retailers (away from "techies")
  - Retail training programmes
- Make DI accessible
  - 'Quick-response' helpline
  - Ensure DI always present at key strategy & functional meetings
  - Weekly DI podcast
- Control distribution
  - Universally available 'highlight material'
  - Dedicated, bespoke and coordinated DI projects

A Revolution of Retail Processes

Organisational structures are static. They serve no purpose in our everyday retail lives.

What organizational structures do, is to spawn the processes that bring the retailer to life. They allocate roles and responsibilities, and they define, control, facilitate or obstruct the relationships and collaborations within the business.

> Traditional hierarchical structures & processes were built for a retail business to work efficiently in one specific way. That way is linear.

The overriding objective of the traditional hierarchical retail business is to develop, buy and deliver products into the shop to sell. In the Age of Discovery, supply struggled to keep up with demand. Money was wasting, competitors were benefitting, as long as product was not in the shop, so the linear process was built to get as much product into the shops as quickly as possible.

The intricacies of product design were not required to sell, so lateral collaboration was not a priority, particularly if it slowed down or interrupted the linear flow and dynamic. Departments such as buying, sourcing and logistics grew strong and powerful pumping the blood of new product through the business.

Today successful mass-market value brands still find success in this model. Price allows their assortment to be relatively unchanged, with less need for product designers, whilst economies of scale are built around a powerful buying team.

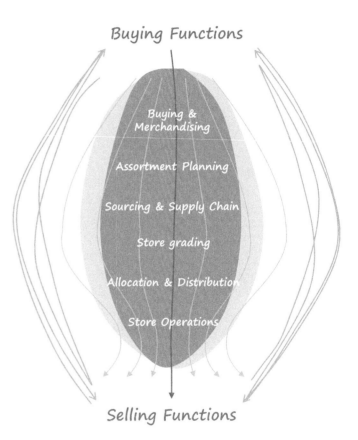

© 2021 vm-unleashed ltd.

Sketch 28 The Linear process flow

From linear processes to lateral processes...

Now in the Age of Disruption, in our saturated markets, the linear pumping of products from the factory to the customer is simply no longer enough for most retailers. For those still focused on linear processes, or with a structure so rigid that they cannot change, the output progressively becomes more unprofitable, the linear process becomes less viable, and at some point in time, it shuts down.

Lateral processes

The customer requires products with added-value. They require added-value in every touchpoint with the retailer, from the product and its availability, to the shopping experience and additional customer services. Adding value requires consideration. It requires thinking and working laterally at strategic parts of the linear delivery process.

Added-value comes from working with data intelligence. Data on the customer, about competitors, about market trends and about sales patterns and a myriad of other considerations. The key to enabling and facilitating the lateral added-value processes is the organizational structure with data intelligence at the centre. Where data intelligence is the customer focus.

Lateral processes must begin with the customer and data. They must end with the customer and data.

For those traditional businesses that can make the change to working laterally, then there is still a way to profit, alongside the new retail businesses with their nimble, laterally integrated processes, for whom linear buying processes were never a priority consideration.

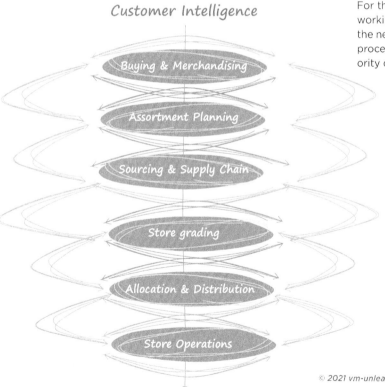

Customer Intelligence

- Buying & Merchandising
- Assortment Planning
- Sourcing & Supply Chain
- Store grading
- Allocation & Distribution
- Store Operations

Product Intelligence

© 2021 vm-unleashed ltd.

Sketch 29 Lateral added-value processes

To continuous, circular processes

The evolution of the volume linear process, with the addition of lateral added-value processes, can morph into the ultimate value circular process.

What this means is that the whole linear process is considered without a beginning or an end. The retailer of course begins by developing products, producing them and then distributing them to customers. But now every function in the business is centered on creating a continuous loop that feeds into next cycle of events.

That cycle can be built around the calendar year, where seasonality is the driver for product change. This is the traditional norm, but there is no reason why the whole circle cannot be built around the most logical dynamic of your business, and of your customers.

In businesses with high frequency customer purchases, anything from fast fashion to fast food then everything from menus and recipes, to colours and lengths of dresses can be built on a monthly, a weekly, daily or even hourly cycle. For products such as kitchens or cars, then the 'linear cycle' will be longer.

One thing is for sure, the most significant increase in dynamics, is the dynamic of change itself. All circular processes whatever their speed, have 'sped-up' in recent times. They are keeping pace with customer demand and lifestyles.

The cycle is built around the buying and selling process as always. But it is built around a continuous one. Lateral processes feed into every stage of the process, always beginning and ending with the customer.

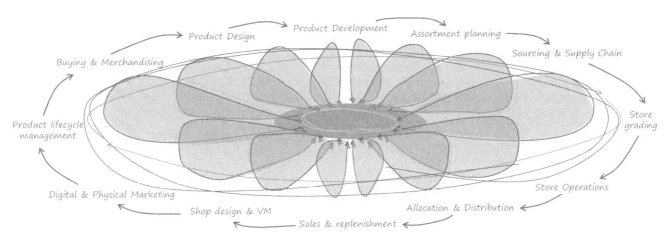

© 2021 vm-unleashed ltd.

Sketch 30 The circular retail process

Zara: moving from linear to lateral processes

Zara disrupted the balance of linear and lateral processes in its buying and merchandising and supply chain operations. It was a synchronized strategy. It had to be, because linear processes and lateral processes must work together, whatever the balance, the priorities or timings.

The decision to enrich the lateral input into the product development process, through analysing competitors, devouring fashion cat-walk shows, listening intently to shop colleagues and analysing customer buying behaviours, could only add value to the business if it were matched by a much simplified and faster linear process. Spending time and effort to design the correct product for the customer would have been pointless if that product could not be brought to market quickly. And the next wave, and the next and so on.

It is a balance that has made it so difficult for competitors to copy and match the Zara strategy.

In many ways adding lateral processes is not so difficult. There is a wealth of analysis for those who want to exploit it. Lateral intelligence can be added. But it cannot simply be bolted on to the existing linear process. Some competitors flatter themselves with their newfound ability to research and create their assortments in new and dynamic ways but are operational stunted and held back from fundamental improvements by a linear buying and supply process that is still long and complicated.

The linear processes can often be a 'waste of time, and an added and frustrating distraction. Ironically, they can add to the total buying and merchandising timeframe.

Zara's strategy was not to shorten linear operations and increase lateral inputs. It was to deliver the best possible products quickly and continuously. A shorter linear process and enriched lateral processes were the only way to achieve this.

Primark: buying power & buying time

I make no apologies for featuring Primark again. There are several retailers that I feature more than once. The explanation of course is that they are very good at different things. Better to have best practice focus than a diversity of mediocrity.

Primark is of course highly successful. It sells volumes of clothing at low prices. 'Love them or hate them' it is a model which works well for them, and which makes millions of customers very happy. It has a very powerful buying team and many long-standing relationships with trusted suppliers.

As with all best practice retailers it has come to understand its customer very well. Primark has always invested, not just in adding value to product and retail environments but also in understanding customers. It analyses sales, reviews products and takes counsel from its shop managers and in particular its highly influential 'section managers.' In Primark it is the 'section managers' that are largely responsible for making buying decisions for their own store assortment.

Primark's assortment is focused on what their customer wants. The business knows that the customers wants seasonal change and a coating of seasonal colours and adornments but that they also fundamentally like the familiar shapes, styles, silhouettes. Lateral added-value is always added but generally through intelligent, strategic and often subtle updates. The design team is relatively small, the buying team is relatively large.

The retailer has powerful buying functions and the linear process of pushing product to shops is strategically vital, but even though product changes are not dramatic each season they are always developed to make best-sellers, as relevant and attractive as ever. A strong traditional buying process that is nonetheless a circular process for today's world.

The Z to A of retail disruption

Eleni's New York: crazy cookie circularity

When I was in New York a few years ago I came across some wonderful food businesses that took my breath way. They were small business, with small shops in Soho and Chelsea Market.

Eleni's cookies absolutely epitomizes the continuous invention and selling opportunities that lateral processes represent.

The base product, cookies, are largely continuous, delicious but the same. However, the dynamic of choices is astounding. There are the favourites of course, but then flavours and designs of the days, the week and the month, flavours and designs to mark seasonal events, celebrations, and to reflect what is happening in the news, the music charts or the world of sport. The temptation is spectacularly vibrant and imaginative.

This model in many ways could not be further from Primark. But they don't need to be, should not be, the same. For sure the basic ingredients of the cookies or the cakes need to produced in appropriate volumes. The process is linear. But the adding of value in the product development, recipe and adornment phases is as lateral as it comes. The research into themes, designs, flavours, decoration, branding and marketing are continuously alive, adding value at key points of the linear process. And of course, the dynamics of the lateral and simplicity of the linear processes are perfectly made for product customization, for which the brand is rightly famous.

Because its customers are frequent visitors the circular process from inspiration, concept, design, development and delivery must be short. In these small and agile businesses, the organizational structures are appropriately light, balanced and customer centric.

No doubt they also use a variety of data inputs, from the physical shop colleagues personally profiling daily customer interactions, to digital customer data mining of its sizeable digital businesses. All happening whilst the satisfied customer remains blissfully oblivious.

Linear & lateral responses to change

The need to change retail processes has become very evident during the COVID lockdowns and the shift to working from home. This trend seems set to continue even after the option of returning to commuting becomes a reality once more.

The customers' commuting behaviour will dictate massive changes to retail processes. Retailers will need to adapt their hourly, daily, and longer planning timeframes.

If you are a commuter business supplying morning and evening 'rush-hours' then the repercussions are initially existential. Commuter businesses that will survive and flourish will need to adapt to variable daily commuting times and potentially very busy Mondays and quieter Fridays and so on.

At the other end of the commuter journey, workers who are now at home during the day represent the opportunity for process changes across a variety of businesses. Home delivery, for grocery, fast food, cafes & restaurants can revert to a more balanced daily cycle rather than evenings and weekends. Retail businesses need to re-appraise all their process timings.

Nor will changing customers patterns be just about frequency and timings, but also the products appropriate to new lifestyles. Linear processes across these businesses will need to be as efficient as possible, even more so than now, whilst lateral intelligence must be enriched to identify new customer types or buying patterns and product preferences.

The demographic profile for many businesses may well be shifting from an anonymous sea of faces where linear efficiency is king, to a more regular and diverse customer base where lateral intelligence and agility are the keys to success. Improved lateral accuracy will allow retailers, cafes and restaurants to predict with more certainty, and respond with more efficiency, always learning for the next time.

The Z to A of retail disruption

027

FIND YOUR COMMERCIAL BALANCE OF LINEAR AND LATERAL PROCESSES

Customer research:
Strategic and operational changes

Your business makes money by doing something that the customer likes. They buy things. That may have been strategic, or it may have been accidental, but at least you were smart enough to respond.

What your customer wants is somewhere on the spectrum of volume to added-value. It will undoubtedly be a combination of the both. You need to have the correct processes to deliver what your customer wants. The correct balance of linear processes to push volume and lateral processes to add-value.

Do you have that correct for now? Are you missing opportunities every day? Are your market, your customer and your competitors changing the balance of volume and added-value? You need to know.

Consider what processes you should have. Build those processes. And find out if you need to change your organizational structure so you can make these processes happen.

Actions

- Define your volume linear needs
  - Analyse data intelligence
  - Define what volumes your customer requires
  - Consider if you waste money from over supply, or lose sales from under-supply
  - Identify predictable supply variance and unpredictable variance
- Make the appropriate changes to your supply chain
  - Build reliability as a priority, productivity as a given
  - Build flexibility if required
- Define the added-value of your product, and the potential additional added-value you could add for your customers
  - Analyse data intelligence. Ensure you ask your customers, and you ask your non-customers.
  - Define what elements will add-value and demand
- Develop an action plan to introduce processes for new added-value features & attributes
  - New internal processes
  - Adapting existing internal processes
  - New skills, training, resources
  - New collaborators and partners
  - Build customer focus into processes
  - Build data Intelligence requirements
  - Make appropriate organizational changes
- Develop similar process action plans for non-product initiatives to add value
  - Shopping experience, services, packaging.
  - Marketing, customer communication & personalization
  - Supply chain & availability
- Develop an exit plan from current processes adding little or no added-value

028

SYNCHRONISE YOUR PROCESS FREQUENCY AND TIMINGS WITH YOUR CUSTOMER

Customer research: Strategic and operational changes

Most things in the world are organised annually. From the beauty of the seasons to the beauty of your tax bill.

We have become conditioned. We conform.

What you produce and sell as a retailer may be suited to a circular process that is not annual. What will define this is your customer purchasing patterns. Their perpetually changing purchasing patterns.

You must align your processes to your customer purchasing. You need to be in harmony and synchronicity with your customer.

Actions

- Understand the buying behaviours, patterns and cycles of your customers
  - Analyse data intelligence, market research
  - Benchmark competitors
  - Consider the whole of the buying process from initial research and browsing through the selection and payment
  - Consider usage behaviour and patterns after purchase
- Define the most appropriate process durations and timings
  - Product development
  - Marketing & communication
  - Sales and selling
  - Creating & refreshing selling environments
  - After-sales services
  - Lifetime services
- Develop an action plan to change the duration and timing of internal processes
  - Adapt existing internal processes
  - Adapt and renegotiate colleagues' hours, periods of working
  - Integrate internal process with potential new timeframes
  - Integrate with partners and collaborators

Lateral Process Loops

The development of lateral process loops ensures that the inputs and outputs of processes are well-informed, correct and coordinated. We need to develop the 'intelligence input curve' and the 'retail input curve.'

The 'Intelligence Input curve'

The first stage of the loop is to input all available and appropriate data intelligence into the process to ensure that the project team is fully aware of all the relevant issues and considerations that will help them to deliver the best possible output. Inputs could range from customer data mining to product trend research, from competitor benchmarking to sales analysis, focus groups to customer profiling. This will all depend on the output of the process loop.

The 'Retail Input curve'

The second stage is the development of the retail deliverable, with the relevant team absorbing the intelligence and interpreting it into their output. The final delivery should be as close as possible to the intelligence brief.

Process loops can cover large scale projects, such as the development of a new product assortment, or a flagship shop, or a 'shop of the future' initiative. But they can also include micro-developments such as a specific 'screw' for a table, or a lighting system for a shop, or the sourcing and development of a sustainable piece of cotton beading.

Process loops can exist within each other. This ensures that the same data intelligence is available for the largest and smallest deliverables within the same project. It also ensures that the development and delivery processes are coordinated for the planned completion date.

It is always worth remembering that the largest 'showcase' deliverables, from assortments to shop designs, are the result of many smaller integrated deliverables.

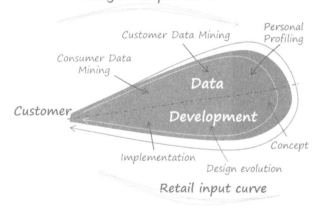

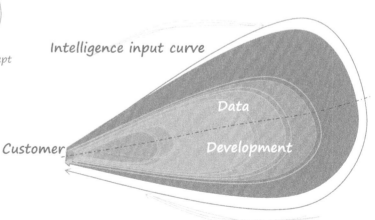

Sketch 31 Generic process loops & enclosed process loops

The "Product Design" process Loop

Focus groups
Product analysis
Competitor benchmarking
Product Trend research
Sales data
Market analysis
Data
Development
Product sub-category
Product silhouette
Product styling
Customer
Product enhancements
Product materials
Product attributes

The "Shop Grading" process Loop

Customer analysis
Customer profiles
Market shopping trends
Location sales trends
Actual sales data
Location demographic trends
Data
Segmentation model
Development
Shop grading
Customer
Shop closures/ openings
Shop clustering
Clustering model
Shop investment refresh/re-develop

The "Shop Event" process Loop

Competitor analysis
Event product sales
Upcoming calendar events
Seasonal buying trends
Customer promotional mechanic take-up
Events sales trends
Data
Marketing calendar
Development
Event product recommendations
Customer
Promotional mechanics
Shop/service costs delivery
Channel & shop allocation
Event theme/design

© 2021 vm-unleashed ltd.

Sketch 32 Process loop examples

Process loops can take any shape or form. They can cover whole departments or be limited to a detail on a single product.

Data Intelligence inputs will vary considerably depending on what the deliverables are. Part of the process is deciding what the intelligence inputs should be.

What is required to refine next seasons ladies' trousers will be very different to the data required to carry out a shop grading strategy, or an events calendar for shops.

It is the role of the data intelligence department working with function leaders and project leaders to define the precise research and data intelligence required.

The Role of Support Functions. 'To Enable not Disable.'

Retailers, as with businesses in any industry, need support functions to operate efficiently.

The IT department is today's most important ally, ensuring everyday operations and new initiatives progress smoothly. It is followed, not far behind, by HR. Technology and people form the foundations for any good retail business, physical or digital. Other key collaborators may include Finance, Legal, Property, Sustainability, Ethics, PR, Heath & Safety and so on.

It is yet another tragedy of retail businesses, when the hard work of creating modern organisational structures and fluid process loops come to nothing, due to the support functions inability to work with the same enlightened principles and mentality. It happens. We all know that. We have all seen it.

As the retail functions of a business grow, the support functions must grow, adapt, or shrink, depending on their relevance to the evolving business, and the requirements of the various retail functions. These may require more IT support, or different IT support, less people or different people, legal experts in physical shop regulations or legal experts in digital copyright laws. They are quite different specialisms.

You would not ask a knitwear buyer to design a shoe, or a social media copywriter to build an event stand. It is prudent to ensure the same logic is applied to your support teams.

It is natural for a retail business to focus on the development and process of its core retail functions. However, the inappropriate development of the support functions can have as serious an effect on the processes of retail as if no development had happened at all.

Under-resourcing can squeeze the organisation as the functions attempt to bridge the communication and efficiency gaps as they collaborate. The whole process resorts to a linear model as cross-collaboration becomes impossible.

Inappropriate resourcing creates bottlenecks as high-demand resources struggle to satisfy the needs across the business. Everyday processes and new initiatives stall where the resources cannot reach. Ultimately the organisational structure distorts, and processes have to be diverted simply to allow any collaboration at all.

Over-resourcing is expensive, and also inefficient. Legacy resources particularly, attempt to justify their existence by adding unrequired complexity and bureaucracy to everyday processes, whilst drowning new initiatives in preparation and contingency. The whole organisation becomes bloated with retail functions pushed apart by the burden of collaboration. Process flows take the longest possible routes, the unofficial routes, to avoid the logical but impenetrable direct lines through support functions.

The perfectly resourced retailer has grown its support resources in-line with its retail function requirements. Everyday activities are supported efficiently, whilst new initiatives are welcomed with a flexible mind-set and approach. The support resources support and strengthen the principles of the organisational structure and facilitate collaboration through the most direct and desirable route.

The retail business is a living organism. The support functions support the skeleton and allow the vital organs to connect, to create a healthy environment for everyone. It never fails to astound me how support functions often remain stubborn and intransigent, as retail functions struggle to operate, even to the point of causing serious commercial harm and hardship. Everyone, including support functions, are in this together.

The under-supported retailer

- Lack of support resources
  - Inability to support retail functions
- Inefficient everyday support
- Slowing down new initiatives

Squeezing the organisational structure
Stopping the process flow

The inappropriately-supported retailer

- Lack of correct support resources
  - Inability to support all retail functions
- Inconsistent everyday support
  - Stalling new initiatives

Distorting the organisational structure
Diverting the process flow

Buying & Merchandising
Product Design
Product Development
Assortment planning
Sourcing & Supply Chain
Allocation & Distribution
Retail Operations
Shop design & VM
Digital & Physical Marketing
Business Analysis

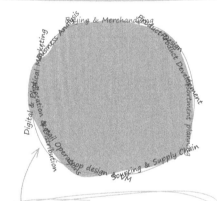

The over-supported retailer

- Inefficient amount of resources
- Inflexibility to support retail functions
  - Ponderous everyday support
- Drowning new initiatives in red-tape

Bursting the organisational structure
Stretching the process flow

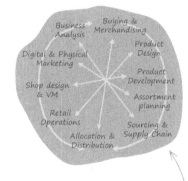

The perfectly-supported retailer

- Correct balance of support resources
- Flexibility to support all retail functions
  - Efficient everyday support
  - Flexing to support new initiatives

Supporting the organisational structure
Facilitating the process flow

Sketch 33 The Role of Support Functions

029

RESOURCE YOUR PROCESSES CORRECTLY

Internal analysis: team feedback

Continuous processes and unique project processes both need to have the correct data intelligence inputs. And it goes without saying that each process needs the correct retail resources to deliver the output.

It is just good practice to review continuous processes on a regular basis to ensure that both data intelligence and retail resources are appropriate

Actions

- Review existing continuous processes
  - Assess quality of outputs and opportunities to improve
  - Speak to team members. Ask customers.
  - Define problem areas
  - Identify need and impact of additional data intelligence or retail resources
  - Agree how often to review process resourcing
  - Assess the need for process management
- Make changes to data intelligence inputs and retail resources as required
- Set up new processes always with due diligence on the correct data intelligence and retail resource requirements

030

INVEST IN PROCESS MANAGERS

Internal analysis: HR & operational initiatives

Believe me, I'm the last person to openly encourage more management. I have seen businesses grind to a halt with over management. However, I have also seen chaos, widespread chaos, caused by team members and managers trying to do their work and manage processes at the same time.

The problem is usually time. In under resourced departments there is not often the time to do your regular job, without worrying about organizing additional projects. What happens is nothing changes. The time for disruptive change, even for the better, is not available so more of the same happens.

Actions

- Review existing continuous processes
  - Define where managing the process is the problem with the process.
- Assign an appropriate manager for the process.
- Assess the need for dedicated process managers within individual functions or departments, or cross-functional.
  - Train dedicated functional process managers in the detail and knowledge concerning their department
  - Train cross-functional process managers with a wide-ranging intelligence programme.
  - Support project process managers with their own input of data intelligence

The Digital-first Retailer

What does digital-first, or being digitally led, actually mean? They are the buzzwords of the moment, the latest in a lengthening line of technology originated expressions that have in turn become essential to retail. The days of the dot.com bubble, the advent of e-commerce seem distant now, almost vintage expressions in this ever-accelerating world. But necessary for retail evolution and development, nonetheless.

It is the supercharged increase in digital retail sales that has prompted a spiraling interest in new ways to organise businesses and their processes. It is the key for every retailer now, irrespective of their relative sales from digital and physical channels, to think, breath and live like the best of pureplay. To put digital considerations of every kind at the forefront of their strategies and operations. To be digitally-led. To be digital-first.

The general conclusion in today's markets, in today's Age of Disruption, is that the new principles and processes introduced by pureplay digital retailers are now the best ones for every retailer. Because being digital-first is more than just being a digital retailer. Pureplay processes are for everyone.

Digital-first is about coordinating human creativity with data technology. It is about creating deep customer relationships, the ultimate customer connections, and about planning and managing the supply and distribution process in rapid time, with lightening reactions and responses.

It is about replacing the hierarchical structure, with a customer centric structure, creating data intelligence departments and DIOs, transforming linear buying processes into lateral added-value processes, replacing linear work-flows with process loops and developing a mentality for perpetual activity and change.

If you have already being doing these things then you are either strategically, or inadvertently digital-first. For everyone else, what are the attributes and benefits of this new-thinking?

Precision data

Data should be behind every decision across the business. You need to be obsessive about understanding everything. You need to be obsessive about the customer.

The key word is precision. The combination of consumer research, customer mining and personal profiling is at the heart of this precise understanding of the customer.

> *Our actions can be precise and decisive, if intelligence is clear and focused.*

Customer Intimacy

It is no surprise that Pureplays are the new best practice model. Their obsession with the customer allows them to anticipate and respond to behaviour and buying patterns.

This allows them to create the deepest and most profitable connections with customers. They are intimate in their knowledge. They can communicate on a personal level and sell to them in a completely symbiotic way.

Traditional retailers need to think and operate in the same way. They need it for their new digital channels, but they need it also to coordinate customer connections across all channels.

This is the big win. To be intimate with the customer, period. Channel management is a secondary fluid development, but the common intimacy is what will make all touchpoints consistent and seamless for the customer.

Be brave. But learn quickly

Data will give us the insights but not necessarily the clearest and best action plan to pursue. This is nothing new.

I was fortunate enough to meet a very wise many on one of my visits to India. His name is Arunachalam Muruganantham and he has become famous as the man who saved millions of women's lives in his native country by developing a sanitary towel steriliser for villages and communities. He was successful through the support and backing of some of the world's largest philanthropists. There has even been the making of a Bollywood film based on his story, 'Pad Man.'

He said to me that the largest department in any successful business is the T&E department. Do you know what it is? After a suitably pregnant pause he explained. He said I would better recognize this department as R&D, research and development. But to the everyday eye, it was T&E, the 'trial & error' department. The simplicity of this observation is true. And even in the data-led Pureplay enterprises we still need plenty of T&E initiatives.

Pureplays are brave, but they are not stupid, because risk is countenanced by high-speed trials and quick responses

Digital-first businesses take actions with precise data. This minimises risk. They monitor the result of actions with more analysis and assessments. There is no such thing as a wrong action, just ones that sometimes don't work. Every action is a learning, and every action is primarily without risk if the repercussions are tempered by correct and rapid reactions.

Digital-led businesses operate processes that allow speed. They are not hampered by archaic organizational structures, or primeval protocols. To maximise opportunities and restrict the impact of mistakes they act quickly.

Reboot the mind-set

We talk about replacing hierarchical organizational structures and linear processes. This is important as it physically removes many barriers to working in more fluid and intuitive ways. What it also does is to change the mind-set of those in the system.

A digital-first mindset is ultimately the prerequisite for significant changes to a retail business. That change in mind-set cannot happen within the confines of a traditional hierarchy and with linear volume processes.

There is an element of 'chicken and egg' here. Someone with a different retailer mind-set must make the changes to the organization, that then allows the wider employee bases to think in new ways. This is the power and the importance of entrepreneurship within a business. It is the beauty of new retail businesses grown from passion and an inherent desire to add customer value to whatever they do.

Common objectives

Traditional business silos, and departmental agendas naturally create different objectives within businesses. When the structure is hierarchical with a small power base, then many unhealthy personal and team agendas fight for favour at the top table.

Rivalries abound and individual and isolated performance can take precedence over the wider business community objectives.

This continues to be an issue when digital retail is clumsily bolted onto the side of physical retailers. Omni-channel requires the integration of processes and operations. However, what it requires also are fair and common rewards and acknowledgements of value and worth.

A common point of contention that creates division within a business is the allocation of 'sales' and 'returns' across channels. Whilst click&collect and shop returns for online sales are essential for omnichannel, they can distort sales performance data without rewarding time and effort. Click&collect adds to online sales, whilst shops take time to find deliveries and serve the customer. Shop returns are sometimes attributed to shop unsold inventory and effect sales performance data, whilst online still registers a sale. As KPIs for colleagues usually include these KPIs an unfair playing field can easily develop. These areas must be dealt with. Fairness must rule. A common objective must be restored.

We come back to the balanced organizational structure with the customer at the centre. In this scenario the customer patronage and activities and the KPIs attached to this obsession are the only meaningful measurements.

> *Retail community KPIs are most important, as they are influenced and stimulated by everyone, with rewards for everyone.*

Of course, different departments and operations have their own performance KPIs. On the distribution side, units picked per labour hour and deliveries per van per week, will be priorities, whilst the size of the active customer base and conversion rate, will be the objectives of the marketing team.

But overall, the retailer objectives should be simple, they will be customer focused, before sales focused. They will be efficiency focused before profit focused.

> *Big KPIs are built from many small KPIs.*

It is essential that we are all rewarded for our individual KPI achievements, but also for community success in the big KPIs, and all genuinely and graciously acknowledged as being partly responsible for those KPIs.

The return of cooperation

There is still much to be applauded in businesses such as the John Lewis Partnership and the Co-op. They instill a community reliance where everyone knows that they all suffer and benefit together. They are a partnership and a cooperative of people.

And this really is at the heart of a digital-first business and its commercial success potential.

> *Ironically digital-first success is built on human partnerships.*

This really takes a little time to sink in. Of course, successful digital businesses benefit from the intensity and accuracy of data, and the speed of processes and communications, but they benefit most from the re-invention of the employee community.

This community has singular aims, and collaborative objectives. It has mutual respect and common rewards. It has many roles but one mind-set. It is the future of intelligence which leans heavily on the experience of old-fashioned respect.

Yoox: artificial intelligence in real assortments

Being 'precise with data' and 'gaining intimate customer insights' are key parts of being a digital-first retailer. We are rapidly moving to whole new levels of accuracy and commercial benefit. Initiatives fueled most often by the development and application of artificial intelligence, AI.

AI is also being used to inspire and influence assortments so close to the point of production that the linear process is almost blending into bespoke operations, inspired by the unprecedented richness of the AI lateral inputs.

YOOX is an Italian online fashion retailer created in 2015 that is a pioneer of such processes. Interestingly and appropriately, the name YOOX is composed of the male (Y) and female (X) chromosome letters linked by OO, the infinity symbol or "the 'zero' from the binary code, the fundamental language of the digital age".

Many thanks to the Yoox website for explaining that one.

YOOX uses advanced algorithmic tools, that allow the design team to review and analyse real-time, image-led content from across social media and online magazines in key markets, with a special focus on fashion influencers. The brand then combines this insight with internal data on product sales, customer feedback, purchasing trends and text searches to create what it refers to as "dynamic mood boards" to support the creative process of the internal product team and allow it to respond rapidly to customer trends.

Collections developed in this way, have become the retailer's best-selling brands and have also resulted in lower returns. Future initiatives will include the integration of additional data into its algorithm, including sales and customer-experience insights from the previous collections.

ASOS: making Topshop digital-first

The acquisition of former Arcadia brands TopShop, TopMan, Miss Selfridge and HIIT by online fashion superstar Asos, gives us a striking insight into the different approaches that traditional and pureplay retailers take with the same brands.

Fundamental to the Asos model is to transform the brands into digital-first and allow them to benefit from their leading online experiences. Clearly the brands are intrinsically popular, but with Asos overlaying what they do best and integrating them into their online platform, there is potential for a true renaissance. Asos has identified the strengths and weaknesses of each of its newly purchased brands and set out a plan of action for the next months.

The approach is refreshingly customer focused. Within the Asos customer segmentation Topshop has apparently been tagged as fitting its 'scenester' customer persona with strengths in denim and day dresses. It has also identified that what Topshop and brother brand Topman lack is 'inclusive sizing', which Asos plans to address, as well as revitalising both brands' footwear ranges.

Miss Selfridges is aimed at a younger audience, and Asos plans to create Miss Selfridge products for every milestone in a young woman's life, such as proms. Commercially it plans to retain an entry price point lower than that of its own Asos Design label and add a tall range to complement the petite offering.

Asos apparently aims to expand the HIIT activewear label to include more menswear and add premium technical and performance products for a greater range of sports activities.

Being decisive and quick to act is clearly an intrinsic part of the Asos digital-first model. Understanding in depth and detail what your customer wants, down to sub-category level allows these fast decisions and actions to be made with absolute confidence. There is an excellent interview with Nick Beighton, chief executive of ASOS in Retail Week. A fuller account of their plans for the Arcadia brands. Well worth a read – "How ASOS will make Topshop live up to its name again" February 2021.

The Z to A of retail disruption

In the Style: socializing celebrity collaborations

Online fashion phenomenon, In The Style, is not unlike other online fashion powerhouses Boohoo, Missguided and Asos, but has carved out its own particular 'digital-first' approach, namely through the clever combination of celebrity collaborations and the highly influential role of social media.

The brand recognised that young social media users copied what their favourite stars wore and spotted a gap in the market to create a brand based on collaborations with the celebrities themselves, rather than to just use them as influencers.

In The Style's differentiation also comes from the fact that the collaborations are longer term, developing into mutual relationships, and the collaborators have more control over designs than would be the case with other fashion brands.

The brand started with 'The Only Way is Essex' star Lauren Pope. Then launched collaborations with a host of celebrities, using their fame to drive sales. Stars from reality TV programmes, 'Love Island' and 'I'm a Celebrity... Get Me Out of Here' have apparently been particularly successful.

In The Style has also used social media very effectively to cement the idea that the business is built on friendships and the relationship with its collaborators is much more than financial and contractual. In the Style often posts exclusive pictures of its collaborators, and shares posts, comments and likes across social media.

The brand has 2.7 million followers on Instagram with 1 million active customers. Engagement rates are high. It has also launched its TikTok channel using videos of its stars.

In the Style will probably remain smaller than some of its competitors but has carved a unique niche in the market, capitalising on social buzz and using collaborations with celebrities to create trends rather than copying them.

M&S MS2: familiar but 'never the same'

Retailers don't come much more traditional than Marks & Spencer, and its reputation is still potentially an asset, but only in the context of operating like a modern digital-first retailer. 'MS2' is a business wide initiative that aims to bring together M&S' product and digital capabilities to be digital-first.

Invisible to the shopper, M&S outlines the plan for a new way of operating, creating a single integrated online, digital & data team supported by stores and a refocused 'product supply engine.'

- MS2 to combine online, data and digital trading in one team adapting to an online model
- To herald 'a step-change in online product, presentation, pricing and social marketing including recognition that the online business will need a focused range.'
- To deliver a mandate to drive for more rapid fulfilment
- To maximise usage of one of the best customer databases in the UK to drive digital customer engagement and loyalty
- To make seamless online/in-store ordering, click-&-collect
- To run domestic and international online as one

The MS2 initiatives will also be supported by the relaunch of the Sparks loyalty programme and the deployment of in-store technology to improve productivity.

MS2' ultimate aim is to 'flip the model.' To act like a pureplay retailer. To respond to product trends spurred by influencers and Instagram demand. To think about range and promotions differently, to think about end-to-end supply chain differently, to think about media spend and marketing differently. To seize the momentum in M&S.com and online sales increases and to apply it across all channels.

The Z to A of retail disruption

031

BE PRECISE

Internal strategies

Be very precise about what you want to achieve from your actions and processes. Be very precise about what data you need to succeed in those processes.

Be clear what the end-point is.

Actions

- Plan activities precisely
- Do not allow activities to be diverted.
- Coordinate data specialists and retail specialists to identify exactly what data intelligence is required.
- Do not overload decisions with too much data – be ruthless.
- Stop when you reach the end-point.

032

BE QUICK

Internal operations

You must ensure that everything you do, whether in the prototype phase or the actual delivery phase is done as quickly and as efficiently as possible.

It is important to remove barriers to speed, both technological, or through the protocols, obstinacy or inefficiency of people and processes.

Actions

- Define fast, efficient and realistic time frames for processes
  - Set milestones
  - Resource realistically and correctly
  - Monitor and report progress
  - Employ professional process managers
- Remove technological bottlenecks – be ruthless
  - Remove legacy technologies
  - Habitually update technologies
- Remove human bottlenecks
  - 'Set a fire' under IT directors and managers
  - Clearly communicate and agree personal expectations of input and timings
  - Agree correct resource levels
  - Monitor and encourage process lag
  - React to achieve set times
- Improve process efficiencies
  - Monitor and take feedback on processes
  - Continually learn and adapt
  - Focus on incremental 'time-gain'
  - Focus on 'handing over the batten' exchanges
  - Focus on internal communications

033

BE BRAVE

Internal strategies

It is important to balance the opportunities of trying new things, which the risks of getting things badly wrong.

Fight always against the 'well we've always done it this way, mentality' but avoid the 'he who hesitates is lost' blind leaps.

Actions

- Properly risk assess everything
- Balance 'what's the worst thing that can happen' against 'what's the best outcome' optimism
- Set 'pivotal measurement milestones"
  - Quick precise assessment of action impacts
  - A contingency 'risk minimization' action plan for every eventuality at every step
- Be fast, act fast, react fast and shop fast if necessary.
- Keep a 'balanced' context within the wider picture
- Always look to the next opportunity

034

REWARD EACH OTHER

Internal strategy

Creating a community can be easier said than done. Filling our ranks with philanthropic individuals helps but being rewarded is so important.

Take the selfishness out of rewards, by ensuring that group achievements lead to individual rewards, whilst individual achievements lead to group rewards.

To achieve this the rewards process must be seen as fair and transparent to everyone.

Be creative but relevant with KPIs. Balance commercial KPIs with wider KPIs on efficiency, added-value, and the positive interactions with colleagues, partners and customers.

Finally, reward individuals and teams primarily through their guaranteed wage and benefits, with additional 'feelgood' incentives the icing on the cake against complacency.

Actions

- Be precise and unequivocal in defining KPIs to be considered and rewarded at every level from business wide to individual
- Ensure individual rewards are made up of individual KPIs, departmental KPIs and total business KPIs
- Make it possible for individuals to be rewarded for individual actions
- Make it possible for individuals to be rewarded for group achievements.
- Put in place a faultless process for KPI measurement
  - Clear objectives
  - Realistic objectives
  - Precise measurements
  - Impartial review and complaints
- Transparent and social acknowledgement of success
  - Social sites, pinboards, internal apps for communication of activities and achievements leading to rewards.
  - Do not communicate directly the reward unless it is open for everyone to compete
- Set scale of permanent wage levels on the growth in skills, experience and company benefit, not just years of service.

The Perpetually Active Retailer

The main reason why retail organisations and processes become unwieldy, inefficient and inappropriate is because the businesses themselves are not built for change.

Creating fluid structures and the potential for added-value processes means nothing if there is not the culture to always drive improvements. At the very least to keep up with best practice. Even in new enterprises there can be a temptation to 'glorify' in the efficiencies of the current state of the art processes, without considering what should come next.

Remember every business was new at some point. Even the ones not around anymore were often leading edge once.

Retail businesses do not have a great history of being built for change. It may seem strange to say that of an industry that is seen as being so dynamic, so full of new products, styles, designs and showcase shops, but in essence it is the truth.

Of course, if you work in a busy shop the pace is fast, the energy of an endless stream of demanding customers pulling you from one situation to another. And for sure, if you work in a hectic buying office the hourly cycle of supplier meetings, sample reviews, design drawings, and assortment plans is enough to make your head spin.

But behind the frantic facade, many retail businesses are built on the erroneous assumption that, in the big picture, nothing really changes that much. The complacency is based on the mis-guided security that we are still somewhere in the "Age of Evolution," where the pace of evolution is slow and manageable.

But as every year goes by, this assumption becomes more outdated. Only when forced by such seismic disruption as the arrival of the internet and e-commerce do businesses stir. Even then, it requires the 'stella' rise of pureplay competitors and a slide in market share and stock market value, to begin the scramble to bolt-on solutions to existing functions and operations.

The heralding in of the 'Age of Disruption' has shone a harsh light on the inability of many businesses to evolve their organisations, their processes, and of most concern, their mind-sets. The mentality of many of the great retail empires is still based in a 'more of the same' mode. The reality now, is that fundamental and continuous change is essential to being a successful retailer.

You won't be going anywhere if the wheels have fallen off! Always keep moving somewhere.

In most cases, to be fare, it is not as though businesses are not trying to change and improve. The main issue is that the changes are sometimes unplanned and uncoordinated. Retail functions which are run as separate 'silos' often instigate changes that adversely affect other parts of the business. Changes demanded from higher up in the business can fail to find agreement and traction across the relevant silos. Changes are attempted without the correct research or resourcing.

Improvising, irritating & interrupting

These represent dangerous scenarios which can cause negative disruption and damage to efficiency & productivity.

'Damaging dynamics' come in three types. They IMPROVISE, IRRITATE and they INTERRUPT.

The ongoing changes that are essential for improvement can be carried out in a logical systematic way, or they can be improvised in a 'knee-jerk' reactive way.

Disconnected teams with a linear operational focus restricted to their own functions often create changes that can detrimentally impact other roles up and down the process chain.

Whilst not being catastrophic, over time these improvisations build into frustrations for team members and stress points in the processes.

Quite often individual functional actions prove to be more damaging as no actions at all. To every action there is a reaction. Not always a good one. Take the advice of Einstein.

Improvising
Disconnected teams with operational linear focus

Irritating
Disconnected teams with uncoordinated new initiatives, amounting to little improvements. The burden of innovation on the same people who manage from day to day

Sketch 34 Improvising & Irritating

Severe irritation is caused by larger changes, which are more 'official' in origin. When these are attempted with the same lack of functional coordination, or cross functional collaboration, then the impact causes severe problems for the wider teams.

The irritation can be compounded because changes at this level require more time and commitment from existing team members, as well as external resource. If neither are able, or available, then the efforts to deliver change will seriously disrupt ongoing processes and cause problems with delays to deadlines and the quality of the output.

When significant strategic and operational changes are instructed the repercussions can be very serious and cause damaging interruptions to the existing process flows. Such interjections are often led and delivered by external teams with limited consultation with the relevant internal teams. The worst scenario is when these external initiatives are independently forced onto the existing teams and into the existing processes.

The interruptions can be so severe, that this ultimately instils a culture of 'bland acceptance' resulting in stagnation and apathy to any further initiatives irrespective of the potential benefits.

At this stage, the wheel's really have fallen off. Nothing changes at all, new direction is impossible, without wheels in motion!

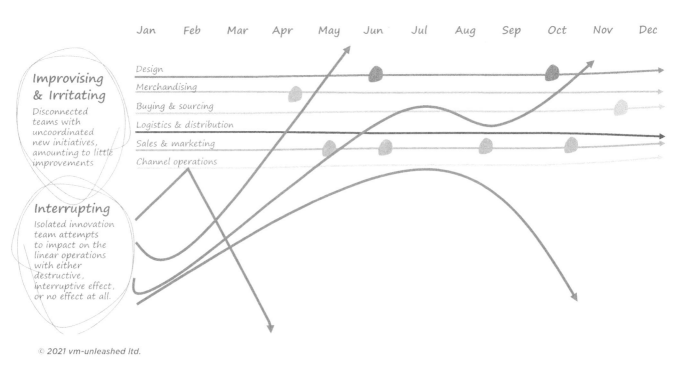

© 2021 vm-unleashed ltd.

Sketch 35 Improvising, Irritating & Interrupting

Evolving, Enriching & Expanding

Retailers need to be dynamic on three different levels. I call them the 3 'E's.' EVOLVE, ENRICH & EXPAND.

The minimum requirement for survival is to constantly 'evolve.' This is the ongoing process of every part of the business striving to get better. People strive to improve their knowledge and skills, technology strives to be more responsive, processes strive to be more efficient.

It is easy to overlook the importance of the steady drip of improvement, but without the momentum that it provides it is almost impossible to drive more significant changes in the business.

To change direction the wheels always need to be turning!

The second level of dynamic within a retail business is to 'enrich.' Enrichment is still focused on the existing functions and processes, but it looks at how to grow, not just improve.

Enrichment may introduce different principles, different ways of working, new skill-sets, technologies, inventions that can take the existing organization, and processes to new levels. Not just evolving efficiency and expertise in what we do, but changing what we do, who does it, and what we produce.

This involves enrichment of the quality of the product for customers, enrichment of the working process for the organisation, and enrichment of the skills and expertise of the workforce.

The third level of dynamic is to 'expand.' This level introduces strategic initiatives to drive the business in new and profitable directions. It may require significant changes, additions or reductions to the organisational structure and the working processes. It requires investment in strategy and capitol.

All three levels must run alongside each other. The relative frequency of each, and the resources required by each, ensure that the small movements empower the big changes, and the big changes define the direction of everyday improvements.

The exact frequency of initiatives depends on the business

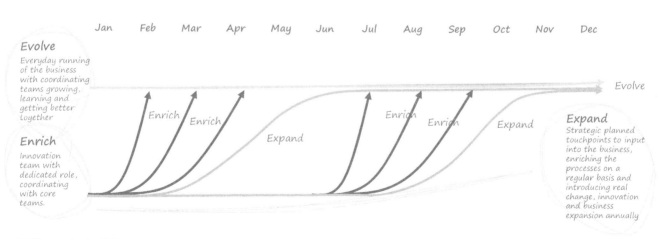

© 2021 vm-unleashed ltd.

Sketch 36 Evolve, Enrich, Expand

proposition, the product sectors, and the category dynamics. Always, the periodic input of enrichment is absorbed into the ongoing evolution of the business so that the result is an ever-evolving, ever-richer process.

The output of the expansion initiatives are coordinated so that they add-to the existing processes or evolve independently as new processes that will continue to the enriched and evolved.

A linear mentality consigns all changes to history once they have been implemented. As every month passes, they become more remote and are never revisited again. The circular model ensures a continuous building of expertise and efficiency where previous enrichment and evolution of the processes are always improved further whenever there is a further strategic requirement to change direction or add additional processes.

Circularity, built around the calendar year, built around the product buying schedule, and built around the seasonal sales patterns, ensures that processes are always efficient and relevant to the needs of colleagues and customers.

All successful changes require coordinated organisational structures and process flows, and appropriate resource support. All successful changes must consider the people required to make change a success.

Perpetual cyclical change

The perpetual processes within a retail business, continuous operations and changes for improvement, should always be viewed within the context of being circular.

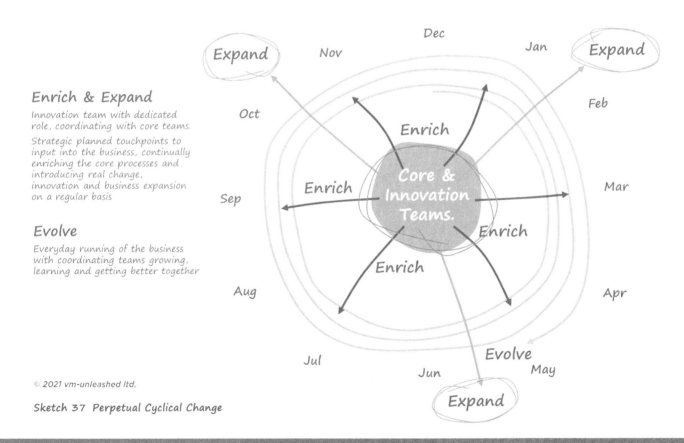

Enrich & Expand

Innovation team with dedicated role, coordinating with core teams.

Strategic planned touchpoints to input into the business, continually enriching the core processes and introducing real change, innovation and business expansion on a regular basis

Evolve

Everyday running of the business with coordinating teams growing, learning and getting better together

© 2021 vm-unleashed ltd.

Sketch 37 Perpetual Cyclical Change

Employees: The Balance of Diverse Excellence!

Some people are good at change and others are good at 'doing the same.' Some embrace the excitement of tomorrow whilst others savour the reassurance of today. Retail businesses require a good balance of both kinds of people. The important thing is to appreciate this.

The people who are amazing at making your current business successful today, are probably not the ones who will drive its future directions and further successes. This means that to add enrichment and expansion, we need to employ additional teams and individuals. This is not just a matter of resource, this is a matter of mind-set, a matter of refreshment.

The structure of the retail organisation is changing, and so too is the skill-set of its employees. So too are the people required to run the business. What is essential at the top of the business is a balance of vision and pragmatism. So much of good retail is about the "balance of diverse excellence."

This combination of viewpoints is essential to manage the everyday business, whilst always seeing opportunities and planning for the future. In essence, one half manages evolution and introduces enrichment, whilst the other identifies ways to enrich, and sees directions to expand in the future.

The combination could be between an MD and a Brand Director, or between a CEO and a Chairman, or any combination of top executives. In very rare circumstances you may even find one person who has the individual balance within their own personality. But based on the premise that "two heads are better than one" it is likely to be a partnership. A partnership of equality.

A Head for Innovation

Every retailer must have a 'Head of Innovation.' But this is not some technologically driven whizz-kid firing random ideas at his shocked audience of traditional retailers. This is a forward looking, commercially aware individual, who sees the future across not only technology, but people, channels, customers, products, services, and collaborations.

The 'Head of Innovation' leads an appropriately sized but relatively small 'Innovation Team' which collaborates with both internal functions, and resources, and collaborates with external innovators and entrepreneurs.

Ideas for innovation will come from external relationships, but also from inside the business. It is essential to find ways to encourage and absorb those ideas and turn them into realities.

It is difficult to force innovation from the outside. It is simply wrong to force ideas from the outside when they are already present within the internal teams.

Certainly, the 'evolve' changes and initiatives should be driven by your existing employees. Only people close to the current processes have the daily insights into where the problems and weaknesses are. These ongoing efficiency and personal development improvements should be suggested and instigated by the team members themselves.

It is important that there is an internal process that allows teams and functions to discuss new initiatives, and a viable way to support these steps with the appropriate technology and training, funding and external resources.

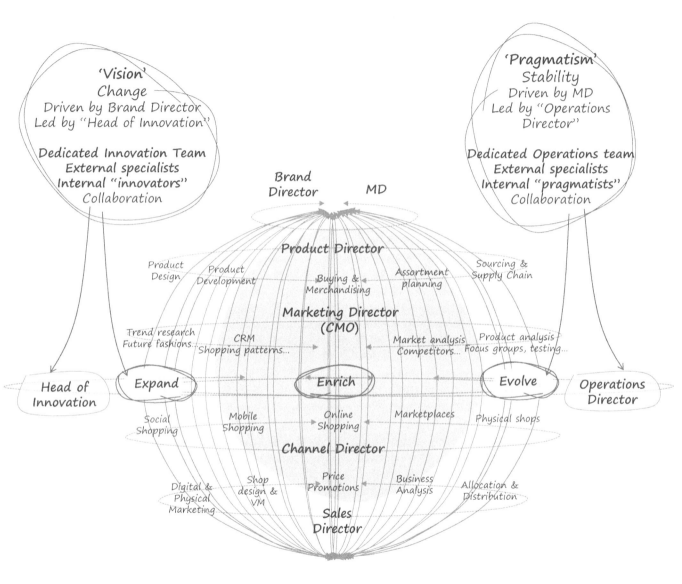

'Vision'
Change
Driven by Brand Director
Led by "Head of Innovation"

Dedicated Innovation Team
External specialists
Internal "innovators"
Collaboration

'Pragmatism'
Stability
Driven by MD
Led by "Operations Director"

Dedicated Operations team
External specialists
Internal "pragmatists"
Collaboration

Brand Director
MD
Product Director
Product Design
Product Development
Buying & Merchandising
Assortment planning
Sourcing & Supply Chain

Marketing Director (CMO)
Trend research Future fashions
CRM Shopping patterns...
Market analysis Competitors...
Product analysis Focus groups, testing...

Head of Innovation
Expand
Enrich
Evolve
Operations Director

Social Shopping
Mobile Shopping
Online Shopping
Marketplaces
Physical shops
Channel Director

Digital & Physical Marketing
Shop design & VM
Price Promotions
Business Analysis
Allocation & Distribution
Sales Director

Sketch 38 The Balance of Vision & Pragmatism

The 'enrichment' of the current processes should be driven by a combination of internal functional teams and the internal 'Innovation Team.' It should be a collaboration that sees joint meetings and workshops on a regular basis. Part of the role of being a team member should be to continuously look beyond the existing way of doing things, to research innovation and rationalise what could be relevant to your own area.

The Innovation Team's function will be to look at innovation potential across the business, to research in-depth the potential opportunities and then to discuss with the relevant functional teams. The implementation must be collaborative.

Part of the 'Innovation Team's' mandate in their ongoing research is also to appraise more fundamental additions to the business. This 'expansion' of the existing business scope, assortment, services, channels, collaborations should be presented into the highest levels of the business, the Brand Director and CEO. The implementation should be performed by a dedicated team, liaising with the relevant functions, and delivered with appropriate new and existing resources.

Collaboration on implementation will need to be with both internal and external partners. Internal resources must be given the opportunities to use change for their own personal development and prestige. But external expertise must be utilised where specialist knowledge is not within the business, where the specialism is outside the internal remit, and where commercial speed and scope require external scale.

Change is always a balance of diverse excellence. It is also a matter of subtle diplomacy.

Innovating your teams

If you ever arrive at the scenario of external partner teams being more important than your internal teams when it comes to your retail processes and their performance, then you have some serious decisions to make.

In all eventualities, your internal teams should be indispensable. They should be invested in as the priority, with time, training and renumeration.

Balancing their practical and emotional needs is not always easy. Existing internal teams should not be duplicated or shadowed by external partners. Internal teams should not be split or separated by new projects, and internal teams should always have communication channels with the Head of Innovation.

Innovation projects should have regular meetings with internal teams and external partners. Within the internal teams, individuals can be given the opportunity and responsibility to allocate part of their workload to innovation projects, liaise between their own internal team and external partners, and train towards more expertise in the innovation area.

External partners should not just be proactive deliverers of solutions but reactive providers of internal expertise responding to the situations and enriching the opportunities they discover.

Internal teams should be developed through appropriate training and experiences to fit into, and benefit from, the wider challenges of a culture of change and innovation. They need to be fit and capable for the wider customer markets, not isolated from commercial realities.

*To **evolve**, teams should be continually trained in latest best practice, use of software solutions, and market & customer analysis.*

*To **enrich**, teams should be exposed to latest technologies and innovation within their specialism, competitor innovations and future trends*

*To **expand**, teams and individuals should always be given the opportunity to become a permanent part of any new initiatives and streams, ahead of external alternatives. They should be given all appropriate training.*

Maintaining & attracting the right people

A business without a culture for change and an appetite for innovation can quickly become an island. People who live on islands become isolated from reality and the rest of the world. Adventurous people leave the island, whilst the unadventurous remain. The only people who come to an island are people who want to relax and enjoy the quiet life.

Successful retailers are not built with people who want to relax and enjoy the quiet life!

Dynamic retailers that constantly want to evolve, enrich, and expand have two huge benefits. Firstly, their strategy will make them competitive, ahead of the market, and commercially successful. Secondly, they will become and remain an attractive place to work for the right kind of people.

If managed correctly, change gives internal employees the opportunities to improve themselves, to experience new things and to embrace innovation. It allows them to interact with external best practice and to be promoted to new roles & responsibilities. Innovative retailers also value curious and ambitious people and tend to reward them well.

Dynamic retailers also attract the attention of potential employees from competitors, and from external innovators. Good relationships between the internal Innovation Team and external entrepreneurs and innovators create a healthy cross-fertilisation. External collaborators are attracted by the opportunities within an exciting retail environment, whilst retail specialists leave to join the suppliers.

Lush: Nurturing beautiful happy people

Even those customers who would never consider crossing the threshold of a Lush store, never mind investing in a bath-bomb or a slice of specialist soap, are charmed and engaged by the customer experience they find.

I've accompanied many clients and colleagues to Lush stores and what astounds them is the life, energy and enthusiasm of the store teams. From a state of embarrassment, the doubters are soon lost in the depths of the store, listening intently to their guides and trying their hand at skin treatments, immersing themselves up to their elbows in baths of beautiful solutions.

The question universally asked is "How do Lush as a business achieve this?" The answers are easily available. Just ask. Any sales assistant will happily tell you of their own individual experiences of the business. In many ways this is the key. Complete openness and transparency with everyone.

Clearly the business values its people. And clearly the business values every one of its people. There is a subtle but decisive difference. Stores are run for the benefit of the individual staff mix and their personal situations. Of course, there is a framework of operations, however within that the store management have the freedom to manage their staff in a way that fits their personalities, interests and their commitments outside their time in the Lush store.

Training is ever-present but engaging and personal. Store managers deliver constant face-to-face training, communicating new products, new Lush initiatives and discussing the subtleties of customer care. The team have a training liaison offer and the link to head office is maintained by travelling trainers and regular opportunities to visit factories and local community initiatives

"Happy People make Happy Soap" The balance of personal training and self-education is a precious mix. Apparently, all personnel are constantly encouraged to self-learn. The starting point is the deliciously names "Lushopedia" full of facts and background of the brands products, philosophies and activities.

And maybe above all the selection of the staff is the key to the success of Lush. Although "selection" would not be accurate because the workforce is more "drawn" to the brand because they associate with its values and initiatives. Top to bottom everyone believes in the brand values and shares a passion for them. The concept behind the product, the ingredients sourcing, and production are paramount. The communication of various charity initiatives such as Charity Pot and the Slush Fund are highly visible.

However, it's the emotional and physical involvement in the values that drives the loyalty and engagement. Many staff "walk the talk," are involved in local charities, and even travel overseas to participate in initiatives funded by the brand. Lush is a community through the length of its supply chain. From the first drop of inspiration to the last drop of charity

The brand involvement is best illustrated by the fact that staff are allowed and encouraged to talk about ethics, the environment and the world with the customer. As much as about the product. You can believe everything you're told in a Lush store. Because being honest with the customer is a fundamental mantra.

One would imagine that same ethic runs through every conversation in the company, from the board room to the stockroom. But there is certainly magic-a-plenty in the shops themselves.

I am eternally grateful to the colleagues at the Lush flagship shop on Oxford Street in London. Whether i visit on my own, or tour the shop with clients or retail tourists, they never let themselves or the brand down. Energetic, enthusiastic, they are also curious and eloquent in how they communicate the Lush values and their own personal interests. In London? Always pay a visit. Better, book a personal shop tour with a Lush colleague guide. Yes they exist.

The Z to A of retail disruption

035

BE HONEST.
HOW GOOD ARE YOU AT CHANGE?

Internal research and soul-searching

We can all see the need to change and improve. It has become an urgency in this competitive world. But we must be honest with ourselves. Are our attempts to change and improve actually causing more harm that good to our existing teams and processes?

We need to ensure that our improvised actions do not irritate and interrupt our existing processes to a stand-still.

Actions

- Carry out an impartial and thorough examination of how improvement projects occur within the current business
  - Analyse recent projects – motivation, concept, initiation, planning, consultation, budgeting, resourcing, implementation, collaboration, delivery, application, impact, monitoring, analysis, roll-out
  - Interview and discuss:
    - Project initiators
    - Project team members
    - Project managers
    - Recipient team members
    - Senior executives
    - External partners
- Define the effectiveness, common areas of success, common areas of failure in improvement projects
- Identify the scale of 'informal' projects
- Identify the level of 'appliance' and 'longevity' of initiatives

036

BUILD A SINGLE STRUCTURE & PROCESS FOR MAKING CHANGES

Operational planning & procedures

It is important to separate your mind from specific changes you want to make or tried to make. Just focus on the process.

It is essential that you create an agreed process for proposing, developing and implementation changes. It is important that this process covers different scenarios. Small scale process evolutions, medium scale enrichment of processes, and large-scale expansions in the business.

Actions

- Set out 3 clear processes for initiating change
  - Internal team/functions
  - Cross team/functions
  - Business wide
- Define stages for the process
  - Submission
  - Consultation & Appraisal
  - Planning, resources, collaboration
  - Implementation, training and hand-overs
  - Appraisal & roll-out, next steps
- Allocate responsibilities and management for each process
- Create 'ideas and recommendations' channels & tools

037

DON'T RE-INVENT THE WHEEL

Internal review process internal operations

Without a proper process for change good things and bad things happen randomly and quite often invisibly, until a problem occurs. The worst of this is that good ideas poorly implemented are thrown out, good implementations not publicised or embraced are forgotten, and forgotten good initiatives are repeated over and over again.

It is essential to correctly monitor, analyse and put a formal end to 'change projects.' Have a unanimous and clear next step including the absolute end.

Just, don't lose track, or lose the benefits, of really good initiatives.

Actions

- Set up a central, coordinated and impartial project coordination and appraisal team
  - Populate it with good experienced change managers
  - Put one of them, who you trust the most, in charge
- Create a regular series of meetings
  - Consider new proposals
  - Monitor ongoing projects
  - Appraise finished projects
  - End products & define next actions.
- Plan a next step timeline.
  - What learnings can be carried forward
  - Into what work, processes, or new projects should learnings be taken.
  - When should the learnings be handed-over – immediately, at the most appropriate time. Log this.
  - Which stakeholder receives and then owns the learnings, next steps and timeline

038

SPOT YOUR TALENT

Employee monitoring, feedback and HR

There are always amazing talents hidden in the workforce at every level. No two people are the same even in the same job.

It is extraordinary, and rather sad, that employee profiles seem to stop when they enter your business. It's as though growth and new skills happened only before they arrived. Or that they are tagged only by formal roles and positions. Get into the minds and brains of employees to understand why they are excellent and valuable assets, not just 'what they do.'

Actions

- Tag your employee's emerging talents. Add these natural attributes to their profiles.
  - Are they excellent organisers?
  - Are they 'roll-your-sleeve-up' doers?
  - Are they creatives?
  - Do they get on with everyone.
  - Are they innovators and disruptors?
- Tag these attributes so they can be found in HR skill searches
- Always consider internal talents for projects
- Do not restrict talent by function or department
- Guard against leaders keeping team 'talents' to themselves.

039

ENSURE NATURAL ENEMIES BECOME THE BEST OF FRIENDS

Hiring criteria & processes, internal processes

We all know those abrasive touchpoints within a retail organization. They are the senior and executive roles whose agendas are often diametrically opposed. Their opinions at loggerheads.

The fact is that even the holders of conflicting positions can and do get along very well. It's a matter of personalities, jovial respect and friendly rivalry. In fact, these energized relationships lead to some of the most vibrant and positive areas of a business.

You have to make friends from the enemies. Hire these people to give them every chance of getting on, in their own way.

Actions

- Identify which functions and roles traditionally create the most negative friction in the business. You know them.
  - Brand directors and Operations Directors
  - Designers & merchandisers
  - Buyers and allocators
  - Store operations and visual merchandisers
  - Sales and marketing
- At senior levels, ensure that the opposite camp are involved in the hiring process. Create relaxed situations for interviews and discussions
  - Consider personality, chemistry and temperament as much as skills, expertise and experience
- Ensure that areas where opposite camps meets and work together are ultimately managed by a senior impartial party
- Encourage and stimulate as much 'out-of-work' fun and occasions for personalities to bond and friendships to form.

040

INTEGRATE INNOVATORS

Hiring criteria & processes: internal processes

Disruption and change can be so much fun and can make work so much better and successful. But it scares people to death, and the people who bring change are viewed with suspicion and outright hostility.

Ensure that Heads of Innovation, and new faces, are integrated immediately and cordially into the wider retail community

Actions

- Hire innovators who are human as well
- Hire innovators who understand and enjoy retail
- Hire innovators who 'listen considerably more than they speak.'
- Introduce the friendly face of innovation to as many situations as possible. Make them 'part of the furniture.'
- Always research and present the benefits of change

041

TRAIN EVERYONE IN INNOVATION

HR & Learning & development teams

Employee workforces are full of inspiration, if you look deep enough. To be honest you don't need to look that deep.

Embrace , encourage and involve employees in all stages of the evolution process. Ask their opinion on proposed ideas, work with them to implement and ask for their honest feedback.

But most important of all. Arm them to be innovative.

Actions

- Develop content and activities with rewards which focus on innovation and disruption, for both the new employee initiation programme, and ongoing training programmes.
- Develop a dedicated internal app, or a content stream in the existing app focused on innovation and change
  - Train employees in latest software solutions
  - Expose teams to latest technologies
  - Communicate innovation within their specialism
  - Show competitor innovations
  - Show future trends
- Internally advertise places on new project initiatives
  - Allow project sabbaticals to develop new skills

042

NO MORE TIME FOR 'HERE & NOW'

Hiring criteria & processes: internal processes

Let me make a clear distinction between those that struggle when dealing with change, and those that obstruct it.

These are two completely different scenarios.

I am not the most digitally skilled member of my age group, I need to be shown how to do things, several times. But I fully embrace and enjoy innovation. It is exciting. For those who embrace but struggle they must be helped and encouraged.

But for people who obstruct the wider good, it is clear they are in the wrong place. Or the right place but at the wrong time. There is no option but to part company, if their personal philosophy is at odds with the business culture.

Actions

- Set up training to educate and help people with the adoption of new processes, and in particular new technologies
- Develop learning programme with a range of tech and non-tech deliveries
  - Self teaching apps
  - Step-by-step desktop/ tablet training modules
  - Face-to-face demonstrations
- Allow internal re-location for 'best-fit' skills profiles
- Develop a step-by-step programme for 'innovation blockers' with an end-game conclusion.

The Retail Business Funnel

'The journey to being a perpetual retailer' has taken us on a path through propositions, organisational structures, process flows, functional teams, support teams, innovations teams, and external collaborators, all bound together within a dynamic business model which is digital-first.

We have been bringing together the stability of the organisation, with the dynamics of retail markets and customer behaviour patterns.

It is always important to build every step of the retail business strategically and proactively rather than to make uncoordinated changes and additions as you go along. It is not possible to know what the future holds, but we can assume it will be different. Retail business planning needs to allow for change even if we do not know precisely what those changes will be.

Build from solid foundations, which are balanced and stable, yet still allow for movement in the future. Construct retail function resources and processes that work efficiently, with the flexibility to change and evolve in response to commercial opportunities. Ensure that dynamic actions can be taken to improve, enrich and expand the business in new directions.

Most importantly, define your vision and proposition around the customer. Through every change you make, both strategic and enforced, remain loyal, with a passion, to those core values. Construct a balanced but flexible business model. Always begin with the customer and end with the customer.

They will thank you for it. In turn you will thank them.

Whether a physical shop only retailer, pureplay or omni-channel, the need to plan for change, within the parameters of your proposition, will be a pre-requisite for survival and success.

The balanced business funnel will give you the three key attributes for success — stability, flexibility & agility.

It is a dilemma that established retailers born in a different age, created without flexibility and balance, need to face head on. Too often, we see organisations required to sacrifice their stability to be flexible, because the processes themselves are inflexible and static.

We live and operate in a world surviving on retail quicksand.

This is the reality of the disruptive markets we now operate in. It is the same for all retailers, old and new. Some will be able to adapt better than others, some will be built specifically to thrive in such conditions, others will disappear beneath the surface.

We hear a lot of talk about being digital-first, the importance to embrace the mind-set, principles and processes of the pure-plays. Whilst this is true, of course, it is important to understand why.

This is not a channel battle with digital good and physical bad. It is not a clash of terminology as pureplay take on 'bricks 'n' mortar.' It is simply a reflection of the new doing things better and more appropriately for today's markets and customers than the old.

It is just an industry getting better. And who wouldn't want to be part of that type of industry. No matter how long you have been a part of it.

Indispensability
- A strong consistent vision, with dynamic customer focused initiatives attracts a loyal customer base

Focus
Maximise the reliability of an organised business, whilst injecting new inspiration for the customer. Putting the customer at the beginning & the end of the business activities

Customer

Internal & external Innovators

Agility
- Retail functions continuously evolving and improving
- Innovation & retail teams introducing enrichment to processes
- Innovation team initiating new strategic direction, product & processes

Change
To be able to continuously evolve, enrich and expand the business to anticipate and react to small and large changes in the retail marketplace.
Allows unhindered dynamic.

Retail functions

Flexibility
- Retail functions with efficient processes and flexibility to change
- Support functions adding stability to everyday processes, and capability to flex and adapt to support change

Process
To be able to modify the business function model for responsive changes to assortments, channels, markets, technology and customer demographics.
Allows flexibility in a framework of stability.

Support functions

Organisational structure

Stability
- A clear, unwavering vision
- An attractive balanced proposition
- An organizational structure built with balance & equality

Structure
To be able to move the whole business in-line with fundamental market evolution and customer behaviour trends.
Maintains stability through all movements.

Proposition

Customer

Sketch 39 The Retail Business Funnel

3. Excel in ...

Astute Strategies

Defining 'Astute Strategies'

Creating a balanced organisation, flexible process flows, and a culture for change will benefit you little, unless you channel these attributes correctly into the brightest opportunities.

Every retailer will have different opportunities that will depend on the product and service sectors that they represent, the markets in which they operate, their level of ambition, and their business strategy. Some opportunities will be common to all.

The first astute strategy consideration is not to focus your attentions on product functions, but to think beyond your internal divisions. Internal divisions can soon become isolated silos, and a focus on specific initiatives by silo will only increase the divisions within your business. This is not a good thing.

Deliver precise strategies for your customers. Strategies that will make you essential, indispensable and irresistible to them. The benefits of your strategy outputs should primarily be for the customer. The strategies will generally be delivered cross-functionally. They will benefit those functions and the ways they integrate their thinking, principles and processes. Everyone benefits when strategies are not retail function focused.

Do not define strategies by 'I need to make my buying process more streamline.' Articulate the strategy as 'I need to make my products closer to what the customer wants!' The project resulting from these ambitions may well will involve streamlining your buying processes and include benefits to integrated processes across related functions.

Apply your ambitions and energy to the things that really add benefit and make a difference to the customer. For me, the following areas represent the biggest opportunities for your astute strategies.

Your channel strategy including collaborations, your product proposition, and your supply partners. Your sustainability initiatives, your shops and communities, the people in your business, and your ethical values as a business – ESG.

I would also consider that the application of technology across every area and function should be a focus of your astute strategies. But absolutely don't work with technology as a function. It is possibly the worst discipline to regard as a function and to isolate. But the fact is, it is so important, so pervasive to every element of retail, that it cannot always be considered just as a facilitator of other strategies. But it must always be viewed in the widest sphere of application, facilitating and bringing functions together, rather than looking at functional processes in isolation.

For all astute strategies, prioritise the likely benefit impact depending on your overall business strategy, and the current levels of practice and skills excellence within your business.

For a new businesses, particularly from non-retail origins, product propositions may be a big opportunity. Brands born on the crest of a wave of disruption, initially thrive through energy, and the novelty of innovation, but will quickly need to learn and incorporate some fundamentals of retail buying & selling. Conversely, the need to expand, to capitalise on new channels, collaborations and market disruptions, may well be the priority for established businesses.

Enrichment of current practices is an opportunity for all. It has the capacity to transform established processes, whilst adding commercial stability to disruptive ones. Enrichment has the potential to bring together the functional 'nuts and bolts' with emotional innovation and energy.

To evolve, to enrich and to expand, requires a common and coordinated approach to forming and delivering 'astute strategies' at every level of every retail business.

The Five-year strategy

The five-year strategic plan is a bedrock of business, and retail businesses are no exception. However, the COVID pandemic with its unpredictable repercussions, illustrates how implementing even a six-month strategy can sometimes be almost impossible.

The new retail landscape shows the need to be 'astute' in the implementation of dynamic strategies on the three levels – evolving, enriching and expanding.

The requirement is to balance strategies that embrace change continuously, as well as those that guide short-term initiatives towards a longer-term goal.

The five-year strategy is a periodic re-appraisal and affirmation of the vision of the business. It responds to the times we live in, customer trends, technological advancements ensuring that change is always within the parameters of the vision.

The 6-month, one-year or five-year plan are all valid. What they all require are agile organisations and astute strategies that have both the stability to withstand severe external pressures, and the flexibility and dynamics, to be able to change. To change quickly to grasp emerging opportunities.

Stability, flexibility and agility are essential in any era. The post-COVID era is no exception. It is an extreme.

Touchpoints: *'Taking it to the Customer'*
The customer relationship is shifting from distinctive channels to a continuously changing number of touchpoints.

Product propositions: *'The Crowning of the King'*
Product is still at the heart of retail but its role as "absolute king" is changing.

Supply Partners: *'In the same Boat Together'*
The move to digital channels highlights the opportunities for technology applications across totally new supply chains.

Sustainability: *'Making More from Less'*
Responsibility for sustainability has shifted from the marketing department to every department across a retail business.

Retail hubs: *'Places in our Hearts & Minds'*
In its formats and in its functions, the essential shop will need to evolve its role, enrich its experiences, & expand its capabilities.

Retail People: *'The Shopkeepers of Today'*
The new wave of retailers have a different outlook on how to manage their staff, nurture their loyalty, productivity, and skills.

Technology: *'The Great Facilitator'*
Technology has changed everything, and its applications and intelligence still develop at an ever-quickening pace.

Ethical Values: *'Performing on a Different Level'*
There is more to life than owning things. There is more to retail than making money. The customer understands this.

	Touchpoints	Product propositions	Supply Partners	Sustainability
Evolve The ongoing process of improvement. People knowledge and skills. Technology applications. Process efficiency.	• Improving existing channels – their efficiency & functionality • Stock availability • Single brand touchpoint experiences • Cross-channel supply chain integration • Click&Collect & returns to shops • Home delivery	• Agile collection planning • Flexible assortment planning • Buying & merchandising principles • Product design • Sourcing & buying • Market references • Allocation planning • Improved support services proposition	• Improve current supplier liaison • Re-energise new supplier selection • Evolve supplier workers charter • Increase factory visits & checks • Re-vamp supplier negotiations • Improve sample checking criteria	• Increase awareness of materials & processes • Reduce internal waste and CO2 emissions • Select sustainable materials • Assess suppliers sustainability criteria • Evolve sustainable micro-collections • Re-use, re-sell un-sold stock • Re-cycle, donate remaining materials • Employ & evolve sustainability ticketing'
Enrich Strategic injections modifying and adding scope and benefit to ongoing processes. Introducing different principles, different ways of working, new skill-sets, technology interventions.	• Transparent inventory data for shops/channels and customers • Last mile flexibility including sustainable eBikes, couriers, collection options • Dark stores & micro-distribution centres • Multi-functional shops • Video product demonstrations, shop tours, advice & customer service via shop video technology	• Added value attributes • Broader design influences • Online/technological product research • Re-defining brand style focus • New size architectures • Fabric/materials training and awareness • Fabric supplier engagement • Production developments • Evolved subscription services as part of proposition	• Develop unique/exclusive suppliers • Local supplier development • Absorb supplier product knowledge • Develop informed raw material collaborations • Increase flexible volumes/lead-times • Employ earlier payments & joint cost burden	• Improve education in raw materials, recyclable, re-usable, harmful processes • Develop assortment planning/ collections built around sustainable criteria • Product origin driven assortment plans • New, used, recycled, upcycled driven assortment structures • Move to 100% re-cycled materials • Avoid 'toxic' combinations of raw materials
Expand Introducing broad strategic initiatives to drive the business in new and profitable directions. Requiring changes to the organisational structure, principles and processes.	• Fully integrated workforce at all levels working flexibly across channels • Fully flexible product, allocation, delivery, collection & returns • Coordinating DTC channels, 3rd parties, marketplaces and retailer channels • DTC omnichannel • New routes to market – social/rich media/streaming • New 3rd party collaborations • Seamless RFID product tracking	• Product lifecycle evolutions • Expansive customer collections • Design/ style/ cultural/ influencer collaborations • Proprietary product R&D • 3rd party brand partnerships • Producer collaborations • External product service partners	• Develop vertical supply integration • Increase owned factories/suppliers • Engage with raw material suppliers • Supply chain integration • Product & customer data sharing technology through the supply chain • RFID inventory tracking at every stage of supply • 3D printing as part of the supply chain	• Build circular economic relationships between product functions and collaborators • Build supply capability for new, unsold, used product • Build sales channel capability to re-sell existing product, up-cycle existing product/ materials • Invest in sustainable support and supply businesses

© 2021 vm-unleashed ltd.

Sketch 40 'Astute' strategies.

Retail Hubs	Retail People	Technology	Ethical values	
• Improve maintenance & cleaning • Refine store grading & clustering criteria • Evolve stock and replenishment processes • Upscale visual merchandising • Upscale window treatments • Intensify and focus promotional activity • Prioritise customer service	• Evolve management & employee organisation • Employ awards for commercial KPIs • Evolve training & improve career path development • Consult & communicate across broader issues • Employ feedback sessions/channels	• Improve technology reliability/remove legacy • Increase cross-business systems compatibility • Usability training • Social media-training • Roll-out remote working essentials • Back-up physical shop system essentials • Evolve operations & training apps • Supply customer wi-fi	• Achieve KPIs in non-exploitative way • Efficiency over cost reduction for profit gain • Add KPIs other than financial performance • Ensure fair wage/rewards for all employees • Achieve Buying/Initial margins honorably • Re-invest % of profit into employees • Apply sustainability considerations	**Evolve** The ongoing process of improvement. People knowledge and skills. Technology applications. Process efficiency.
• Enrich personalised relationships with customers • Cross-channel hubs for product and customer service queries/problems • Develop social integration & involvement with local communities, events & charities • Apply social media local area integration • Adapt utility space for customer workshops, local business and customer use. • Employ local shop rewards and loyalty benefits	• Develop trust building initiatives • Front line staff re-prioritisation • Enrich training in product and production • Integrate customer service across channels • Performance rewards based on wider social added-value KPIs –and customer satisfaction • Develop enhanced staff areas	• Shop colleague automated scheduling • Individual shop colleague personal tasks, "help" and communication tool • Wider customer payment options – mobile, self-checkout, self-scan... • Roll-out digital screens – imagery, video, interactive, demos, colleague training • Develop rich-media and social media selling • Colleague customer profile awareness • Develop discussion-based search engines	• Review performance KPIs of all job functions to reflect added-value responsibilities • Prioritise full price sales • Reduce volumes of unsold product • Match supply with demand • Manage use of resources/ waste recycling • Drive loyalty through added-value products • Fair employee & supplier wages and standards • Initiate supplier charters • Initiate sustainability objectives	**Enrich** Strategic injections modifying and adding scope and benefit to ongoing processes. Introducing different principles, different ways of working, new skill-sets, technology interventions.
• Shops built with flexibility, as shops, dark stores, rental space & offices • Shops as social and community hubs • Shop manager empowered as "The New Shopkeeper" • Devolution of power to shop teams as the front-line brand interface • Working office hubs for regional teams • Flexible shop leasing, locations & pop-up capabilities	• Develop the 'Passion Supply Chain' • Focus on the financial and mental wellbeing of people • Become a product & customer focused organisation • Omni-channel colleague role flexibility from head office to shops and digital channels • Maximise colleague efficiency and customer reach	• Facilitate digital-first business strategy • Seamless channel & data integration • AI demand planning, availability prediction • Personalization of cross-channel touchpoints • B&M digital visualisations & process streamlining • RFID supply chain product tracking • Inter-channel & partner data communication tools • Digital & shop CUI optimisation tools	• Develop a sustainable Business Model for Profit • Commercial growth via Business growth • Set Growth KPIs across wide social and ethical parameters • Circular model, re-use, re-pair, re-cycle • Develop a unique sustainable proposition • Work with natural resource capacities, not intensive. • Commit to ethical partnerships • Commit to investing in local shop communities • Link investment conditions to ethical/sustainability KPIs	**Expand** Introducing broad strategic initiatives to drive the business in new and profitable directions. Requiring changes to the organisational structure, principles and processes.

Touchpoints: *'Taking it to the customer'*

The relationship is shifting from distinctive channels to a continuously changing number of touchpoints. These touchpoints cut across digital and physical channels. They are used by the customer in the moment, often with little predictability.

> *Speaking of channels is irrelevant. It is one brand delivering retail services to a transient customer.*

The touchpoints are used by the customer in two fundamental ways. For inspiration and communication with the retailer, and to buy from the retailer. The customer flits across these touchpoints as and when they please.

With such freedom and choice, it is now time for retailers to be proactive, and to 'take it to the customer.'

Get the fundamentals right

Before attacking the complexities of channel and touchpoint integration, it must first be the priority to ensure that all your touchpoints are independently, as efficient, as reliable and as engaging as possible. That they are working.

Address the fundamentals with a 'zero-tolerance' approach to anything other than best practice. Ensure that digital channels load quickly, present themselves in a logical and intuitive way, allow the customer to navigate where they need to go, but with relevant stimulation to lead them to what they really want.

Ensure physical shops are convenient in location, and open at convenient times. That the environments are clean and attractive, allowing the customer to find easily what they came in for, and discover seamlessly what they will leave with.

The choice of touchpoints is myriad, but the one that the customer is currently using is always the most important to them. Make sure that no touchpoints disappoint. Remember to never allow the customer to fail, by failing the customer yourself.

Integrating the customer experience

The next stage of evolution is to begin the process of integrating touchpoints, as marketing tools and as places to buy. In both cases the application of appropriate technologies is the key.

For marketing, integrated customer profiles need to be constructed, bringing together sales data and personal insights from across touchpoints, which can then be easily and continuously available and applied across those same touchpoints to create the best possible relationship with each individual customer.

Appropriate dialogues, suggestions and rewards can be communicated as subtly or as bluntly as is required, through the interactive visual and audio of digital channels, and through intimate conversations with physical shop colleagues.

For selling, inventory transparency and supply chain functionality should evolve with efficiency at every step. Prioritise the data and physical product connections between key touchpoints, ensuring that inventory requests, sales, and availability are accurately coordinated in real-time.

Evolve

The ongoing process of improvement.
People knowledge and skills. Technology applications.
Process efficiency.

Areas of consideration:

- Improving existing channels – their efficiency & functionality
- Stock availability
- Single brand touchpoint experiences
- Cross-channel supply chain integration
- Click&Collect & returns to shops
- Home delivery

Summary of opportunities:

- To own your own channels
- Give the customer the best possible experience by individual channel
- A single best practice brand experience across every channel touchpoint
- To never fail the customer. Focus on product availability and prompt and efficient service and services
- To evolve and better integrate the cross-channel supply chain such as click & collect, home delivery, and shop returns

Enrich

Strategic injections modifying and adding scope and benefit to ongoing processes.
Introducing different principles, different ways of working, new skill-sets, technology interventions.

Areas of consideration:

- Transparent inventory data for shops/channels and customers
- Last mile flexibility including sustainable eBikes, couriers, collection options
- Dark stores & micro-distribution centres
- Multi-functional shops
- Video product demonstrations, shop tours, advice & customer service via shop video technology

Summary of opportunities:

- To integrate your own channels
- Integrated and transparent inventory management across channels – see where the product is
- The integrated and efficient movement of product across channels from supply to warehouse to shop and to home
- Enriching and making consistent the customer service proposition across shops.
- Using same people flexing across channels, not channels flexing across different people

Expand

Introducing broad strategic initiatives to drive the business in new and profitable directions.
Requiring changes to the organisational structure, principles and processes.

Areas of consideration:

- Fully integrated workforce at all levels working flexibly across channels
- Fully flexible product, allocation, delivery, collection & returns
- Coordinating DTC channels, 3rd parties, marketplaces and retailer channels
- DTC omnichannel
- New routes to market – social/rich media/streaming
- New 3rd party collaborations
- Seamless RFID product tracking

Summary of opportunities:

- To integrate across own and partner channels – DTC and DTP
- To develop new channels to market such as pop-up shops, event social selling and rich-media selling
- New routes to market through collaborations and partnerships – partnerships in own shops, partnerships in other retailers and marketplaces
- End-to-end, front-to-back inventory management capabilities

Sketch 41 Touchpoints: Evolve, Enrich & Expand

Ensure that the capability to transport inventory from its absolute current location to the desired destination for the customer is always accurately reported, calculated, communicated, monitored, and implemented according to the customer's wishes.

A brand is often defined as something that delivers a consistent experience. Before running into an ocean of complexity firstly be satisfied with eliminating the weaknesses and inconsistencies from your most-important conduits of supply.

Click & collect is an important and relatively new touchpoint and should be a priority for many retailers. By eliminating the final-mile delivery you reduce costs, whilst driving footfall into shops. Similarly, the 'return orders to shops' capability also serves to drive footfall. Ironically, it is dissatisfied customers that are providing the biggest momentum to physical shop visits, and impulse purchases.

Enriching the experience

Enriching the touchpoint experience is not just about entertainment. Firstly, it comes with the achievement of efficiency & reliability. Channel and touchpoint transparency, and the integration of functions, will allow the business to move from a reactive distribution chain, to being a proactive retailer.

Experience is about developing and evolving transparency and integration, not just of products, but for touchpoints and customers themselves. Full integration of your own touchpoints with those of your support businesses facilitates one of the most important customer experience facets – 'accurate expectation management.' In an informed availability scenario, the delivery can only exceed expectations.

Further enrichment of inventory data will enable retailers to anticipate the location of products, rather than simply monitoring the status quo. This will minimize reactive deliveries, reduce costs and carbon footprints. Placing the product where the demand will be is a major step to making touchpoints attractive, and their experiences rewarding.

In a digital-first world, last-mile logistics also promise to deliver innovative and cost-effective solutions for both customers and retailers, working with precise timeframes and location hubs.

Owned and third party eBike and peddle bike options will support local shops and communities, where collections by customers, and neighbourhood community groups, will also be encouraged and facilitated. A sense of shop ownership will be engendered. It will become the 'local touchpoint' for the brand.

Physical shops will evolve to integrate deliveries-in and deliveries-out, turning stockroom space into delivery hubs, or converting to 'Dark Stores' and micro-distribution centres.

Colleagues across the business will no longer bear the brunt of the 'demarcation of channels,' or location ownership. Customer service specialists can satisfy physical customers face to face, and digital customers through zoom and specialist demonstration portals. Local shop workers can become the local delivery workforce following customer demand in the store, and into homes, with the same service ethics and brand personality that they demonstrate over the shop counter.

Enriching touchpoints is about freeing up the static resources of channel focused businesses, to deliver a new flexibility and fluidity of people, places and products.

Expanding into new 'touchpoints' of opportunity

The new directions of retail expansion come from exploiting the efficiency and fluidity of your internal business, opening-up and developing new ways to the market. New ways to touch the customer.

New touchpoints for selling, from online editorials and social media to rich content platforms and streaming media can also be supported and supplied by the same fluidity and efficiencies in operations that fulfil existing physical shops with products.

Collaborations with partners as facilitators across all areas of the business will be the key to expansion. The old barriers of competition are already beginning to fall away.

Brands which naturally support a wholesale network of partners, are further exploiting the Direct to customer (DTC) opportunities, supplying merchandise as well as communicating brand values and vision directly to the customer. They will begin to 'bundle' and 'package' individual products into attractive customer facing propositions. Brands becoming merchandisers.

High street retailers, with decades of isolation from competitors, will forge new alliances to fill each-others physical and digital spaces, to sell their own products side-by-side through each other's shops.

The imaginative and innovative retailers will absolutely 'take it to the customer' by partnering with event organisers, leisure and travel operators, sports teams and venues, TV programmes and film producers, media platforms and influencer sites. They will sell and deliver instantly and directly to the customer in the physical and digital space via a single footstep, or a single touch of a screen. The brand and product relationship will be seamless.

> *Touchpoints have already become our retail world. Flexibility, efficiency, fluidity and reliability will be the benchmarks to success in this ever changing supply and delivery landscape*

The loss of traditional retail control

The single physical channel was relatively easy for retailers to control. At the very least they knew where, and roughly when, they were going to 'come into contact' with the customer. And they knew it was on their patch. It was on their terms, under their rules. The retailer held all the cards.

The internet, e-commerce and the moving to new channels has changed that completely. The proliferation of retail possibilities has just added to the complexity. It has also accelerated the loss of control that traditional retailers once enjoyed. The stability of power, based on the buying and selling of product, has crumbled away.

The complexity behind multiple touchpoints, has also magnified the range of skills, expertise, and tools required to be competent, proficient, and to excel across channels. Best practice has managed to buy-in, and evolve internally, many of these skills and processes. However, even the most successful have concluded that some of the more specialist pieces of the skill-set jigsaw cannot be developed easily, and cost-effectively, within the business itself.

The multi-touchpoint retail environment has necessitated a new Age of Collaboration.

Mastering the 'six stages of the buying process' is still at the core of keeping customers happy. It is just that 'discover, select, pay, collect, receive & return' just got a lot more complicated to fulfil. This complexity is behind the need to collaborate. The evolution, and revolution, of the six stages has given the customer unbelievable choice and flexibility in how they carry out their retailing activities. The retailer needs to respond.

It is symptomatic of the shift to saturated markets, with supply outstripping the demand, that retail businesses are now embarking on ever more flexible ways to satisfy the elusive customer. To build custom and loyalty. They must, and they are, 'bending over backwards' to accommodate the customer at every twist and turn of the retail journey.

Retailers are 'losing face.'

To cover all the necessary touchpoints that your customer demands from you, as retailers you are going to have to rely on more touchpoints which are owned by your collaborators. Possibly more than you own yourselves.

And when it comes to 'face-to-face' interaction with your customers there is an ever-increasing chance that the customer will be interacting with the face of your collaborator, and not your own carefully crafted and branded face.

The probability at least for now, is that the interaction of customers will remain mainly with touchpoints that you own, and

as a result the 'face-to-face' interaction will be with your brand. However, one of the most rapid areas of development which is really 'turning the retail tables' is where digital interface collaborators who are currently only selling your product, are also becoming the distributors of your product. These familiar, and unfamiliar, partners are now also the delivery face to the customer. Literally at the customer's door.

This is not new if we consider wholesale partners in the physical world. But in a digital world retailers are facing the prospect of being relegated to product suppliers in a sea of customer touchpoints over which they may have very little control.

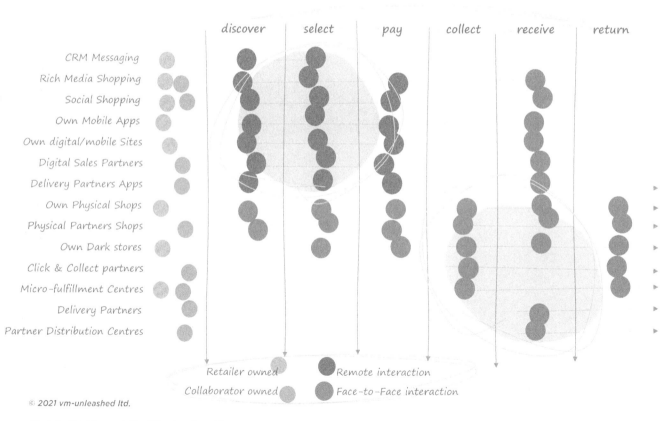

© 2021 vm-unleashed ltd.

Sketch 42 The retailer "Losing Face!"

Essential Collaborator Touchpoints

The loosening of the grip of established retailers on the customer facing service and delivery processes has opened the way for non-retailers to enter the retail market, exploiting the touchpoints that have emerged.

New retailers are not being born out of buying & merchandising, they are emerging from touchpoints.

> *New retailers are being born out of retail touchpoints.*

Not only that, but from footholds across services, logistics, technology or deliveries the new collaborators are expanding themselves into product development and retailing itself.

What could be more of a seismic shift, than a retail industry based on customer touchpoints and not on buying product? Where services and technology, and not the products they sell, are defining the successful 'retail' brands.

What could be more terrifying for traditional retailers? In such a scenario, 'sleeping with the enemy seems a more favourable alternative to simply sleeping on the job!'

> *It is time for collaboration. It is time for retailers to collaborate with the very businesses that threaten their existence.*

Fighting for 'Touch-holds!'

Modern retail is so complex and competitive, it is no place to be on your own. If all your potential protagonists are turned against you, then it can be a lonely place.

If you do not exploit collaborations and partnerships, then your competitors certainly will. So, it is best to have the innovation, experience and technology that such partners represent, on your side instead of against you.

Now is a good time to examine your historical relationships and consider how to approach new ones. The fact is that with the physical castle walls breached, some retailers who have been "lording it" over their traditional partners for many years, need to start making peace in the new power game.

A little humility might go along way to securing a 'touch-hold' in this new retail hierarchy.

Playing ball with the protagonists

DTC Brands

If you work with brands, sell their products, collaborate with them on new initiatives, then you know what an asset they can be. However, as retail was the partner with all the cards historically, it was not difficult to alienate brands.

Now they have plenty of cards of their own. Direct to Customer (DTC) channels and touchpoints are attractive to brands. They can control the brand communication and retail standards, manage media platforms effectively.

They can also select which retail partners to align with, alongside their growing portfolios of directly owned shops. It is not a good idea to be on the blacklist. Without them you will lose a considerably amount of footfall pulling power.

Competitors

There is strength in numbers. Competitor retailers may not have always been thought of as allies. But with potentially different physical geographies, and nuances of market position, 'competitors' can be excellent partners.

At the very least it is good to work together on location footfall initiatives. Traditional battles between serious competitors could be fierce, until only the last one was left standing. However, even the winner was usually weakened for the next battle ahead. Wars are largely futile. It is time to move on. Time to stand together and not fall divided.

Suppliers

The relationship between retailers and suppliers has been under the spotlight. How different retailers reacted to suppliers during the COVID lockdowns became the litmus test for retailer integrity. Did they honour or cancel orders, pay invoices quickly or hang on to the cash?

Under any circumstances, treating suppliers unfairly may seem like a good short-term solution but the mistrust it generates can create long term problems with future relationships.

Do not make an enemy of the people who make your product.

Suppliers, growers and manufacturers happen to be some of the most important people you could possibly do business with.

Physical landlords

The relationship between retailers and landlords is also a topical subject. To varying degrees, we have seen cooperation and empathy, and mis-trust and intransigence in the COVID lockdowns. We will see what happens when the legislation protecting retail tenants and rent holidays comes to an end.

Landlords do not make good enemies either and can make life difficult in the short term. In the longer term we all need to compromise and work together. Landlords may turn to other types of tenants. But for those that continue to rely on retailers to fill their properties, the drastic reduction in retail partner supply will hopefully lead to more symbiotic and balanced relationships. The reality of empty shops and streets will be a sobering proposition for all parties.

Logistics & Distribution

Logistics is an industry resurgent as digital retail presses the button on investment to get products from suppliers to warehouses, to shops, and directly to customers. Logistics is so critical to retailers now that any disruption of the relationship could be catastrophic, whether the relationship is between a local retailer and a local lorry-driver, or a billion-pound state-of-the-art logistics business and a large retail chain.

This new distribution world will require relationships with agile and fleet-footed newcomers, as well as the traditional logistics powerhouses. The world of logistics has never been so diverse or promised such rich opportunities.

Marketing

Mastering the complexities of new social media channels and traditional marketing channels is essential to your brand's exposure and communications. It is more important than ever to develop collaborations with agencies, influencers and advocates, and to work tirelessly to keep them strong & vibrant.

Without these key partners, not to mention many others involved in both the front-end and back-end of business, retailers risk losing more than just face. They will potentially also lose brand pulling power, customer loyalty, scale of offer, distribution efficiency, market exposure, shop convenience, operational efficiency and customer engagement.

It is not just functionality that will be affected but also the emotional connection with customers. Retailers are at the centre of a whole range of opportunities. But if they do not continually sell themselves as attractive propositions to partners, as well as to customers, then they could soon be wondering how they are simply going to sell anything at all.

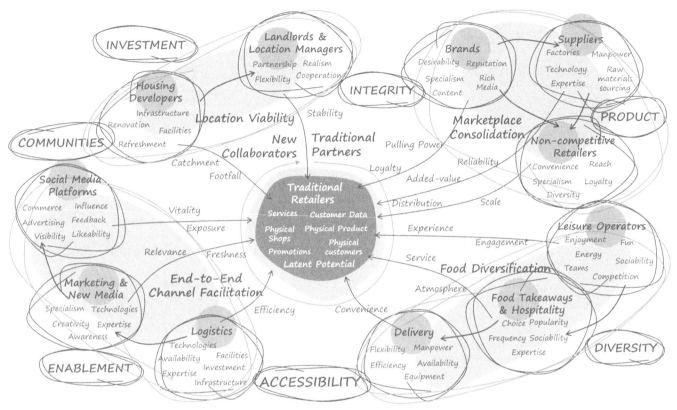

Sketch 43 Traditional Retailers "The new focus of attention!"

Smart and efficient retailers can leverage their assets, and through forming intelligent relationships can make themselves once again the centre of the customers' attention.

By working with social media partners, and logistics businesses they can add efficiency to their end-to-end facilitation, projecting themselves far ahead of their own capabilities.

By working with housing developers and landlords they can assure location viability for physical shops.

They can achieve marketplace consolidation by working with their brands and suppliers and through forming mutual relationships with competitors and complementary retailers.

Retailers can diversify their proposition supported by expertise in other sectors. From financial services to food & hospitality, a strong retail brand can deliver choice and value to an existing loyal customer base.

Better to be the 'focus of attention' amongst many partners, collaborating and compromising, than 'centre stage' in a one man-show that nobody wants to see anymore

The Hut & Homebase:
Two heads are better than many

It may be that the likes of Amazon, and Next, get much of the publicity for the development of e-commerce platforms that are both the basis of their own online retailing empires, as well as being available to third parties to use for their own independent retail businesses. Amazon famously makes much of its profits from hiring out its unique technology platforms.

However, the Hut group is quite possibly an even more astounding business in terms of the scope of services, across technology and logistics, that it offers to 3rd party retailers, as well as being the basis of its own e-commerce business. THG (The Hut Group) has been on an acquisition spree of late adding many beauty brands to its portfolio, however it's THG Ingenuity platform has been the focus of enormous investment, that is now bearing fruit.

In the scramble to deliver best practice e-commerce services to customers, some very well-known businesses were left behind. As every year passes the ability of such brands to catch up and compete, under their own steam, diminishes. The Hut groups services allow the fastest possible, and most professional route to quickly and seamlessly joining the omni-retail fray.

THG services platform is complete from end-to-end. Its compelling proposition exemplified by its deal with Homebase, one of the UK's largest DIY and home retailers. The retailer will have access to THG Ingenuity's proprietary end-to-end ecommerce solution. This will include web development and hosting, global fulfilment and payment infrastructure, digital channel and proposition management, brand building, strategy and even providing digital content for their digital sites and social media from The Hut Group's own content studios.

The potential is now very much real to outsource the whole of the brand communication and interaction chain from visual introductions to logistical fulfilment. Such scale of collaboration requires a parity of respect and acknowledgement. Where is the value? A brand without the ability to interact with its customers. Or a logistical thoroughbred with nothing to deliver. Who is the retailer?

Homebase, having lagged the market will be potentially catapulted into best practice. Importantly it allows Homebase to focus on its assortment and its brand building, channeling its internal teams without distraction.

The model shows the collaborative approach to modern retail. A brand as a product producer, and an end-to-end facilitator, is the combination that creates the compelling combination. With many traditional retail skills in the supply chain and sales operations becoming redundant, it opens the way for brand passion and product innovation to steal the market.

Ocado: Believer in people & technology

Ocado now describes itself as a specialist in automation and robotics; big data, the cloud, web and app development, algorithms and smart optimisation. It is one of the world's leading, most technologically advanced e-commerce facilitators.

Its Smart e-commerce platform supports retailers such as Marks & Spencer with front-end interfaces, fulfillment warehouses with store pick technology carried out by hundreds of its famous robots, and last mile technology which includes fleet management, routing, and delivery planning.

However, its fleet of brightly coloured vans are not always driven by traditional drivers. Ocado realizes that the 5 minutes on the door-step is the richest customer interaction it gets. It reputedly hires hospitality staff and even actors to create an unforgettable experience with its brand.

In a highly competitive delivery market, this personal touch might just make the difference. How Smart of Ocado to realise that technology alone, no matter how spectacular, cannot 'crack every customer nut.' Technology 1. Humans 1.

The Z to A of retail disruption

Tesco & AO.com: Physical space collaborators

The biggest and best from both digital and physical channels are gaining more strength together by consolidating their reputations and footfall to create super physical destinations.

AO, the leading pureplay electronics retailer has partnered with Tesco and opened the first of five shop-in-shops. The 200 sqm spaces allow customers to order larger electricals such as washing machines, fridges and TVs for home delivery, while smaller items are available to purchase off the shelf.

AO colleagues are trained to assist customers. Each product available at the shop-in-shop also has a QR code. Customers can scan the code which will then take them to the AO website.

Asda & Co: The more the merrier

Asda, another leading hypermarket' suffers also from a surfeit of space in its megastores. Its solution is to partner with many specialist retail businesses to create shop-in-shops.

Despite its strong non-food heritage, not least the George clothing brand, Asda has stepped back from some of its non-food initiatives and found it more worthwhile to let more recognized brands take the space and bring in the customers. The partners gain footfall in food shops that is becoming unobtainable on many fragmented high streets.

In essence Asda is creating a grocery driven department store. The additional benefits come from the ability to flex and grade the partnerships in any particular location to match the demand. Many retailers now see 'too much space' as a drag whereas for Asda its imaginative approach is becoming a money-spinner driving additional footfall to its square metres.

Friends of Joules. Like-minded marketplaces

Joules has become an established brand with a distinct image and a growing band of loyal customers who buy into its 'all things countryside' ethic and proposition.

The strength of proposition has allowed it to expand from adult fashion into childrenswear, home and an increasingly wider assortment where its strong values and consistent quality allow it to appeal to the wider lifestyle of its customers.

The strong emotional relationship also saw it survive and 'thrive' in the lockdowns of physical retail, as its online sites took the strain offering the same level of personality, reliability, re-assurance and emotional connection.

So where next for this appealing brand? Again, collaboration has been the answer. But whereas some of the larger commercial powerhouses are rightly fueling partnerships in a pragmatic functional way, Joules is pursuing a meeting of hearts and minds to offer something very powerful to its customers.

The Joules online presence is 'morphing' into 'Friends of Joules' where a growing number of smaller and independent producers, manufacturers and retailers are being curated into a cooperative marketplace for Joules' brand advocates.

The categories covered are complementary to the Joules assortment, strengthening its credentials in important clothing & home categories, whilst filling in some niche gaps for a complete lifestyle proposition.

The glue is the same 'local,' 'artisan' and 'crafted' mindset washing a fresh glow of authenticity onto the Joules brand, whilst giving small businesses access to an eager market.

Moving forwards Joules continues to flourish on 3 strategic fronts. Strengthening its own brand proposition, acquisitions of appropriate brand extensions such as Garden Trading, and the further expansion of its Friends of Joules collaborations.

The Z to A of retail disruption

043

MAKE YOUR WORST TOUCHPOINTS BEST PRACTICE

Internal soul searching, customer research & competitor benchmarking

We all know what we do well, and even more so we know what we do badly. But it is human nature to do more of what we're good at. Unfortunately, it means that the gap between your best touchpoints with the customer and the worst gets wider and wider.

Bite the bullet, identify what's really bad. Ask your customers and your colleagues at the touchpoint coalface. Put an action plan in place and just do it.

A good litmus test. When you're finished, it should be impossible to tell whether you began life as a physical shop retailer, a pureplay or a relatively early omni-channel retailer.

Actions

- Select an impartial team to manage the assessment
- Identify the touchpoints in your business and prioritise
  - Website
  - Mobile site
  - Shop exterior
  - Shop design
  - Customer service...
- For each touchpoint identify the best ways to assess and analyse them
  - Customer feedback, likes
  - Mystery shopping
  - Stakeholder team
- Compare with best practice competitors by touchpoint
- Workshops with touchpoint stakeholders
  - Prioritise actions
  - Define action plan
  - Timings & responsibilities

044

ALWAYS KNOW WHERE YOUR PRODUCT IS

Internal analysis & best practice partnerships

This is a lifetimes work, of course. But you need to start now. Hopefully as you evolve as a truly multi-touchpoint retailer and respond to what today's customer wants across those touchpoints an absolute priority must be to know where your product is.

It could be anywhere between the designers drawing board, the manufacturer, the warehouse, shop, customer's house or any number of storage and delivery hubs. It might not even exist yet, but it will soon. To be honest if you don't know where individual products are, where product delivery packs are, you will not have a chance to survive as the months go by. Begin now, invest in partners and systems and processes.

Actions

- Work by category or collection, whatever is most natural
- Assess the identification criteria for each product
  - Prioritise actions to improve the logic and consistency of identification numbers, codes & descriptions
- Assess system capabilities across touchpoints to identify quickly and accurately where product is
  - By touchpoint & channel
  - Identify black-spots
- Assess synchronisation of channel & touchpoint systems
  - Friction points between channel systems
- Carry out an external IT analysis of system incompatibilities
- Identify best-fit external experts and partnerships to improve/coordinate IT

045

DELIVER HOW YOUR CUSTOMER WANTS YOU TO

Customer research & best practice partnerships

The retailers of the world are using every means possible to get a physical product to a physical customer's location. The larger operators are trialing everything, but they will settle on a reduced number of options. You must do the same.

You must ask your customers what delivery and returns services they want. Analyse how they use existing ones and monitor closely what competitors are delivering, literally. Offer them best practice in what they want the most, not average service across too many. Become famous for one delivery touchpoint.

Actions

- Run a customer research programme to find how your customer wants to buy, receive, collect & return products
  - Identify key touchpoints
  - Identify essential touchpoint details for customers
  - Identify priority services
- Benchmark competitor and best practice touchpoint priorities and details of deliveries
- Identify potential USP touchpoint deliveries
- Assembly a taskforce with touchpoint stakeholders and facilitators from across the business
- Identify and hire essential delivery third parties
- Build and deliver market leading delivery services and touchpoints by customer priority

046

DO THE MATHS ON DELIVERY

Internal analysis & best practice partnerships

There is no point offering the world to your customer, if your world implodes because it doesn't make money.

Every option other than customers buying in shops will cost you margin. It may gain you favour, but it will cost you margin. So absolutely do the maths with delivery partner experts to achieve a solution that is viable. It will never be as profitable as you would like, but it must be profitable. It must also contribute to increases in loyalty, frequency of purchase and value across all the touchpoints of your business.

Actions

- Detailed quantitative analysis of actual and potential sales and profit data across channels
- Analyse and calculate accurate logistical and delivery costs across touchpoints
  - Balanced and holistic considerations
  - Accurate channel roles, time and costs
- Identify efficiency and profit improvements
- Analyse competitor models, infrastructure and costs
- Assess in depth customer priority services
- Run a cost improvements viability assessment with external logistic partners with recommendations
- Test a variety of solutions
- Adopt most cost-effective cross channel solutions

Product Propositions: 'The Crowning of the King'

Getting the basics correct is the constant task of the buying teams. Sadly, our shops are full of products that are unbuyable.

'The Product is King' or so the old-adage goes

It seems strange to doubt this statement. After all, retail is the process of bringing the product and the customer together. Product is still at the heart of retail, of course, but its role as 'absolute king' is changing.

Whilst in some businesses it is still everything, in others it is just a part of a variety of services, collaborations and subscriptions that make up the commercial proposition. What the product 'really' is, now has a wide range of interpretations from the physical, the digital, to the virtual.

It is also worth considering, in our saturated markets, with supply outweighing demand, that there are plenty of physical products that are struggling to find any type of kingdom to rule at all. The 'tarnish on the crown' of the product is not just a result of lower demand. It also reflects and exposes how lackluster many products have become.

Generic product. More of the same. Enough is enough

Selling generic products has become a fight to the bottom, where lowest price is often the only differentiator between retailers. In such brutal fights there is generally only one winner. For all other retailers, a range of more sophisticated weapons needs to be employed to survive and to flourish.

As retail brands we need to build assortments that are distinctive and desirable. The products must reflect our vision and our values, our taste, and our aesthetics. The need to constantly evolve our assortments is a priority. In dynamic, disruptive markets it is essential.

We need to enrich our product. We must embellish, enhance, and adorn our products to add value to them. Ultimately, our products must have an emotional connection with the customer, as much as a physical one. The glory must be restored to our product assortments.

Evolving best practice buying & merchandising

Attention needs to be paid across all the features, attributes, and design elements of a product to ensure that it meets the fundamental needs of the customer. A blouse with the wrong length sleeves, a container that is the wrong size for what it is designed to hold, are common examples of a culture of complacency where buyers go through the motions, and suppliers are paid to produce the least acceptable quality and features.

Planning a balanced commercial assortment, means considering different categories, and type of products. Products should play many roles for retailers from basic commodities, collections of essential and desirable products in the style of the season, to eye-catching image makers that set a brand apart from its competitors. For all types, basic mistakes and fundamental errors that create a barrier to sales must be eliminated.

Evolve

The ongoing process of improvement. People knowledge and skills. Technology applications. Process efficiency.

Areas of consideration:

- Agile collection planning
- Flexible assortment planning
- Buying & merchandising principles
- Product design
- Sourcing & buying
- Market references
- Allocation planning

Summary of opportunities:

- Planning a balanced commercial assortment, considering different categories, type of products – basic, core and image makers, silhouettes, colours & designs.
- Coordinating products to create coordinated customer stories
- Buying with merchandising collaboration to define the price points, margins and commercial quantities.
- Shortening & reducing supply chain times
- Making 'every product an online story'

Enrich

Strategic injections modifying and adding scope and benefit to ongoing processes. Introducing different principles, different ways of working, new skill-sets, technology interventions.

Areas of consideration:

- Added value attributes
- Broader design influences
- Online/technological product research
- Re-defining brand style focus
- New size architectures
- Fabric/materials training and awareness
- Fabric supplier engagement
- Production developments
- Evolve subscription services as part of the proposition

Summary of opportunities:

- Adding value to products through materials, design, workmanship
- Embracing a wider, and newer range of design influences
- Using technology & online to reach new influences
- Creating emotional appeal to products through origins, histories, location, endorsement and collaboration
- Increased awareness of production processes & technologies
- Increased awareness of materials and fabrics

Expand

Introducing broad strategic initiatives to drive the business in new and profitable directions. Requiring changes to the organisational structure, principles and processes.

Areas of consideration:

- Product lifecycle evolutions
- Expansive customer collections
- Design/ style/ cultural/ influencer collaborations
- Proprietary product for customer loyalty
- 3rd party brand partnerships
- Producer collaborations
- External product service partners

Summary of opportunities:

- Radically change the buying & selling calendar, the number and size of collections and the lifecycle of collections
- Action new collaborative strategies with designers, celebrities, influencers and other competitor brands
- Development of unique patented proprietary products
- Adapt the product design collaborative process working with external designers/produces in new ways
- Changing the balance of own-brand and 3rd party brand

Sketch 44 Product propositions: Evolve, Enrich & Expand

The evolution of product stories

From our origins in the physical world of retail, we know that products must be presented as groups, as stories to the customer. A display of oddments, even attractive and potentially bestselling oddments, will not attract the attention of the customer if they are part of a visual chaos. Coordinating products to create coordinated customer stories is an important task in the buying and merchandising processes.

Appreciating the evolution of product storytelling in an omni-channel world is essential for buying teams. The advent of digital retail, particularly on smaller mobile devices, has made the customer focus more on individual items, rather than story groups. It is a challenge to work with every product, to tell individual stories in one medium, whilst celebrating the collection and the coordinated theme in another. But it is a pre-requisite for success for omni-channel retailers.

Product teams

Still at the core of retail commerciality, the proposed assortment must balance its aesthetic logic, for physical and virtual touchpoints, with its sales potential. The buyer and merchandiser relationship is therefore even more essential to define the price points, margins, and commercial quantities, in the new complexities of dynamic timelines, diverse customer preferences and omni-channel allocation and availability.

This relationship will become ever more critical as the safety net of the physical store parameters dissolves into a digital world of unlimited real and virtual products. The buying and merchandising teams still need to define the breadth and depth of physical assortments, but now within the wider context of the potential commerciality of virtual and bespoke ranges.

Enrichment of the product, requires enrichment of the product teams.

The product must be customer orientated. It should reflect the world around them, and the places where they, work & play. Increasingly customers are influenced by a wider variety of things and buyers and designers need to be ahead of, and in tune with, the customer inspirations.

Enriching the product design team, means ensuring that they continually embrace a wider, and newer range of design influences. The internet, and digital channels can bring inspiration from around the world. This new world of stimulation must be balanced with traditional shop visits and competitor benchmarking.

This wider range of influences and design possibilities also brings added responsibility in selecting the correct trends and buying patterns to produce. Translating fifty influences into five collections is much more difficult than selecting from ten ideas. The ever more sophisticated role of retail intelligence, customer research and data analysis has a big part to play in the enrichment and accuracy of the product design process.

The product team, with responsibility for buying as well as creating, also have a more complex role to play in their awareness of changing production processes & technologies, and the options of raw and fabricated materials, and fabrics in the case of fashion and home furnishings.

A growing web of international and local suppliers has widened the possibilities of more efficient processes, and of more complex and diverse product finishes and attributes. Awareness and a discerning eye, coupled with confident decision making are increasingly important attributes for the buying team across any category of products.

New raw material developments, and a return to older practices of growing and supplying materials, all underpin the responsibility of buyers to balance the spreadsheets, whilst adhering to sustainability, and supplier protocols relating to working conditions and pollution levels.

The role of a buyer is a complex one. They must be supported in growing their skills and expertise, supported by production and creative specialists.

Only through enriching the buying team will a retailer be able to add value to products through new materials, and unique workmanship. The buying team will only be able to add emotional appeal to products through their increased understanding of the origins, histories, location of designs and influences.

The customer is looking for more added-value and distinction. The onus is on retailers to evolve, and enrich, their product teams with education and collaborations.

Expanding the strategies behind product buying

Innovative strategic decisions regarding the structure of assortments, the production processes and the relationships with suppliers are required more than ever. The disruptive market, and innovation of competitors, requires the input of the whole retail business from the boardroom down, to plan and execute the future direction of assortments.

Amongst the strategic opportunities is the radical changing of the buying & selling calendar, the number and size of collections, and the lifecycle of collections.

The buying trend from two assortments a year has accelerated to an incessant turnover of new designs. However, this momentum is now being questioned and re-appraised as customers and society recoil against the increased and over-whelming implications of waste and pollution from an endless stream of buying variations.

Buying & merchandising decisions are ultimately becoming the remit of strategic and ethical decision makers at the highest level of retail businesses.

Strategies focused on new collaborations with designers, celebrities, influencers and other competitor brands need to be put in place to evolve the assortment and align it with the wider brand positioning and values.

Unique & proprietary products

The adoption of a more collaborative culture should also open the possibilities for creative product design partnerships working with external designers and producers in new ways. The shift will reflect strategic changes in the balance of own-brand product, and third-party brands, and should see the initiation of competitor amalgamations of resources and ideas, combining shop space and production capabilities.

The scramble will also be on to develop unique patented proprietary products. This is the extreme of distinctive product development where a design becomes ubiquitous with an activity, a customer group and ultimately with a brand. Unique proprietary products are literally worth their weight in commercial gold.

There are many ways that retailers can restore the crown to its product proposition. Make it the king again amongst competitors and for the customer.

To stand out from the crowd, a product needs to be essential. Functionally and emotionally essential. An essential retailer needs to be developing and selling essential products.

The balance of product stories

Whilst it isn't possible to go into depth across all areas of buying & merchandising within the covers of this book, it is worth reflecting further on the opportunities surrounding product stories. In a truly customer centric retail world it is these stories that will be key to attracting customers and stimulating sales.

As we have said, product storytelling originates from retail in physical shops where products need to be grouped. They need to be grouped for visual impact. They need to be grouped for coordination of colours and similar styling, grouped to encourage multiple purposes. They also need to be grouped to help shop colleagues and customers understand the assortment.

Traditionally, one story consists of multiple products.

This striving for multiple sales through product grouping inadvertently creates problems in other areas. The stories look incredible when seen in their perfect state. However, to deliver the perfect state into physical shops requires a high level of supplier coordination, shop allocation sensitivity, delivery correlation and shop display operations. Even then, the perfect state becomes its own worst enemy. Best sellers sell quickly, stock fragments, and shops struggle to maintain cohesive displays.

No matter how attractive they look, traditional stories are also traditionally one-dimensional. When that dimension is broken the stories, and the products they contain, can lose their context, their identity, their raison d'etre and their selling potential.

Visually orientated product stories segment the whole assortment into blocks. Ironically, the stronger the visual stories the greater the barriers between different blocks. As a result, traditional product stories push most products away from each other. They do not bring them together.

In the digital world, the focus is much more on individual products. The limits of the digital interface, and the way the customer buys online have helped to mould this. As such the individual product contains the most important stories, not the product groups themselves.

Digitally, every product should consist of many different stories.

It is the products themselves that must become rich and deep in stories. They should create rich and deep relationships with the customer. Products are now multi-dimensional. They are flexible and adaptable. Products in the digital age should be able to come together in many ways, as their stories combine and coincide.

This digital approach results in fewer barriers between products. They co-exist. They work together in many ways. Grouping of products no longer needs to be only pre-determined by distant designers, months before the products are on sale. Product stories can react to customer trends, interests, and influencers. They can react to sales.

The digital touchpoints facilitate this flexibility. Smart, conversational, and visual search engines will group and present products in as many ways as they are identified and tagged into the system. Product stories can even be personalised by responsive interfaces which means no two customers are experiencing the same stories, the same grouping.

Having multi-faceted products with deep stories, does not mean they should not be conceived as part of initial visual groups. It means they have the potential to be part of many groups. Sometimes definitively part of one story. At other times, in fact simultaneously, products can be part of many stories. Products, and product groups have just become a whole lot more interesting.

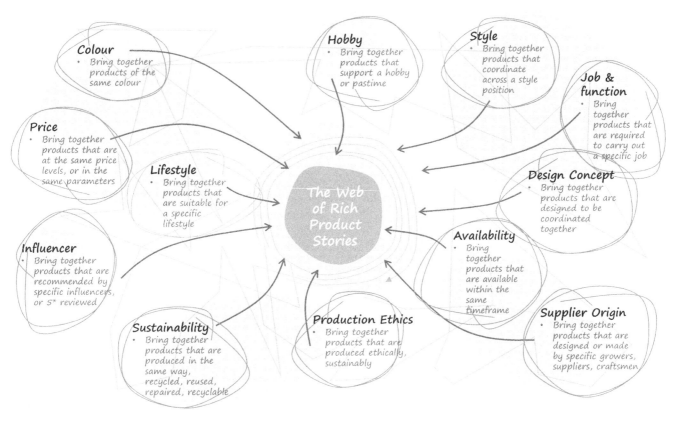

Colour
- Bring together products of the same colour

Hobby
- Bring together products that support a hobby or pastime

Style
- Bring together products that coordinate across a style position

Job & function
- Bring together products that are required to carry out a specific job

Price
- Bring together products that are at the same price levels, or in the same parameters

Lifestyle
- Bring together products that are suitable for a specific lifestyle

The Web of Rich Product Stories

Design Concept
- Bring together products that are designed to be coordinated together

Influencer
- Bring together products that are recommended by specific influencers, or 5* reviewed

Availability
- Bring together products that are available within the same timeframe

Sustainability
- Bring together products that are produced in the same way, recycled, reused, repaired, recyclable

Production Ethics
- Bring together products that are produced ethically, sustainably

Supplier Origin
- Bring together products that are designed or made by specific growers, suppliers, craftsmen

Sketch 45 The Web of Rich Product Stories

Individual products have a variety of stories to tell. Their potential is to be as inclusive as possible in as many customer journeys as possible.

For the sake of traditional buying and merchandising processes, and physical displays in shops, products will have an initial story priority. They will be conceived as part of a visual story.

However, that story should not even be a priority concept. It should just be an initial concept – where the story begins. The buying and merchandising process should consider products as part of several different stories, even several different physically grouped stories. In this way it can be flexible and relevant in many ways, not just one.

When we consider the dynamic and simultaneous possibilities of the virtual world, then products can come to life in many individual ways for so many different customers.

Turning on the style

Style is difficult to define, but in the hands of experts, expert designers, and expert customers, grouping by style has a magic attraction.

Grouping by style can be done deliberately in specific collections or themes, but style cuts across pre-determined groupings. Grouping by style promises to be one of the most flexible and personal ways of presenting products together.

Where there are aesthetic choices to be made, there is style. Style can be an essential product, and product story feature, from fashion to furnishings. It is also increasingly important in the selection of everything from cars to kitchenware, recipes to ingredients, toothbrushes to mobile phones, music to film genres, homes to hotels, garden plants to holiday destinations.

Style in its customer focused orientation can be translated to 'taste.' Customer 'taste' is becoming the definitive element in the customer's choice of products to buy, and who to buy them from.

Style is a difficult thing for algorithms and technologies to get their microprocessor heads around. Much analysis and logification is being done, visual search engines developed to help bring products of a similar style together. However, one way or another, people are still currently the key to grouping by style, and the flexibility and personalization that this offers.

As a result, the pre-determined grouping by style including the use of colour, pattern, materials, shapes, silhouettes, enhancements, adornments and so many other agile aesthetics, will continue to be essential for many retailers.

The opportunity also lays in an increased empathy and inclusion of 'style' across wider collections and themes. Ultimately only two 'style DNAs' are important. Only two 'tastes' are important. The 'taste' of the brand, the retailer, and the 'taste' of individual products.

The imaginative, sensitive, and accurate 'tagging' of individual products by stylists is the starting point for flexible and personal grouping by style. Algorithms can enhance this logic and learn quickly from customer buying patterns and preferences. They can learn what patterns and journeys the customer takes from A to Z, and every twist and turn in between.

Technology can use 'tagging' as its signposts to understand and then predict and influence the customer's next turn in their journey through style. The organic new groupings are allowing the customer to be their own stylists, to build their own aesthetic groupings, using the building blocks of the original stylists only as a point of entry, a starting point.

This rich style analysis can be amalgamated to find common style journeys and product links. It can also be used to identify individual customer 'styling gurus,' who can be approached and collaborated with, as style advisers, collaborators and influencers for other like-minded customers. They are the incarnation of a 'popular taste.'

This collaboration of human creativity and machine intelligence, is clearly a powerful tool for responsive digital retail touchpoints. It can also be an essential learning for physical shop colleagues from visual merchandisers to sales assistants.

The knowledge can help visual merchandisers construct spontaneous visual story groupings based on pre-determined style groups, and the known buying patterns, preferences, and combinations from customer stylist journeys and style gurus. The knowledge can also be transferred to new product group planograms, or by more informal product guidance and suggestions, allowing the visual merchandisers to apply their creativity.

Importantly, the same processes can be used to present compelling and logical categories. Style can be as much about logic as creativity. Taste can be 'bland' or 'full of flavour' yet equally attractive to different customers, on different journeys.

Style knowledge can also help sales assistants and personal shoppers to walk in the footsteps of 'style gurus' as they lead the customer on a journey of buying possibilities, based on the customer's individual taste and particular style preferences.

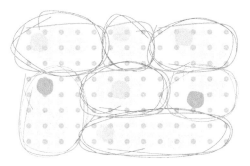

Predetermined Stylist Product Story Groups
- Traditional product story design process
- Trend & market analysis
- Stylist & designer led
- Buying & merchandising teams

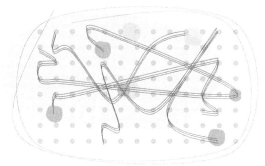

Spontaneous Customer Style Journeys Product Story Groups
- Organic customer journeys
- Instigated by customer brief
- Led by personal shopper/sales assistant
- Guided by style guru aesthetic product links

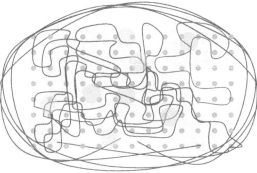

Responsive Customer Style Guru's Product Story Groups
- Customer style shopping journeys and preferences
- Product style tagging
- Algorithm customer aesthetic journey analysis
- Delivered visually by VM teams

© 2021 vm-unleashed ltd.

Sketch 46 Style Product Grouping

Whilst there are not an infinite number of ways to group products by style, there are many. That overused expression, Eclectic taste is the blanket expression for every individual's good taste.

Good retailers pre-determine style grouping in whatever formal or informal way is correct for their brand. Best practice retailers then use technology to understand and respond to how customers are grouping products, by what taste attributes the customer is prioritizing.

AI technology can analyse the way customers are browsing and buying products, correlate style tags to create new product grouping based on how the customer shops across channels. Shop VM teams and online space planners can create new space plans to recreate these trends.

Spontaneous customer journeys can also be created in real time both in shops and online by responding to customer style likes and dislikes, either verbally communicated or analysing product responses.

The sales assistant can then guide customers across predetermined style boundaries directly to individual style products, whilst online hierarchies and layouts can respond to individual style decisions.

This knowledge can be transferred as intense and continuous learning training, and by ear-piece real-time guidance.

Stylists leading customer style gurus, leading visual merchandisers, leading sales assistants, leading customers, who then lead the stylists in the next wave of products. A 'style' virtuous cycle. Perpetual good taste!

What is style?
Style is essential.

The rules behind product story grouping

Despite the customer potentially taking such a leading role in product grouping, either actively as style gurus, or inadvertently through facilitating responsive digital experiences, it is still very important for retailers to control the balance of product stories they present to the customer.

It is even more important for retailers to control the balance in a market of many digital touchpoints which are all, to varying degrees, responsive and personalised. There is a risk of brand values being eroded in the free-for-all chaos of customers trying to find what they need, what they want. Customers respect a strong and consistent 'style' proposition. They may like to take the lead, but they do need authority and consistency.

The fact is most people love the idea of choice, but the vast majority cannot handle it. To a certain point, we want to be told what to buy. That is still the role of retailers, even if we decide at some point to ignore their advice. The customer is always right, even if they do not always know what is best, or most tasteful!

Nike: presenting the illusion of infinite choice

'Choice' really is the most peculiar of things. People love the concept of it, but in reality, only a few can manage the responsibility of it. As a result, many retailers have felt compelled to offer vast assortments of diversity only for customers to fight for the remnants of a few best-sellers.

It is a conundrum with profound consequences not only for retail performance, but also in terms of the wasteful and damaging practices for the wider environment.

'Offering the world' has been Nike's solution for a number of years. It is most visible in its NikeID shop-in-shops. I love visiting the 'special place' in the London Nike Town flagship shop. Before my eyes it has grown from personalized 'sneakers' to a wide variety of personalized sports & fashion items.

Of course, the premise is personalization. You can have whatever you want. Once beyond the special customer entrance rope, you have the attentive and exclusive attention of your sales specialist.

Personal service. In the case of trainers every possible detail of personalization is discussed from the base materials, the sole design, the grip pattern, the colours, the logo, the owner's name, the laces and the shape, material and colour of the aglet at the end of the lace. Same aglet, complementary aglets?

The most common question from customers after this most personal of tours is, 'What's everybody else having?' Therein lies the beauty of the puzzle. Brands like Nike thrive on offering the proposition of infinite choice. A proposition that would be commercially unsustainable, where it not for the fact that, in reality, Nike only needs to plan for a very limited number of product variations. The illusion of making profit, in reality.

The Z to A of retail disruption

Fishs Eddy: the non-accidental storyteller

If you're a regular visitor to New York, then please tell me that you visit the retail gem that is Fishs Eddy, in the Flat Iron district.

The shop sells all manner of kitchen and dining ware. It is storytelling at its most idiosyncratic. The story of the brand's origins gives you a clue to its assortment strategy. The founders stumbled on a warehouse crammed with crockery, excess to requirements, and apparently the owner said, 'take the lot!'

Every step of the shop opens a compelling product story. The delivery is uniquely Fishs Eddy using old wooden crates, boxes and tins, giving at atmosphere of charming chaos, but the stories themselves are as strategically commercial as those planned in any retail buying office across the globe.

The shop is pinned by authoritative categories, spanning the wall spaces, for glasswares, kitchenwares, plates. Floor focal fixtures for kitchen utensils and flatware, that's cutlery to us, are utterly compelling. But these categories are not regimented although you can buy a set of six matching dinnerplates.

The joy is to mix & match within categories and across categories, combining anything that takes the eye. There is an onus on the customer to have the eclectic eye, but occasional structure does help with the conventional approach.

Tables are also stacked high with coordinated themes across varieties of categories, New York themes, floral themes, vintage themes. Even the smallest surfaces have single price cup displays, classic diner white opportunities, and the trademark ceramic rubber glover displays. Beneath the chaos lies magic, and behind the magic a cunning combination of commercial categorization and irresistible and unpredictable charm.

In many ways, this concept, with origins in the ceramic manufacturing industry is an excellent template for the flexibilities of the modern omni-assortment, where it is the common 'taste' of the customer that defines the final choice. Buy with logic, display with imagination, but allow eclectic taste to define the day.

Anthropology &More Stories: fluid patterns

Whilst digital channels offer the most fluidity and flexibility for bringing individual products alive, by including them in a variety of immersive and responsive groupings, the physical space has also been re-invented by some retailers as a more dynamic and spontaneous vehicle for product stories.

H&M found success in its Scandinavian regimentation of classic shop groupings. It was therefore a delightfully refreshing evolution when its '&more stories' concept landed with its unpredictable and very personal way of telling stories.

The shop design itself is open and free, lending itself to many changes of furniture and mannequin combinations, graphics are often printed photo-copies, using clips and pins to secure them. There is a wonderful temporary and transient feel to the space, reflecting the assortment itself.

Stories are rarely obvious and require investigation. The product blocks and densities often belying or hiding the story beneath. The stories are deeper, coming from the creative vision, a designer's philosophy, the origin of the fabric, the place where the shapes and folds were inspired. The customers themselves are not confined by the restrictions of space. To shop requires a curious mind and a confidence in style.

The glorious, if slightly more classic world of Anthropology, is also crafted and created by the wider eclectic tastes and undulating combinations of its designers. Products that should have no commercial importance such as vintage drawer handles and papier mâché animals collide with monographed mugs and handmade jewellery, all bound together with impeccable and laser consistent taste.

The freedom given to VM to interpret the product stories adds to the individualism of each shop floor and the anticipation of assortments waiting to be discovered.

My understanding is that each shop VM team are given a design brief for the seasons props, and window displays, and a budget. Beyond that each team converts their shop into an out-of-hours workshop where they can create their own interpretations. It is not just customers that can re-imagine the proposition to their specific taste, to reflect their individual style persuasions.

The Z to A of retail disruption

Marks & Spencer: old pigs & new tricks

Before you possibly glaze over and turn over, at the Marks & Spencer reference, particularly if you're from the younger generation, you should be aware that it has been for many years at the heart of product innovation.

Its role of honour include being the first chain to have sold fresh chicken in the 1960s by developing the 'cold chain' process. Maybe not sexy enough, but it is also worth noting that everyone's favourite pink and porky chewy sweet, 'Percy Pig' recently racked up his 30th birthday acquiring 250,000 Facebook followers.

Marks & Spencer has recently re-established a specialist food innovation hub, whose goal is to create industry-leading products once more. Apparently, the hub has a transversal team comprising packaging, nutrition, product innovation and business development so that initiatives can be developed and delivered in an integrated way and be quick to market by avoiding traditional silo frictions.

The innovation hub also tracks emerging trends and insights and collaborates with external partners to add disruption to the production processes, the way the products are manufactured, the supply chain and the integration of technology and sustainability to the proposition.

The integration of product development & marketing has before been at the vanguard of M&S thinking. They were the first retailer to have a marketing director at board level, as the Stuart Rose era took food storytelling to a new level with its "This is not just...this is Marks & Spencer..." Who can forget those Valentine's Day chocolate ads, and maybe the innovation hub will re-invent the art of M&S storytelling once more.

Crate & Barrel: the emotive power of words

Whilst it's time to celebrate 'American Greats,' when it comes to product assortments & storytelling, it is worth remembering that the principles of assortment construction, the link to visual merchandising & displays, and the development of product stories all owe a great debt of gratitude to Crate & Barrel.

Crate & Barrel were, for me, the first retailer to be truly customer-first in the buying process. Assortments were not built from buying deals but were constructed back into the buying process with a clear commercial and visualized customer vision driving every decision.

They invented 'buying for space' The concept today is second nature, but someone did it first. It was Crate & Barrel.

They segmented their shop space into areas, and they conceived product stories for the customer.

They envisaged powerful categories, they imagined coordinated themes, they saw powerful hero product displays and they constructed stories around the customer lifestyle. Most importantly, they took space, linear metres, and they built real product display blocks to communicate visually and commercially the product story they had conceived. Then they bought the product to fill that space & tell the story.

In effect Crate & Barrel invented visual merchandising as we know it.

They also showed how to communicate powerful stories through emotive words. Floor displays were themed around 'The Cozy Night-in' or "The Business Lunch' with simple graphics setting the scene.

Whilst furniture sets used black text on white board to tell the story of the set in-front of you, from children playing on the rug by the fire, whilst Mum & Dad sat back and read their Sunday newspapers on Autumn days, to the perfect Thanksgiving meal complete with table displays, decor & ornaments, coordinated seat covers and occasional furniture. Truly innovative and mesmerizing 'storytelling' at its best.

The Z to A of retail disruption

047

WIDEN YOUR INFLUENCER HORIZONS

Market research & customer research

When you work in a commercial conveyor belt it is so easy to stop looking for influences. It is so easy to stop looking outside the window and just replicate the tried & trusted.

The fact is, many retailers and their buying teams today are way behind the customer when we talk about inspiration and diverse and exciting influences. You have to be ahead of, or at least side by side, with your customer. You can even collaborate and partner with you customers on sharing inspiration. It's your call. But you've got to get out into their world.

Actions

- Create several customer focus groups
- Identify their influences
  - Physical and online competitor brands
  - Bloggers, vloggers, celebrities, influencers
  - Media, style, fashion, trade influences
- Create influencer groups from the focus groups
- Plan interaction points with the groups
- Re-plan and prioritise influences for future assortment design & development
  - Balance of different sources
  - Key influences
- Assess current suppliers and their level of product inspiration input
  - Plan closer collaboration on design, manufacture including sharing knowledge, influences and training

048

TURN OVER THE PAGE OF YOUR CALENDAR

Customer research & competitor benchmarking

Deadlines, deadlines, deadlines! Buying teams lives are run by them. But are they the correct ones?

Again, its easy to get immersed in the same processes and timings. But often the timings are dictated by the wrong things. Chief executive strategy meetings, resource availability, factory production slots, shipping schedules. What about the customer?

It is literally time to ask your customer what they want, when they want it, and how often they want it. You need to adjust your buying calendars to suit your customers wishes. You might find it a refreshing change in the buying team offices as well.

Actions

- Competitor & best practice benchmarking of product calendars and product deliveries and stockturn
- Customer focus groups and research on frequency of purchases and preferred assortment timings
- Detailed assessment of historical sales patterns by weeks and months by category and collections
- Develop assortment delivery calendar
- Work backwards through the B&M process to achieve the new assortment calendar
  - Manufacture & shipping
  - Product development
  - Sourcing
  - Research & design
  - Strategic & financial planning
  - Sales performance reviews/range reviews

049

IT'S STORYTIME, BUT NOT AS WE KNOW IT

Internal brainstorming, customer research and benchmarking

Your category management and buying processes are, to a greater of lesser extent, driven by the grouping of products. Stories, as themes or categories are important parameters for buying structures and quantities. But buying across one dimensional stories limits the stories of individual products.

You need to move your mentality to delivering several layers of storytelling for every product. You need to provide products that have many selling points and many product scenarios.

Actions

- Competitor & best practice benchmarking of product story strategies and story type balance across channels
- Assessment of best practice individual product story telling
- Customer focus group product story priorities
  - Product coordination preferences
  - Product information priorities
  - Product buying triggers
- Create a calendar of product story telling opportunities
- Define product story details by category and collection type
  - Identify story levels and priorities
- Plan story telling across channels
  - Digital information & product communication
  - Physical shop stories, coordination & displays
  - Story telling across social channels and marketing
- React in season to best selling stories across markets

050

WORK WITH YOUR ENEMIES

Competitor benchmarking & partnerships

When you are a brand, when you design and develop your own product, you are competitive, and you are ferociously independent.

However, the customer is driven more now by the convenience of availability rather than the historical independence of brands.

To attract the customer both physically and digitally it is time to start working with your competitors. Working with your worst enemies because they are attracting the same customer. You need to share the greater spoils of partnerships. Grit your teeth and get to know your competitors and how you can work together. They won't be any worse than you are.

Actions

- Identify competitors and complementary brands with mutual reasons to collaborate
- Identify areas of collaboration:
  - Research & development
  - Manufacturer & shopping costs
  - Economies of scale/raw materials
  - Complementary collections
  - Complementing assortment strengths & weaknesses
  - Complementary physical distributions
  - Logistics & distribution costs
  - Physical shop sharing
  - Shop in shops
  - Cross-selling across channels
- Identify collaboration options
  - Informal partnerships
  - Mergers & acquisitions

Supply Partners: 'In the same boat together'

The relationship with suppliers has never been so important. The COVID lockdown exposed the dangers of weak supplier integration, whilst the move to remote digital communications highlighted the opportunities for technology applications across new supply chains.

Trust between some suppliers and retailers hit an all-time low as orders were cancelled and payments frozen. The repercussions of such actions will set back the industry, unless proactive action is taken to re-build relationships and increase safeguards for suppliers.

Retailers wishing to evolve supplier relations would do well to begin with opening new dialogues and taking measures to personalise individual relationships as far as possible

Evolving the ethical supply chain

Customers no longer separate in their eyes the practices of the retailers they buy from, and the suppliers selected by the retailer. It is important for retailers to take an ever-more active role in the monitoring and implementation of human rights, employee conditions, and sustainable initiatives in those suppliers.

Bad practices, at home and abroad, will ultimately reflect poorly on the retailer. It is in their interests to establish a better understanding of their suppliers, through the development and application of supplier charters and impartial monitoring. These agreements must cover working practices and conditions, child labour, potential slave labour, payment, working hours, working environments, air & water pollution safeguards.

It should become normal practice for both suppliers and the retailers who use them, to take a more active role in the social and ecological issues of the areas around factories and the places where workers live. In the best cases, this can include housing, sanitation, healthcare, education and job security.

Evolving a better relationship will have a variety of commercial benefits from increased efficiency and reliability to a better collaboration on the quality of product sample standards and checking procedures, and the added-value of the final product.

Enriching product quality & consistency

The enrichment of relationships will also help to add genuine value to products through the consistent additions of high-quality adornments and embellishments, in the battle to produce non-generic products. The development of exclusive supplier relationships with formal safeguards on both sides would stimulate a richer exchange of ideas, deeper understanding of customers, worker cultures and skill-sets.

An important element in building trust is the fairer burden and spreading of costs, such as those involved in purchasing raw materials, and accessing specialist production skills. The relationship with manufacturers should be evolved further to include special and exclusive relationships with growers and the providers of raw materials. A spreading of cost responsibility, and a guarantee of consistent added-value product supply.

The COVID lockdown and the need for flexibility has also accelerated the development of relationships with local suppliers who can deliver shorter lead-times, as well as bespoke and responsive products. Local supplier physical adjacencies will also facilitate and inspire closer working relationships and collaborative working.

Evolve

The ongoing process of improvement.
People knowledge and skills. Technology applications.
Process efficiency.

Areas of consideration:

- Improve current supplier liaison
- Re-energise new supplier selection
- Evolve supplier workers' charter
- Increase factory visits & checks
- Re-vamp supplier negotiations
- Improve sample checking criteria

Summary of opportunities:

- To create a better relationship of trust and reliability based on open communication and negotiations.
- To establish a better understanding of suppliers, through development and application of supplier charters, covering working practices, child labour, working conditions, payment and hours, working environment, air & water pollution safeguards
- To collaborate on product sample standards and checking procedures

Enrich

Strategic injections modifying and adding scope and benefit to ongoing processes.
Introducing different principles, different ways of working, new skill-sets, technology interventions.

Areas of consideration:

- Develop unique/exclusive suppliers
- Local supplier development
- Absorb supplier product knowledge
- Develop informed raw material collaborations
- Increase flexible volumes/lead-times
- Employ earlier payments & joint cost burden

Summary of opportunities:

- Develop exclusive supplier relationships and safeguards for a richer exchange of ideas, cultures and burden of costs
- Create a common culture of product strategy & knowledge
- Develop local short lead time suppliers to complement distant suppliers, and bespoke opportunities
- Extend relationships to collaboration with raw materials suppliers and growers to extend supply chain responsibilities

Expand

Introducing broad strategic initiatives to drive the business in new and profitable directions.
Requiring changes to the organisational structure, principles and processes.

Areas of consideration:

- Develop vertical supply integration
- Increase owned factories/suppliers
- Engage with raw material suppliers
- Supply chain integration
- Product & customer data sharing technology through the supply chain
- RFID inventory tracking at every stage of supply
- 3D printing as part of the supply chain

Summary of opportunities:

- Develop an end-to-end owned vertically integrated supply chain
- Extend the vertical chain to raw materials growers and suppliers
- Invest in the development of recyclable materials
- Develop a circular closed-loop supply chain that incorporates recyclable raw materials, recycled materials and recycled products, bespoke, made-to-order and virtual assortments

Sketch 47 Supply partners: Evolve, Enrich & Expand

Expanding the depth and breadth of the supply chain

The supplier base and the supply chain offer some of the biggest opportunities for decisive strategic expansion in the retail industry. An industry based on margin exploitation, volume orders and high customer demand is learning the need for new principles and practices.

The development of vertical supply integration including owned factories, suppliers and distribution offers the possibility of greater efficiency, higher flexibility and the ability to create a branded end-to-end process.

The rise of digital retail has shifted the focus, and the priorities, of the customer to the product delivery to them, as much as the physical shop location and the visual display of it. Satisfying this change in physical interactions will require a much closer collaboration between retailer and supplier. Traditional logistics to warehouses for distribution needs to be complemented with the potential for delivery direct from the producer, the supplier, to the customer. This relationship could ultimately extend to bespoke products, and the facilitation of 3D printing of products where appropriate and feasible.

The more flexible timing of production that is increasingly demanded by customer behaviour also necessitates closer collaboration and risk management between producer and retailer as well as an extended relationship down the supply chain to include relationships with growers and material suppliers.

The whole process ideally expanding to a circular model instead of a linear process flow. Lateral added-value processes added at the supplier, the manufacturer, and the delivery stages of the process, as well as in the buying & merchandising processes of the retailer itself.

The 'Passion supply chain'

The vertically integrated model can be expanded as far as required or beneficial to include plantations, farms, energy suppliers and owned raw material supply chains.

An important emotional output of this operational strategy is to ensure that what the customer receives captures the passion of the original brand vision. The vertically integrated and managed chain is the best way to ensure that every partner in the supply chain understands, feels and works with the same common passion for what they are doing. The passion in the vision of the business, and the passion of the loyal customer can be bridged by the potential to develop the seamless 'Passion Supply Chain.'

Investment in technology to integrate with suppliers and transform the supply chain are an essential. Common or compatible IT software and systems allow partners through the whole supply chain to identify individual products and progress the automated transfer of documents and the sharing of virtual samples. An initiative such as 'AI product sample checking' would slice weeks off a lead-time and remove the costs of duplicated and repetitive hand checking.

Applying RFID technology for end-to-end product tracking not only revolutionises the supply chain transparency from factory to distribution centre, but to micro-warehouses, dark stores, stockrooms, shop floors and to the customers' home.

RFID technology in essence also adds the customer to the supply chain. Digital shopping has increased the proliferation of returned products. These may be viewed as 'failed sales' or as dynamic supply chains for new sales to alternative customers. RFID technology adds transparency to the supply chain, making inventory visible and available in double-quick time.

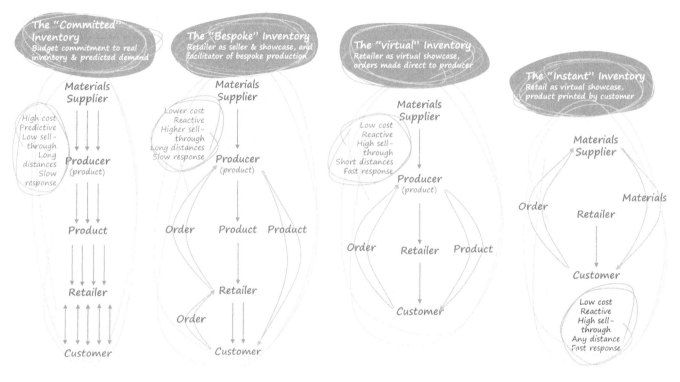

The "Committed" Inventory
Budget commitment to real inventory & predicted demand

Materials Supplier

High cost
Predictive
Low sell-through
Long distances
Slow response

Producer (product)

Product

Retailer

Customer

The "Bespoke" Inventory
Retailer as seller & showcase, and facilitator of bespoke production

Materials Supplier

Lower cost
Reactive
Higher sell-through
Long distances
Slow response

Producer (product)

Order   Product   Product

Retailer

Order

Customer

The "virtual" Inventory
Retailer as virtual showcase, orders made direct to producer

Materials Supplier

Low cost
Reactive
High sell-through
Short distances
Fast response

Producer (product)

Order   Retailer   Product

Customer

The "Instant" Inventory
Retail as virtual showcase, product printed by customer

Materials Supplier

Order   Retailer   Materials

Customer

Low cost
Reactive
High sell-through
Any distance
Fast response

© 2021 vm-unleashed ltd.

Sketch 48 The evolution of inventory

The evolution of inventory

Agile retail businesses are shifting the supply chain to support a major strategic and operational focus on new inventories. The traditional approach of producing an inventory which is then sold, as much as is possible, is being transformed into an approach where a partly, or fully, virtual inventory is showcased as much as possible, and then produced to order.

The enablers of the new processes are built around delaying final commitments to designs, styles, materials, colours and sizes until the latest possible moment.

Bespoke inventories use local suppliers and fast response times to refresh and replenish the assortment in shops with the most up-to-date sales data and analysis. Virtual inventories respond to individual requests and orders from the customer, whilst the advent of instant inventories will potentially put the production of the product directly into the hands of the customer.

'Right here. Right now'

The development of non-supplier, supply chains is a dramatic but feasible innovation using 3D printing technology and on demand production technologies.

In essence, this is the ultimate in personalised or bespoke shopping. Only when an order has been received will a collection of raw materials be transformed into the appropriate product, which will then be available in the right place at the right time. That being... right here, right now.

If you are reading this book as a physical product then it will be as a result of POD, 'print on demand.' The book exists as a digital file, which springs into action in the hands of a selected few digital printers. The product is produced and shopped within minutes.

Similar technologies are widespread and growing for products such as t-shirts and commodity fashion. Production on demand is no longer just in the market for personalized t-shirts and 'stag-party' sweatshirts. It is a tool for mass-production for international brands. Where mass-production can be flexible and responsive. The impact on efficiency, sell-through and as a result commercial profit is equalled by the efficiency in the use of raw materials and the drastic reduction in waste.

POD is one of the most exciting areas of retail and potentially one of the most lucrative for retail businesses who can get their heads, their agile organisations, and their astute strategies around it.

'Slow boats to fast technologies'

Supplier relationships, and the supply chain, are being transformed from a world of big sheds and slow boats to one of small lead-times and fast technologies.

Reducing 'space & time' supply

In more traditional buying and merchandising processes, the single element that prevents increased sales, better sell-throughs and lower markdowns, is time. The distance of time, the remoteness of time, are the realities of a buyer's predicament in a traditional supply chain model.

We need to reduce the space between the processes. Reduce the time for the whole process.

The further ahead of the time when a product hits the shops, that the design research has to be carried out, that the final product decisions need to be made, then the greater is the chance that it will not be the right product for the customer. The popular colour may have changed since the initial research, the preferred materials to be used may be different. Time changes everything. Time can be a blessing or a curse depending on how you manage it.

The time between the initial design research and the product landing in shops must be as short as possible. The physical and virtual distances between the collaborators must be the working minimum. To create more time, that we can use less of.

The 'Inspirational lag' is created between the stages of inspiration and development. Retailers should work with virtual tools to ensure that this relationship is as efficient and accurate as possible. To reduce the lag.

The 'Accuracy drag'" is a result of the production and distribution processes. It is here that closer physical adjacencies can reduce delays and maximise responses, whilst virtual technologies can replace the physical movement of products altogether.

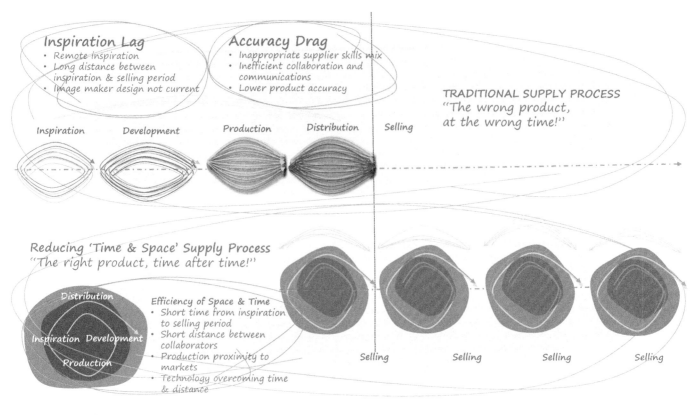

Inspiration Lag
- Remote inspiration
- Long distance between inspiration & selling period
- Image maker design not current

Accuracy Drag
- Inappropriate supplier skills mix
- Inefficient collaboration and communications
- Lower product accuracy

TRADITIONAL SUPPLY PROCESS
"The wrong product, at the wrong time!"

Inspiration   Development   Production   Distribution   Selling

Reducing 'Time & Space' Supply Process
"The right product, time after time!"

Distribution
Inspiration Development
Production

Efficiency of Space & Time
- Short time from inspiration to selling period
- Short distance between collaborators
- Production proximity to markets
- Technology overcoming time & distance

Selling   Selling   Selling   Selling

© 2021 vm-unleashed ltd.

Sketch 49 Reducing space & time Reducing the 'Inspiration Lag' and the 'Accuracy Drag'

Customers buy products that are part of the 'here & now.' The more current and relevant to that moment when the customer stands in the shop, or views their browser, the greater the product value and attraction.

The two 'kill-joys' are the 'inspiration lag' and the 'accuracy drag.' These are both elements of the supply process that suppress sales and margin.

The "inspiration lag" is the delay between the original product inspiration and the time the product hits the market. With every weeks delay the product becomes a paler shade of the original inspiration. Alongside this the internal retailer passion for the product is lost, as excitement gives way to exasperation and frustration as the development of drawings and re-detailing swamps the process. This is reflected in the product.

The "accuracy drag" is the time it takes to produce and ship the products. Inappropriate supplier skills and communications again slow the process and introduce inaccuracies and mistakes into the product.

The 'role' of the product, and the 'demands' of the supplier

The reduced 'space & time' supply chain using virtual tools to reduce the 'inspiration lag,' and closer physical location adjacencies to shorten the 'accuracy drag,' should be used to create a supply chain cycle for each wave of product. The cycle becomes more refined and precise as each wave of product goes through the supply chain.

The cycle can also be used in different ways to save time and space depending on the role of the product passing through the supply chain. The traditional segmentation of products by 'role' is still very valid for the supply chain planning process.

Image makers are important to attract customer and to show to the world that a retailer is up-to-date. They need to be delivered absolutely at the right time. Their window to sell is short. Ultimately, they will not sell in large volumes.

Seasonally planned best sellers also have the 'flavour' of the season to make them current and desirable. They represent a good breadth of products and sell in good volumes. They need to be delivered on time, but their window to sell is longer.

We then have core, continuous lines that do not change significantly, if at all, from one season to the next. These are always in-stock and are replenished on an ongoing basis. Over time they sell in very large volumes.

Buying in the correct volumes for each product role certainly mitigates the risk of unsold stock and optimises product investments. Sensible principles to follow, and in a modelling exercise the reality of sales against predicted stock synchronises perfectly.

In the real world, we must introduce the unpredictable whims of the customer. Individual products, and sometimes whole themes and designs sometimes miss the mark. On the one hand this is part and parcel of the buying and merchandising process, however it re-enforces the fact that the shorter we can make the buying & merchandising process then the more relevant, attractive and sellable the products will be.

By adapting the supply cycle according to product role the buying team can focus on the parts of the chain that offer the most value to each type of product. In this way maximum impact can be made in the correct way to each product, whether an image maker, best seller or core product. It also means that energy and money is not wasted on improving parts of the supply chain that will result in little improvement to product, sales and profit.

The astute retailer will develop three different variations on the supply chain cycle across its suppliers. Each supplier should be focused on products of one role type. And every product should clearly be designated as an image maker, best seller or core product an its very inception as an option in the buying office.

The process requires collaboration across buyers to ensure that similar products with the same role and requiring the same supply cycle can be coordinated as much as possible. There may also be consistencies and cost benefits from cooperating on materials, production processes and factory timings.

Ultimately for the customer, products arrive as individual items and as visual stories. They will also have stories behind the origins of the raw materials and in this transparent retail world the stories behind their supply chain journeys will also be of interest. The story behind an efficient and sustainable supply chain, using established suppliers and intelligent technologies is not just of commercial interest to the retailer, but increasingly an important ethical story for customers.

Identifying and making feature profiles of partners in the supply chain is truly creating the most complete virtuous supply cycle.

"Image maker" Inspiration

- Inspiration from the product team is the most important input into the product
- Sources of inspiration are critical – trend agencies, store visits, online research, customer research, industry fayres, product shows, influencer blogs and 'instagramming'
- The collaboration between stylists and product teams is the most important relationship

"Planned bestseller" Development

- Product development experience from the joint retailer/supplier team is the most important input
- Areas of expertise – knowledge of materials, appreciation of fashion, quality of craftmanship, awareness of complexity and cost implications in product enhancement, adornment and styling.
- The collaboration between product teams and suppliers is the most important relationship

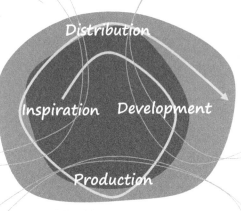

"Core product" Production

- Efficiency from the producer is the most important input into the product
- Experiences of production are critical – quality standards, consistency of work, attributes of raw materials, limitations of workforce skills, cost of changes and enhancements
- The collaboration between producer and raw materials suppliers is the most important relationship

Sketch 50 Inspiration, development, production & distribution

Increasing efficiency and reducing time barriers within the supply chain by creating efficient supply cycles by 'product role.'

Burberry: gaming technology for sampling.

Whilst digital is often seen as a threat to traditional retailers, their principles and practices, the technology that brings the customers' screens to life, also represent opportunities. These are not just confined to adding atmosphere to shops, but the positive effects can be seen deep in the supply chain, adding distinct commercial advantages.

Anyone who has worked in a buying department knows what a nightmare it can be trying to ensure that a precise product vision and specification is brought to life accurately by suppliers often thousands of miles away. The process can involve costly physically visits, or many painstaking transfers of visuals, photographs and crib sheets.

For Burberry, gaming technology is being used to help streamline the fashion design process. The company has developed a new application that merges gaming technology and design to speed up and simplify the process of placing prints onto garments. The internal 3D development team, who had previously built the successful games B Bounce and B Surf, saw an opportunity for their technology.

Apparently, the software places a two-dimensional print onto a 3D product template to show how the finished product will look and provide real time instant feedback. Burberry said the use of 3D is now embedded in its merchandising model and has become a staple tool in the process of print engineering.

The application has also reduced paper usage at the design stage by two thirds and Burberry is also hoping that producing an accurate sample with fewer iterations will help cut factory waste. The first products designed using the new technology were available in-store as part of the 2020 collection.

The bottom line is that if the retailer can create detailed and accurate product representations for the customer, for websites and mobile apps, then it is equally feasible that they can do the same for their remote suppliers. If the inspiration is the same then the product itself will be more consistent.

Le Labo: the beauty of live inventory.

It might not take rocket science to work out that 'Le Labo' equates to 'The Lab' in English, however the proposition and inventory concept behind the fragrance brand is super-intelligent, imaginative and commerciality very astute.

Anyone who has visited Le Labo will appreciate the intimacy and anticipation of the customer experience. The shops are designed like vintage apothecaries, if there are such things. The exploration of the fragrances takes place on dark wood creaking floorboards, whilst the fragrance is made and bottled in a white tiled space, with white coats and clinical spotlights.

But retail theatre is not where this concept ends.

The customer selects from a precious range of curated fragrances with single drops delivered onto their wrist. Precious is an important concept in Le Labo where it seams every drop is the work of years.

Then before the customers eyes, the assistant sets to work mixing together carefully prepared and secret combinations of raw scents, using pipettes to slowly fill the customer's bottle. The label is hand printed, personalized and dated. The process is as precious and as personal as it can get.

However, the economics of the process are a retailer's dream. Literally, in essence, the product is made to order. The retailer's investment is made only once the customer has committed. No raw materials are wasted on sales speculation. 100% is saved for a secure purchase. Every drop is paid for.

Whether it is theatre, personal service or the actual fragrance that is the product is irrelevant. As with all excellent brands it is undoubtedly the combination which is critical. However, turning the process of bespoke production from a tedious wait into a spiral of anticipation is genius.

'Genius in a bottle.'

The Z to A of retail disruption

John Lewis: the wellbeing supply chain

John Lewis has launched a supplier engagement initiative called 'Better Jobs' that focuses on the job satisfaction and welfare of employees across its own-brand supply base.

The programme aims to offer suppliers a framework to develop their employee support and engagement programmes. It focuses on seven themes, on which suppliers can engage with their workforce – voicing opinion, progression, reward, security, job design, respect and health & wellbeing.

The scheme was originally implemented with 23 of John Lewis' long-standing suppliers in the UK which 'had already undergone forensic style audits' to confirm that they complied with laws on employment and human rights, and health and safety.' The scheme has also been trialed with 15 of the retailer's Chinese suppliers.

Asos: supply chain transparency

Extended supply-chains will continue to come under more scrutiny with customers expecting the behaviour of all parties to be the responsibility of the retail brand. Fast-fashion giant Asos has published four new commitments required of third-party brands. It asked all brands to sign the Transparency Pledge, to map out all parts of their UK textile supply chain; to identify risks within those supply chains; and to join the Fast Forward auditing programme.

By signing the pledge, launched in 2016 by nine charities including Human Rights Watch and the Clean Clothes Campaign, brands are now committed to 'regularly and publicly disclosing a list of manufacturing sites in their supply chain.'

Ren Studios: the bespoke option for IKEA

Let's face it, at some point in our furniture buying lives, we all love the functionality and the value of IKEA's cabinets and shelving systems, furniture & chairs. However, even with a variety of finishes, the furniture still misses the mark for the more eclectic customers who crave more individuality and personality in the décor for their homes.

Ren Studios is an Australian company bridging the gap between flatpack furniture and bespoke joinery. They are finding a niche injecting personalization into the supply chain of one of the most mass-merchandise of retailers.

The ecommerce business uses IKEA base cabinets, but stocks its own collection of doors, drawer fronts, cover panels, shelving and handles to create unique pieces at a lower price than other bespoke furniture. Customers design their kitchen, wardrobe or living room unit using IKEA's software, and then select bespoke doors, drawers and panels on Ren Studio's site that match up with the IKEA bases. The products can still be assembled using IKEA's original nuts and bolts.

IKEA: 3D-printed accessibility add-ons

IKEA is collaborating with accessibility specialists to design and supply furniture add-ons to make their furniture more usable and inclusive for its disabled customers. It is employing 3D printing to produce and distribute the add-ons worldwide.

The 13 available designs are intended to modify existing products and accessories in the company's extensive range, for example, making small buttons larger on drawers and cupboards, or lifting sofas and chairs higher from the ground.

The Z to A of retail disruption

051

IT'S TIME TO SPREAD THE BURDEN

Internal soul-searching, operational principles

You ask a lot of your suppliers. The news is you're going to have to ask a lot more of them. It is difficult to see how that is going to work with a remote and purely commercial relationship.

There needs to be a new level of trust, a new level of understanding you have probably not entered into before. This will only come through a fair and equal allocation of responsibility, risk and financial burden between you and your suppliers.

A difficult 'pill to swallow' but it is essential medicine.

Actions

- Carry out an analysis and review of existing suppliers
  - Current relationship and potential
  - Exclusive or allied to competitors
  - Skills, specialisms, future thinking
  - Quality of work, professionalism
  - Brand & culture fit
- Assessment of alternative suppliers, profiles and business strategies
- Compile and produce a supplier's charter and agreement outlining best practice working relationships
  - Points of collaboration – data, costs, knowledge
- Approach selected suppliers and negotiate
- Set out a collaboration development plan

052

UNEARTH THE RICHES OF YOUR SUPPLY CHAIN

Operational research & best practice benchmarking

How long is your supply chain? Do you even know how many links there are in the chain and what they all do? Why are they all so important?

It is well worth your while understanding and forming relationships from the cotton or potato farmer to the family of the delivery company The relationships you have with them are essential to supplying your customer. Believe me the ideas and initiatives that will appear will be truly inspirational.

Actions

- With preferred suppliers carry out a qualitative appraisal
  - Heritage & skills
  - Sourcing relationships
  - Specialist knowledge & techniques
  - Marketing knowledge
  - Design and style capabilities
- Consider ways to work together through the B&M process
  - Market analysis
  - Styles and trends
  - Product story contribution
  - Sourcing relationships
  - Speed to market & flexibility
  - Open to buy
  - Brand profiling
  - Marketing & advertising campaigns
  - Brand advocacy

053

EXPLORE EVERY EFFICIENCY AVENUE

Brainstorming, benchmarking, market analysis and prototyping

When many people speak about disruption and innovation, they refer to product development or shop concepts, and new ways to access a market. The same for applications of technology.

Nothing wrong with that but for me the invisible stuff, what the customer doesn't see is the real opportunity. The supply chain sits at the top of my list.

Making product is one thing, but getting it from A to B, or C and then D, that is the new battleground for retailers. Look around you and see what is happening from the extraordinary technologies used by Amazon and Ocado, in warehousing and distribution technologies. Explore the collaborations and agile technologies behind some of the newest listed businesses such as Deliveroo and Uber.

Set up an experimentation lab. Apply its benefits down the supply chain. Your customer may not yet be in the position to receive their product via a 3D printer. But they may be able to soon. Or at the very least such technology may be useful to send product parts across the globe, samples for assessment by buyers and designers.

Have fun. Explore technology and people possibilities in the supply chain.

Actions

- Compile a supply chain innovations team
  - Appoint a leader
  - Define responsibilities & outputs
  - Set-up a research team to assess supply chain innovation
  - Confer and collaborate in intelligence gathering with leading edge external collaborators
  - Constantly monitor best practice in innovation across the widest possible sphere of manufacturing & distribution.
- Set up an experimentation lab
  - Identify incubator partners in supply chain technologies and production techniques
  - Manufacturers & suppliers
  - 3D printers
  - Logistics
  - Distribution
  - Deliveries
  - Smart allocation
  - Virtual assortments
  - Re-distribution and re-sellers
  - Returns mechanisms
- Execute real trials with new collaboration teams
  - Assess & evolve
  - Introduce B&M and supply chain innovation into the existing supply chain processes
- Constantly assess and improve
- Integrate innovations and IT systems across B&M teams

Sustainability: 'Making more from less'

> Greater than the disruptive markets we operate in, is the disrupted world that we live in.

Time has long passed, from when a sustainable initiative was not much more than a smart marketing strategy. Sustainability has now irreversibly developed into something essential to establish commercial traction with many customers.

Responsibility for sustainability has also shifted, from the marketing department to every department across a business. Products are being held up as icons of the sustainable age, and so too are the businesses that produce and sell them. Shaming of exploitative businesses and the wasteful products they sell has gained a momentum that is not going to slow.

For our commercial, as well as our existential security, it is essential that retail embraces every aspect of sustainability.

Evolving sustainable education

The process of evolution begins with education. Increasing the awareness of colleagues, customers and suppliers about sustainable materials & processes is the minimum first level of achievement.

A 'quick-win' overhaul of the complete buying & merchandising process is simply not going to happen. Superficial changes make little difference to either the business credentials of the retailer or the actual impact on the environment, and genuine sustainability.

Fundamental change requires the un-picking of existing process principles and collaborations, whilst additional sustainable alternatives are also explored. This takes time, however it does not mean that the buying teams cannot move relatively quickly to selecting more materials that are recyclable or recycled, wherever possible. This begins with education.

Buyers can also evolve further the development of individual products, ranges and capsule collections that are completely re-cyclable, or re-usable. Moving forwards one step at a time can accelerate into a sustainable pace for change across the entire assortment.

> The important thing is to have a long-term sustainability strategy in place. And to communicate it honestly.

Customers are also realistic enough to know that every change cannot be made in an instant. However, they are fully aware of the 'greenwashing' of businesses claiming to be on the road to sustainability, whilst still clearly driving along the exploitation super-highway.

Marketing campaigns, internal sustainability schemes, charitable collaborations and donations, as well as the harnessing of colleague lifestyle initiatives are all important in communicating to customers that at the very least, the intent to change is a reality within the business.

Often, your customers will listen more to your shop colleagues than they will to the platitudes of senior executives and expensive marketing campaigns. If you are serious about sustainability and communicating it to your customers, then use the social power of your workers to do this. Firstly include them in sustainable initiatives, celebrate their efforts. Communicate and reward their efforts. When your workforce is undoubtedly social media integrated then the good sustainability word about your business will soon reach the customer.

Evolve
The ongoing process of improvement. People knowledge and skills. Technology applications. Process efficiency.

Areas of consideration:
- Increase awareness of materials & processes
- Reduce internal waste and CO2 emissions
- Select sustainable materials
- Assess suppliers sustainability criteria
- Evolve sustainable micro-collections
- Re-use, re-sell un-sold stock
- Re-cycle, donate remaining materials

Summary of opportunities:
- Increase awareness in colleagues and customers of sustainable issues, materials & processes
- Communicate and campaign sustainability and re-use to customers
- Select materials which are recyclable, and encourage suppliers
- Develop products, and ranges that are completely re-cyclable, or re-usable
- Ensure un-sold stock is re-sold, or re-used
- Ensure remaining materials donated to partners for cycling
- Encourage customers to 'buy less!'

Enrich
Strategic injections modifying and adding scope and benefit to ongoing processes. Introducing different principles, different ways of working, new skill-sets, technology interventions.

Areas of consideration:
- Improve education in raw materials, recyclable, re-usable, harmful processes
- Develop assortment planning/ collections built around sustainable criteria
- Product origin driven assortment plans
- New, used, recycled, upcycled driven assortment structures
- Move to 100% re-cycled materials
- Avoid 'toxic' combinations of raw materials

Summary of opportunities:
- Intense education of internal teams, shop colleagues, and suppliers on sustainable/harmful materials and processes
- Transform the B&M process to develop full collections that only use sustainable materials and processes – replace capsule only collections
- Employ more accurate product sampling to increase sell-through
- In B&M process consider a mix of product origins – re-use, re-cycled, re-paired when creating collections and suppliers to use
- Ensure material combinations in products/packaging are re-cyclable
- Move supplier base to those that meet sustainable benchmarks
- Commit to 'producing less!'

Expand
Introducing broad strategic initiatives to drive the business in new and profitable directions. Requiring changes to the organisational structure, principles and processes.

Areas of consideration:
- Build circular economic relationships between product functions and collaborators
- Build supply capability for new, unsold, used product
- Build sales channel capability to re-sell existing product, up-cycle existing product/ materials
- Invest in sustainable support and supply businesses

Summary of opportunities:
- Evolve vertical integration process that is sustainable, reduced carbon emissions, uses & produces recycled materials and low-energy use
- Set a zero-carbon plan
- Build and collaborate to develop complete circular supply production and sales chains for re-used, re-cycled, re-sold and re-paired
- Invest in sustainable businesses
- Convert distribution fleet and delivery vehicles to low energy, electric ,eBikes and employ cycles for local deliveries
- Make more profit from 'selling less!'

Sketch 51 Sustainability: Evolve, Enrich & Expand

Enriching the lives of the sustainable customer

At the customer-facing end of the product supply chain there are also numerous activities that can begin to reduce the impact of waste. Ensuring for example that un-sold stock is sold-on to alternative markets or re-used.

There are already retailers who have created 'sustainable sales chains' to achieve the highest possible sell-through. These begin with full price shops, then the unsold product journeys onwards to discount outlets, local reduced-price shops, community giveaway shops and then to charities. Along the way, unsellable products can be filtered out of the system to be re-made into more attractive new products or deconstructed into raw materials at the earliest opportunity.

Every fibre, and every ounce of remaining material, can be donated to collaborators and partners for re-cycling. These refreshed raw materials can be re-used in any number of ways from making wood substitutes, compounds for industrial use, fillings for sofas, rubber for tyres, hardcore for roads.

There is no excuse for waste, and the customer is no longer accepting any.

The enrichment of the existing buying and merchandising processes should also continue with specialist and intense education on sustainable and harmful materials and processes. Buying and merchandising must embrace the twin goals of reducing waste, whilst increasing the use of recyclable and recycled materials.

Expanding sustainable assortments

Buying & merchandising teams need to work from individual items and capsule collections towards full collections that only use sustainable materials and processes. Heightened awareness should facilitate the design and creation of products that also avoid the combination of materials that together make them un-usable, and un-cyclable in the future. Horror-hybrids.

In the product development process itself, the adoption of technologies to streamline and improve the accuracy of the product sampling processes also have the potential to reduce waste through making more products sellable, increasing sell-through rates. Good for the retailer, the customer, as well as the environment.

A change in material priorities

For product teams that traditionally build collections prioritising fashion trends, colour palettes and high margin materials, the new considerations of the origin of materials, re-cyclability, longer-life cycles and de-constructable combinations of materials will take time to learn.

However, the new considerations can also add creativity and additional possibilities to the collection. The consideration of the mix of product origins – re-used, re-cycled, re-paired, re-cyclable when creating collections can add a relevance to the theme and concept, authenticity to the products, and added-value uniqueness to the styling and finishes.

Sustainability can move onto the front of the product ticket, from the back. Its motif onto the proud chest and not behind the hidden seam.

Buying teams are always on the look-out for new materials to add aesthetic edges and visual standout to products. The new investments in recycled materials is generating an unprecedented number of new materials possibilities. Aesthetic stand-out can be married with unique qualities and attributes and further levels of sustainability to help create innovative and inspiring assortments.

> *Sustainability offers the potential for creativity, and the reality of commercial sales.*

of vehicles running on alternative energies and sustainable electricity.

The linear retailer should evolve into the circular retailer, working in collaboration to develop closed loop production, supply, and sales chains, re-used, re-cycled, re-sold and re-paired product customer propositions.

Packaging & plastics

There have already been many initiatives to reduce packaging. The world outcry at the use of single-use plastics in packaging and the waste it generates, has already brought about new regulations and laws. These will only gain momentum, as will the customers dismay, and refusal to buy from businesses that do not evolve their packaging and marketing materials to sustainable alternatives.

We will also hopefully witness the end to mindless, ineffective, over-produced, and over delivered, signage, graphics, leaflets, ticketing, and other physical communication for shops.

Vertical supply-chains

The evolution through organic growth and acquisition of retailer owned vertical supply chains will facilitate the acceleration of sustainable integration processes, the use & production of recycled materials, alternative energy adoption, low-energy use, and reduced carbon emissions.

Every part of the supply chain will need to play its part in the total commitment to sustainability. Physical shops and offices should be built using sustainable materials, re-usable energy sources, low energy lighting and refrigeration in grocery shops. There will be no hiding place for anything other than a full sustainability commitment.

This is the realisation of the 'zero-carbon plan' for every retail business, with objectives and deadlines. The links of the closed chains will be connected by a distribution and delivery fleet

Sustainability 'lock-in.'

Retailers will encourage all customers to become an intrinsic part of their closed-loop cycles. They will stimulate the beginning of one buying and merchandising cycle, initiated by the re-usable assets of the previous.

> *Sustainability 'lock-in' not price & availability 'lock-in' will be the incentives to customer loyalty.*

Every part of a business will be under scrutiny. The deepest of retail relationships will involve customers, colleagues, suppliers, and shareholders, demanding to know a retailer's conscience, ethical values, and sustainable reality.

Actions speak louder than words. When it comes to sustainability, words alone will be inexcusable if set against a record of inaction and continued exploitation.

Sustainability also offers the potential for retailers and brands to find the elusive brand USP. Whilst R&D and buying teams have been toiling over the look and styling to create something unique and desirable, that USP is now more likely to emerge from the process itself as much as the end result. 'Back stories' will continue to take a front seat, and products with genuine sustainability back stories will be thrust into the forefront of the customers' consciousness.

Beautiful materialism

The silver lining from a new enthusiasm for materials is the imaginative use of existing materials, and the development of innovative new materials. All of them ethical and recyclable.

The world of sportswear is based on aesthetics but increasingly also on the development of new materials. Materials that magically keep you hot and cold, wet and dry, all at the same time. Brands from Nike and Adidas, to Under Armour and Lululemon, are creating brands and sub-brands built literally on the back of new sustainable and recyclable material technology.

In the world of beauty and cosmetics, there is also immense interest from customers and brands to discover pure and natural materials and ingredients that unleash their latent benefits. The trend and desire for natural, organic, sustainable is in marked contrast to the world of petrochemical fabrication that drove earlier surges in toiletries proliferation.

Increased customer curiosity will also lead to more experimentation on what to do with existing recyclables, as well as exploring new recyclables and more natural materials that can be sourced sustainably.

Get up close

Retailers must get closer to where their materials come from because the customer is getting closer. They need to be more knowledgeable than the customer, and transparent. Consumer brands must communicate through their product ticketing, and digital product information the names of producers and suppliers, and in turn their commitment to ethics and sustainability.

Undoubtedly an industry wide 'traffic-light' product labelling standard will be developed allowing customers to see, at a glance, the sustainability level of their purchases. Expanding from current products such as electrical white goods and homes, to everything from food products to home furnishings, from cars to fashion crop-tops.

If a butcher can tell you the name of the farm, the breed and the cow that your meat comes from, then a retailer can tell the customer the name of the grower, the location, the farmer, the distiller, the weaver, the mechanist and the definitive sourcing origins of the rawest of materials across a variety of products.

> *Get realistic.*
> *Get materialistic.*
> *Be sustainable.*

Cyclically integrated materialism

Many production and supply chain processes are not integrated. For those that are vertically Integrated there are benefits in reliability, security, flexibility, and loyalty which assist in commercial strategic planning and efficient productive ROI.

An essential part of vertical integration is the ownership and exclusive partnerships related to sourcing, growing or production of the required raw materials. The cyclically integrated model expands this ownership and responsibility model to include all other avenues and opportunities to control the raw material sourcing, recyclables, and newly developed materials. The system is closed and integrated, with the product development team supported fully in their materials requirements.

> *The new 'Materialism' is the supply of recycled, recyclable, and sustainable raw materials.*

- 3 materials sources – raw materials supplier, materials recycler, new materials R&D
- All elements of the cyclical integrated process are vertically owned
- All processes focused on current essential materials with new proprietary material development
- Less Raw materials suppliers
- All raw materials suppliers working with recyclable materials – sustainably sourced
- Additional materials sourced from trusted sustainable suppliers
- Products designed using only recycled and recyclable materials
- Products designed using materials fundamentally limited to those in the integrated cyclical system
- Next seasons products designed considering recyclable materials from this season's collection, and potential new materials
- Customers incentivised to return products directly to the retailer, in physical shops, or via pick-ups and collection points
- Returned products and materials considered as business assets
- Vertically owned raw-materials extraction and recycling facilities

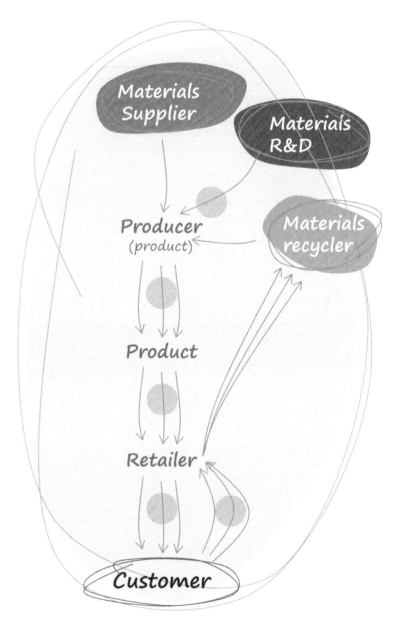

Sketch 52 Cyclically Integrated Materialism

Lifecycles with the customer

The awareness and considerations about the product lifecycle must now be extended forwards to the customer purchase, their relationship with the product, and its disposal. The retail lifecycle must evolve into the product lifecycle.

The solution is to make more use, and more uses, of what the customer buys. To turn away from the throwaway, to embrace and enjoy possessions. The terminology needs to move on from possessions to investments, squeezing every hour of use, enjoyment, and value from them.

Rental is now a life choice, led by technology. We no longer possess physical music but download rental versions. What we buy from apple we rent for life. We rent other people's homes for holidays, rent other people's cars for convenience, we can now rent furniture for our rented homes, rent clothes for occasions.

The motives are flexibility of lifestyle, the ability to change without financial commitment, convenience on every occasion, and the opportunity to use in volume, just not the same things by the same person. Our experience of variety is greater, but our possession of volume is much less.

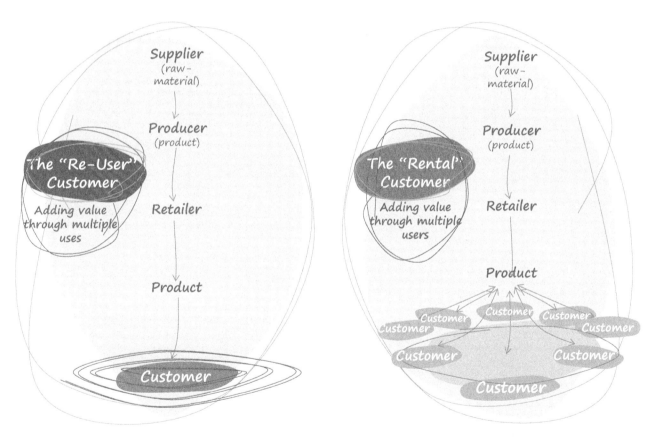

© 2021 vm-unleashed ltd.

Sketch 53 "Added-Value Lifecycles" Re-inventing possessions as investments

Re-productive lifecycles

Product re-production is the new story in town. Innovative retailers, brands and customers are re-working what we think of as production, adding creative value to products and developing a new sustainable landscape for products.

The new initiatives bring together customers, who love their product, and want to continue and evolve its lifecycle beyond the normal timeframe, and retailers who want to increase their length of involvement with the product, after the initial sale to customers. The mutual love of a product forms a deep connection between a retailer and its customers, developing a strong loyalty and advocacy.

For a desirable brand, with a loyal customer base, unique 'bespoke' pieces can fetch a retail price far in excess of the original product. The price for the curation of a unique piece, is well worth the investment for retailers and creative customers.

Cottage lifecycles

The recent trend in home creativity, has accelerated rapidly during the COVID lockdown periods. It has given people the time to fully explore everything from home baking, and knitting, to crafts, painting and clothes making. Instead of shopping for new things. Instead of being creative with new materials, there has been a surge in re-pairing, re-working and refreshing possessions.

Sites such as Etsy have been tapping into this new product development stream, supporting and promoting individual producers, and cottage industries, helping them show off and sell their wares to a wider audience.

Vintage shops display fusion sweatshirts, gym tops and shorts created from distressed sportswear and popular denim brands. Individual products generating attractive prices, combining quality fabrics with fresh creativity. Vintage branding brought back to the streets. Sustainable processes and extended lifecycles, free marketing, and influencer endorsements.

The culture from decades past, to extend a products lifecycle is being embraced and enjoyed. In this lifecycle within a lifecycle, the loyal customer becomes the producer and the retailer as well as the customer. All for the glory of the brand, the promotion of the product and for sustainability.

The "Cottage" Customer

Customer reselling products after repairs, refreshment, customisation, and through fusion & hybridisation of several products

Supplier
(raw-material)

Producer
(product)

Retailer

Customer Product

fuse · repair · hybrid · refresh · customise

© 2021 vm-unleashed ltd.

Sketch 54 "Cottage Creative Lifecycles"

The cyclical supply chain

The cyclical supply chain is a fully integrated model, where functions and processes work together to ensure that new products are produced, and existing products reused, in a commercial and sustainable way.

On the one side, materials used to make products are sourced and developed to be recyclable and recycled. On the other side, existing products are repaired and refreshed for re-use and rental, re-created to make new products for re-sale.

All processes are coordinated through self-ownership, or exclusive and jointly invested partnerships. Suppliers are solution deliverers. The customer is encouraged to integrate with the system through re-using their products, repairing their products, and renting products when they have no regular need of them. The customer is at the heart of the recycling process donating products which will be recycled into raw materials or into new hybrid assortments.

The participation of the retailer, suppliers, producers, recyclers, renovators, and customers is guaranteed and founded on trust, mutual respect, mutual commercial gain and the ethics of sustainability.

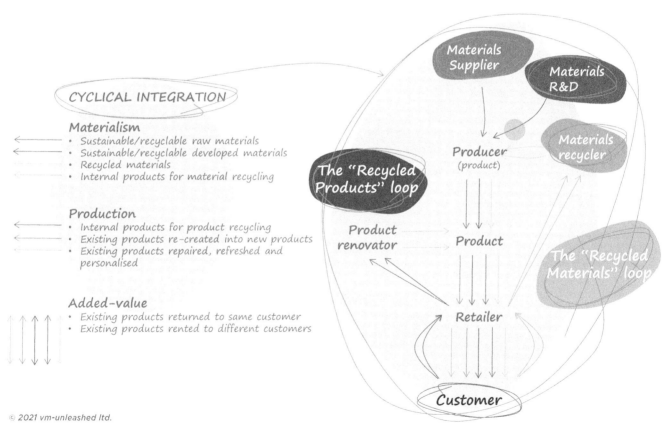

CYCLICAL INTEGRATION

Materialism
- Sustainable/recyclable raw materials
- Sustainable/recyclable developed materials
- Recycled materials
- Internal products for material recycling

Production
- Internal products for product recycling
- Existing products re-created into new products
- Existing products repaired, refreshed and personalised

Added-value
- Existing products returned to same customer
- Existing products rented to different customers

Sketch 55 The Cyclical Supply Chain

Elvis & Kresse: lighting the sustainable fire

Elvis & Kresse is one of those truly inspirational retail brands that you don't come across every day. It is commanding a loyal following and represents a growing number of businesses producing beautiful products with a 360-degree ethical and sustainable philosophy. Their passions are to reduce waste, to conserve resources, to support like-minded charities and to train apprentices.

Their starting point was a meeting with the London Fire Brigade. That chance meeting over 10 years ago revealed that all the old rubber hoses used by the force were simply being thrown away when their useful lives came to an end.

After some exploration of the materials and properties of hose pipe construction the business evolved the processes that are used to this day to create the handbags, belts and purses that are their trademark. The authenticity of the products is captured by the fact that many of the products carry the unique 'stamp' of the fire station where the hose had its first life.

From this collaboration the "Fire & Hide" range has evolved which combines the rubber of the fire hoses with the re-woven leather from factory floors. In a poignant twist, 50% of all profits are given back to Fire Services Support Charities. That's 50%!

The brand also collaborates with Burberry turning 120 tons of leather off-cuts into accessory products sold through the Elvis & Kresse brand.

Elvis & Kresse is also very much a community as much as a manufacturer or retailer. Such an important element of a brand to survive & flourish. It collaborates widely on new designs and offer workshops for customers and craftspeople to learn techniques and design their very own personalised bags.

Ultimately the USP of Elvis & Kresse is the process not the product. This actually creates a stronger brand proposition, where sales are not just reliant on design and trends. Assortment extension does not involve an obsession with shape and look but on new raw products and materials that can undergo the Elvis & Kresse treatment. From hoses the brand now creates product from coffee sacks, auction banners, printing blanket, and military-grade parachute silk. The list grows whilst the Elvis & Kresse brand and USP get ever stronger.

Nudie: living the life of denim

If you want to experience something which is as far away from mass merchandising as it is possible to be, then look at Nudie.

Nudie Jeans is a Swedish clothing brand. They believe in 'an owner for life!' And there are many owners for life out there. You should take a look at their website and the customer profiles and endorsements.

They all believe it takes time to 'break-in' a new pair of jeans. They believe the more you wear and repair jeans, the more character they have. They believe wearing Nudie jeans is an adventure together.

Both brand and customer live and breathe the same philosophy and ethos. They stand firmly behind social responsibility, and against throwaway fashion, waste and exploitation in the supply chain. Every step of every product is transparent in where and how it was made and by whom. This not only includes the environmental credentials of the manufacturer but the transportation route and the sustainability of the logistics.

Nudie jeans are always made from 100% organic denim, made with environmentally friendly production methods. Their life-long repairs, their ultimate recycling and re-use always source the same sustainable materials whether they are being made into clothing for the first time, or enjoying a new lease of life, extending the life of another precious garment.

And of course, Nudie specialise in, and promote, the free reparation of their product and the recycling of materials from products that are beyond repair.

Nudie is beautifully and honestly circular. It uses organic & recycled materials. It sells, and rents for life. It repairs, re-works and then re-invents and re-uses to make new hybrid products.

Not often you pass-on your clothes to your children.

The Z to A of retail disruption

H&M & Arket: renting for the time of your life

Increasingly, rental rather than ownership is becoming part of everyday life, from the music we listen to, the films we watch, the cars we drive and the clothes that we wear. Amongst the leading retailers to move to rental is mass-merchandiser H&M.

Across its brand portfolio H&M leverages the values of the different customers for each brand to deliver appropriate and appealing sustainability initiatives. Despite its 'mass-market' origins H&M does continue to attract plaudits and awards for its genuine attempts to reduce waste.

'Arket' believe that children's clothes need to be designed with a longer-term horizon in mind and handed down when outgrown. It has begun offering products from its children's collection for rent through a new partnership with Amsterdam-based online shop and clothing subscription company, Circos.

Rented clothes can be kept and used for as long as they fit and returned when it is time to size up. Apparently between eight and ten families will share the same piece of clothing. Once the product wears out, the materials will be repurposed to make new products.

H&M itself, has also launched into the rental market with its free men's suit hire service called ONE/SECOND/SUIT. The scheme is intended to help those attending job interviews, and who don't own a suit themselves to make a good first impression. Customers can rent a suit for a 24-hour period

H&M has found an intriguing new angle on the rental idea, in that the sustainable benefits are matched by social responsibility, and the fact that the service is free, an investment in young peoples' potential, their futures and their loyalty.

The service was launched with a 'stirring and evocative film' by American director Mark Romanek that aims to capture the interview nerves and self-doubt many people experience.

After years of development into natural fibres and organic materials, stimulating healthy sales, these new intiatives are focused on the longevity of products and a longevity of customer loyalty. Quite a shift.

IKEA: buying-back furniture for good

As the world's largest furniture retailer, IKEA has a significant impact on the sourcing of raw materials and distribution of products. It has a strong commitment to sustainability, from the creation of its own wind-farm and commitment to renewable energy, to its latest initiative, its furniture 'buy-back' scheme.

The furniture 'buy-back' scheme is far-reaching, as it not just focuses on using recycled, or recyclable materials, but on the core issue behind sustainability – encouraging customers to buy less new products, and by default the need to manufacturer less new furniture.

Products eligible for buy back include dressers, bookcases, shelf units, small tables, cabinets, dining tables and desks. The used products will be bought back at a price dependent on their condition. Those returned as good as new with no scratches will be bought for 50% of the original price, while items with minor scratches will be bought for 40%. Furniture that is well used with several scratches will be bought for 30%.

Customers can then bring the fully assembled product into a store, where they will be found in the 'Bargain Corner.' Alternatively, IKEA has partnered with Gumtree to sell on second-hand products through their website.

There are loyalty benefits of course for IKEA, customers sell back their second-hand IKEA furniture in return for an IKEA voucher. However, credit where it is due. The underlying principle is commendable and focused on encouraging customers to buy less, and with more thought. The voucher will have no expiry date, to encourage customers to only purchase something when they really need it – again stimulating more sustainable consumer behaviour.

The Z to A of retail disruption

Lidl: the carbon neutral cheese supply chain

Apparently chilled cheese is the second largest carbon emitter in Lidl shops. It's one of the reasons why the brand is working with its major UK supplier to create carbon neutral cheddar in 2021. The initiative is a landmark exercise as it involves the whole supply chain from the raw materials and that means the cows that produce the milk. In reality, an ambition much more complex than removing plastic packaging for example. Lidl has said The Carbon Trust will verify the project to ensure the approach taken stands up to scientific principles.

Lidl is therefore working closely with its supplier through a mixture of sustainable farming, improved business practices and the purchase of "gold-standard" carbon credits. Lidl will work directly with Wyke Farms farmer suppliers to help them take action to reduce their on-farm emissions. This work will span feed management, soil and land management, manure management, herd management and energy management.

Chipotle: avocado, the colour of sustainability

If you think of Chipotle restaurants, then you probably have guacamole in the front of your mind. You would be correct as the chain uses and throws away nearly 300 million avocado stones a year. In many parts of the world where appropriate recycling services are unavailable these 'pits' end up in landfill.

In recent years Chipotle has developed a range of leisurewear as part of its proposition. The brand is now using the avocado stones to create a dye for clothes and bags, with each bag using up to about five pits to transform its colour. It's a natural sustainable synergy linking the clothing to its 'core' business.

H&M: walking on banana skins

Sustainability initiatives are not just meaningful ways to be more responsible but can also be eye-catching brand statements. One that did 'catch the eye' was H&M's collaboration with sustainable footwear brand Good News.

The collection was the retailer's first ever shoe collaboration featuring innovative materials like Bananatex, a fibre from banana plants, and the vegan grape leather Vegea.

The range included seven trainers and one pair of sliders in seventies-inspired styles and colours. Each had their own sustainable elements, such as recycled rubber soles and recycled cotton, Vegea and Bananatex uppers. Big initiatives sometimes begin with single banana steps.

Coat Paint: painting a brighter future

Coat Paint is improving the 'seriously flawed' customer experience involved in buying paint. Multiple trips to stores, complex product and colour ranges, wasteful and expensive tester pots and tons of plastic and waste are environmentally damaging and not fit for millennial buying expectations.

With sustainability at its heart, Coat has created peel-and-stick colour swatches, which are 95% less wasteful than tester pots, while its supplies are sustainably made from bamboo and recycled materials. Coat carries a refined range of 36 colours.

Once customers are finished with their paint job, they can either give their leftover paint back to Coat for recycling or use Coat's social media community to pass it on to fellow customers.

Coat Paint demonstrates that it is not just the product that must be sustainable, but the concept itself. Developing less wasteful patches would have been half a story, but creating a community that can exchange and finish off patches really adds sustainability value to the proposition.

The Z to A of retail disruption

054

SET UP AN INTEGRATED SUSTAINABILITY DEPARTMENT

Strategic planning & resourcing

We talked earlier about having a data department. How it was important to have a DIO on the board, and a team of specialists integrated into the functional teams.

The sustainability team needs to be the same. In fact, the sustainability team and the data team should very much shadow each other. They will have overlapping agendas and sustainability data will be one area of knowledge that the data team will cover.

There should be a Sustainability Officer on the board. And his team should be integrated across the business. The integrated presence is important to ensure that the sustainability roadmap is being followed and that the actions are coordinated and on time.

An integrated sustainability team will also be there as a source of information and guidance to ensure that all new initiatives are sustainably coordinated.

It all sounds like another set of bodies, but their role is important if you are serious about sustainability.

All project initiative planning meetings, whether to evolve, enrich or expand processes, should include both data and sustainability specialists to support and inform the project.

Actions

- Allocate sustainability ownership at board level
  - Better an engaged executive, or a new appointment
- Define the role, responsibilities and resources required for a sustainability team
- Define the required sustainability team members
  - Sustainability officer
  - Sustainability consultants
  - Sustainability accountants
  - Researchers
  - Internal communications
  - Data analysts
  - Influencers & marketers
  - Sustainable logistics
  - Sustainability product experts
  - Carbon footprint experts
  - Sustainable operations
- Define the processes and networks for sustainability consultants and managers to work alongside key internal functions
  - Embedded in functional teams
  - As part of new initiative projects
  - Shop development programmes
  - Omni-logistics
- Introduce sustainability awareness as an important consideration for hiring new staff at any level of the business
- Develop appropriate KPIs for the Sustainability team, its colleagues, and for collaborations with internal departments
  - Carbon levels & reductions
  - Travel limits & logistics
  - Recycling & waste management
  - Re-usable and recycled raw materials

055

EDUCATE YOURSELVES & EACH OTHER

Market & customer research, internal awareness programmes

Some 'swanky' new posters on the way to the canteen aren't going to cut it anymore when it comes to sustainability education.

The table of volunteers as you enter the canteen, collecting money and 'bodies' for environmental work is an improvement, and donations are commendable, but the sustainability message, and the actions it inspires need to be engrained within every aspect of the business, not supported and applauded as additional activities to normal business.

Increasingly throughout retailers, and particularly with younger employees there is a ground swell of interest and concern over sustainable issues. They are genuinely interested in what their business is doing. And they want to learn and be involved.

The key to gaining real traction through an internal awareness programme is to cover the subject from all angles and to engrain its ideas into the actions of every team & department. Interaction is key as it is 'teaching each other' rather than passive listening that will create the tipping point where sustainability awareness becomes second nature.

Combine awareness and data of the wider world picture with data, analysis and comparisons of the environmental impact of the business and employees themselves.

Actions

- Ensure that the sustainability research and internal communication teams are coordinated fully with existing L&D and HR teams
- Plan the general education and specific education of teams
- Ensure sustainability is part of ongoing internal communications
  - Newsletters
  - Intranets
  - New colleague training programmes
  - Meeting agendas
  - Shop colleague communication channels
- Ensure that sustainability is a topic on internal chat forums
  - Initiate discussions
  - Encourage feedback
  - Reward initiatives
- Use sustainably advanced partners as advocates
  - Presentations
  - Discussions
  - Workshops
- Initiate and manager volunteering
  - Environmental
  - Waste management
  - Carbon savings
  - Social & community
- Create & deliver sustainable specific workshops for specific departments
  - Buying
  - Shop design
  - HR & shop colleagues
  - logistics
  - Include external partners as well
    - Suppliers
    - Shopfitters

056

KNOW WHERE YOU WANT TO GO, AND CREATE A SUSTAINABILITY INTEGRATED MAP TO GET THERE

Best practice benchmarking, brainstorming, strategy and project management

Your business needs a sustainability map. Avoid the natural inclination to talk about journeys. The main reason is that this is not a linear process, or even a series of linear journeys.

It is circular. It is integrated. It is inclusive.

You need to consider time of course and the steps and milestones on the way to some significant objectives such as a zero-carbon footprint, 100% recyclable product materials and zero waste from unsold products. So set out the objectives and the timeline.

The linear plan soon turns into a map because the routes involve a network of activities to achieve the objectives. There will be a myriad of small events, changes and initiatives that play into the delivery of the major objectives.

You then need to consider all of the stakeholders, the teams and individuals, internal and external partners that all need to play their part in this sustainable plan.

Sustainability is a serious undertaking. Awareness, planning and project management are essential.

Actions

- Strategic planning:
  - Agree where you want to go, as a business, and as individual teams
  - Map each journey with milestones and destinations
  - Map out where the journey must be shared.
- Stakeholders & resourcing
  - Identify stakeholder responsibilities
  - Allocate budgets and resources
  - Define KPIs and ROIs
  - Identify the role of external partners
  - Identify the need for new partners
- Put the product at the heart of the plan
  - Re-imagine the B&M team
  - Re-imagine the supply chains
  - Re-imagine the materials
  - Re-imagine the selling process
  - Re-imagine the post-sales process
- Re-define the 'brand'
  - Re-define the product sourcing strategy as an intrinsic part of the 'brand proposition'
    - Recycled materials
    - Research into new materials
    - Recycling products
    - Upcycling products
    - Renting products
- Re-define the sales channels and the 'selling journey'
  - Full-price shops
  - Discount shops
  - Community 'charity shops'
  - Recycling partners & marketplaces

Retail hubs: *'Places in our hearts & minds'*

COVID was supposed to be the death knoll for physical shops. It was of course immensely damaging and resulted in many shops closing and businesses folding. Customers naturally migrated to digital channels, some permanently and others temporarily.

Despite the whole channel being closed, the physical shop, in its best incarnations has already continued to bounce back. Despite everything, it is still the major channel for many customers, across most sectors, in the majority of markets, across the world.

However, what has survived the seemingly impossible, will not be the same as before. It never will, and why should it be?

Tender loving care

Before you look for magic to turn around the fortunes of your shops, it's worth looking at some more mundane actions to transform the underperforming store.

Firstly, don't expect customers to love you if your shops are dirty and untidy, with broken lightbulbs. You wouldn't leave your houses like that if guests were coming round. Especially guests who were potentially going to give you money. So, as a priority keep your shops clean and tidy. It's not the greatest ambition on the road to being an essential retailer, but it's an alarmingly common evolution for many retailer businesses.

Prioritise a minimum standards, 'zero tolerance' approach to your shop estate and for every shop that you have.

Never fail the customer, so never run out of stock. Keep your shelves full, and make sure all your best sellers are on display, and not in the stockroom.

Ensure that your shop is appropriate and relevant for your customer demographic. Fill your shop with products they want, and not with those that other people like. And just as much as

I am an advocate of visual merchandising, only put in the level that is required for your customer.

If they love beauty and have the time to admire it, then make your shop beautiful. If they don't, then don't waste money and effort on something which at the best will be invisible, and at worst irritating. If they don't want beauty, give them efficiency, order and clarity, with the cleanliness thrown in for nothing.

Curb appeal. Customer appeal

Ensure your shops have 'curb appeal' Wherever you are and whatever you sell make sure you look like a great place to enter from the outside. Look at the distance and speed the customer is passing by. Deliver something appropriate.

Large signs and visual impact for car drivers, with more intimate messages and product displays for the pedestrian, or the person waiting for the bus. Make the message clear, and the product relevant for their journey, their occasion, the time of year.

Clearly communicate what you sell, what you offer, and why you're the best option. Develop a marketing calendar which coordinates seasons, annual events and references to popular news, talking points and opportunities to sell.

Relevance can be more powerful than beauty when it comes attracting customers into your shop

Evolve

The ongoing process of improvement.
People knowledge and skills. Technology applications.
Process efficiency.

Areas of consideration:
- Improve maintenance & cleaning
- Refine store grading & clustering criteria
- Evolve stock and replenishment processes
- Upscale visual merchandising
- Upscale window treatments
- Intensify promotional activity
- Prioritise customer service

Summary of opportunities:
- Ensure that shops are clean, welcoming places, at the very least
- Never fail the customer – always in stock
- Shops are correct for their customer demographic, with appropriate assortment, levels of customer service and services, appropriate levels of visual display
- Shops have correct "curb appeal"
- Promotional activity rewards loyalty and builds loyalty

Enrich

Strategic injections modifying and adding scope and benefit to ongoing processes.
Introducing different principles, different ways of working, new skill-sets, technology interventions.

Areas of consideration:
- Enrich personalised relationships with customers
- Cross-channel hubs for product and customer service queries/problems
- Develop social integration & involvement with local communities, events & charities
- Engage in social media local integration
- Adapt utility space for customer workshops, local business and customer use.
- Employ local shop rewards and loyalty benefits

Summary of opportunities:
- Encourage and facilitate human relationships on every occasion
- Shops become hubs for the whole business, selling product, collecting product, returning product, answering questions and solving problems
- Shops become part of the community, integrated into activities, organisations and events
- Shops collaborate with neighbouring retailers, online and offline, to drive footfall to the location
- Local shops reward local customers and frequency of purchase
- Shops use free space for community space, clubs, meetings

Expand

Introducing broad strategic initiatives to drive the business in new and profitable directions.
Requiring changes to the organisational structure, principles and processes.

Areas of consideration:
- Shops built with flexibility, as shops, dark stores, rental space & offices
- Shops as social and community hubs
- Shop manager empowered as "The New Shopkeeper"
- Devolution of power to shop teams as the front-line brand interface
- Working office hubs for regional teams
- Flexible shop leasing, locations & pop-up capabilities

Summary of opportunities:
- Shops built with a flexibility of space use as physical shops, dark-store storage, eBike space, offices for local meetings and community
- A devolution of power from head office to the shop manager and shop team, supported by training on customer relationship building, product knowledge, assortment building & social media marketing
- New flexible rental agreements with landlords
- A range of physical shops including more "pop-ups" to take the shop to the customer

Sketch 56 Retail hubs: Evolve, Enrich & Expand

Deliver promotional activity that rewards loyalty and builds loyalty. The more immediate and instant the reward the quicker you will get the attention of the customer and the sooner you build some loyalty. What could be better than a free drink on your 18th birthday, a free chocolate egg at Easter?

A little upfront investment will pay dividends when the customer comes back again, just for a friendly chat, or a stamp on their loyalty card. Of course, none of this is rocket science, but in an industry that has shamefully neglected its shops, its staff and its customers for so long, then this level of evolution is a welcome improvement.

Community spirit

Make shops meaningful, by making them part of the community they serve. Instill the important mind-set across the business that shops and shop colleagues are there to 'serve' the customers. The customer is not there to pay your wages or send you on holiday.

The important street battle is no longer retailers competing against each other, but as locations competing against other locations for footfall. In a footfall fight, it is 'united we stand and divided we fall.' Encourage and facilitate shops to collaborate and coordinate as part of locations, whatever the size of your business. Support social media involvement in a town community post publicising events, or a joint promotion. The impact on footfall is much more positive when communications are integrated across a community of shops, rather than uncoordinated, individual retailer initiatives.

Shops are the opportunity for retail brands to be the hubs of customer communities, to create loyalty in a genuine and sustainable way. They should become hubs for the whole business – for selling product, for collecting product and returning product, for answering questions and solving customer problems.

Follow the customer

More living, working, shopping combinations will appear in more diverse locations, employing more imaginative old and new developments and building renovations, driven by the post-COVID desire to work and live more flexibly. Retailers will need to adapt further, by adopting a dynamic and flexible shop estate strategy to 'follow the customer'

Online and offline, to market and to sell, the retailer will now need to be wherever the customer wants them to be. The move to shorter-lease times will be symptomatic of this trend, and also the proliferation of pop-up shops, and marketplaces, and pop-up shopping centres. Even the defining lines between a shop and a pop-up shop will become blurred. Permanent retail shops will be flexible, and dynamic and increasingly transient. Pop-up shops will take dynamic decisions to stay in locations for longer or to move to 'pastures new.'

Further exploitation of the potential of the physical shop depends on a further devolution of power from head office to the shop manager and shop team. This responsibility should be supported by comprehensive training on customer relationship building, conversational skills, active listening, product knowledge retention, visual shop enhancement & social media marketing.

The shop team will adopt a single model, each contributing to, and benefitting from, their involvement in the complete running, and performance of the shop.

The shop manager, once again, will be "the New Shopkeeper."

The customer 'Retail Hub'

A physical shop was originally designed to sell, and nothing else. Its space was viewed in terms of capacity. The space segmentation decisions were limited to how much space was required for the stockroom, and how little space can we give to our shop teams, to sit, to eat and to function as sales assistants.

Today's shop must be a combination of a traditional physical shop, a dark-shop storage area for collections, an eBike parking place for deliveries, a space for colleagues to relax and stretch, a space to demonstrate product for zoom customers, desk space for local managers and regional managers, and offices for local meetings and community.

Storing, and shopping, are the equal and opposite reasons why physical retail will survive.

Excess shop space will be converted at an increasing rate to living space to own or rent, above and under the shop, when space overload hits a certain tipping point.

The retail shop will return to being a destination, a hub of activities appealing to all types of customer. It will remain a destination for shopping, become a hub of the customer community. It must be a solution for retail logistics, and a focal point and meeting place for retail activities.

New shops should be designed for all these possibilities. They should also be designed to incorporate different combinations of space, at different times. For evolution over time, even for different seasonal requirements, weekday and weekend variations and special occasion layouts.

Shopper paradise – for 'those who are born to shop!'

Shopping will still be an essential part of most retail spaces. Sectors that rely on excitement and inspiration, which need to generate impulse will be shopping wonderlands, where the shopping experience is the priority. The Shopper Paradise experience will require space for product displays and media excitement, fitting rooms, interactive areas, social chill-outs, and hospitality refreshment, during the shopping journey.

The colleagues will be highly trained in interpersonal communication and selling skills, product knowledge and awareness of shopping trends and influences. Fitting rooms will be demonstration areas, whilst shops will provide excellent space and facilities for colleagues to unwind, to recharge, and to refresh, and to reflect on the latest buying patterns, best sellers, and new product information.

Destination shopping spaces may be large surface areas in destination shopping centres. They may equally be local destination shops on small high streets. They will all be dedicated to shopping. They will be run and staffed by shopkeepers!

Collection crossroads – for 'cosy click & collectors!'

For the 'cosy click & collector' everything is at the touch of their fingertips, in the convenience and comfort of their own homes. But even digital shoppers need to buy physical products, need to collect physical products and return those very same physical products back to the retailer.

Whilst digital is convenient, it isn't free. The lifestyle of the digital shopper allows plenty of time for visiting the new type of retail store. As a result, the retail store, the click & collect store, and the product return store will continue to be 'alive and kicking.' The Collection and return hub. The Collection Crossroads.

Sketch 57 The customer lifestyle hub: retail spaces to complement customer lifestyle needs

Community hubs – for 'community customers'

Retail space should be built around added-value, where value is not just defined by the potential to sell, but the potential to build lasting and fruitful relationships with the location and the local customer community. Imaginative retailers will find ways of using all areas of the shop for the benefit, comfort, hospitality and lifestyle of the customers they serve. Loyalty will be built on activities. Activities linked to the retail shop space.

Business centres – for 'convenience seekers'

Increasingly space within shop buildings is not required for shopping, or even storage. However, it should still be viewed as a valuable asset for the business. It can be utilized as the local, or regional home for managers, or an available space for other local business and societies. If it is proving difficult to bring together shopping, residents and business-people outside your shop, then bring them together inside your business.

Making the most of space

There is a glut of physical retail space, as businesses go online. The glut is not confined to the number of vacant shops, but also to the square metres of empty space inside those shops that remain open.

The need to fill every available shelf with product, as the only way to make retail sales. As the only way to show the assortment to the customer, has been superseded by the digital channel which now represents the most comprehensive product catalogue, and a convenient way to buy.

Less densely stocked shops now have a vacuum of space, and an even larger vacuum of creative ideas

One solution to make good use of available space is the rising trend in 'space collaborations,' and joint ventures with non-competing retailers co-habiting the space and sharing the increases in footfall. There is also the opportunity to turn over space for non-retail activities, that can easily drive footfall. From local barbers, craft demonstrations and student exhibitions, to fitness classes, space for community clubs and meetings. A dedicated space with a vibrant calendar of footfall drivers, serves everyone better that a desert of sparsely arranged fixtures.

Collaborative retailers are enriching their shops by filling them with the sounds and the personalities of their customers and their colleagues. Engineering ways to make them one and the same, will be rewarded with the loyalty of both.

Ownership of the shop space

Space planning for multi-use 'retail hubs' requires a re-assessment of 'space users' & 'space stakeholders' carried out at a high level by a cross-functional group including retail strategy, customer marketing, business development, omnichannel operations and sales analysts.

This team must be more innovative and open minded than the traditional product allocation team, with a wider stake holding in the potential retail opportunities that physical shops can now offer. Unfamiliar names must also be considered when it comes to putting a stake in the ground for retail square metres.

People will be at the heart of the retail hub, and the shop team will be at the centre of this. HR, training, and learning & development teams should help to create a template for space, and design facilities appropriate for shop colleagues, for training and customer interaction.

Marketing usually control windows and internal POS, if they are lucky. The opportunity for colleagues to be involved in local marketing, social media posting as well as video conferencing and customer demonstrations should be supported by consultation with central marketing, and the allocation of appropriate space and financial support.

Space allocation for the collection crossroads should be carried out after consulting the logistics and distribution teams, considering everything from parking and unloading to the storage space required for delivery cycles and eBikes.

IT will, as always, be an important part of the planning team as the digital-first shop's demands will range across flexible payment options, digital screens and terminals, dark store inventory management and delivery docking systems and technology for video conferencing and video streaming, and free wi-fi for customers.

Wider than ever broadband will form the new foundations on which shops of all shapes and sizes will be built.

	Stockroom	Dark space	Hub space	Colleague area	Experience areas	Services "studio"
Space Use Opportunities & Considerations	• Rates of sales • Delivery schedule • Remoteness • Product processing needs	• Micro-fulfilment centres • Level of click & collect to hold • Level of returns • Shop deliveries • Processing space • Ebike space	• Local hub team office needs • Training space • Potential for community space • Potential workshop space	• Number of staff • Diversity of staff • Importance of service • Sales of store • Personalisation	• Opportunities for customer interaction • Demonstration Events calendar • Changing rooms • Service desks	• On-line demos • Customer zoom sessions • Social media station • Photo set
Space Stakeholders Retail functions responsible for planning and managing areas of "space use" in the evolved shop concept	Store operations Allocation & replenishment Sales Central merchandising Shop manager	Channel operations Shop manager Logistics	Regional manager Local manager Shop manager Colleagues Marketing HR/Training	Regional manager Local manager Shop manager Colleagues HR/Training	Marketing Visual merchandising Shop Manager Colleagues Customer Service	Marketing Customer service Channel operations Shop Manager Colleagues

Sketch 58 Who owns the shop space? stakeholders with a stake in the ground

Considerations on product mix will fall under the remit of product merchandisers, buyers, product designers, sales analysts, regional, local and shop managers. Ultimately display densities and capacities will be quantitative considerations for the merchandisers and space planners.

Retail hubs require many active stakeholders when shops are up and running. Each of those stakeholders should be involved in the initial space consultation process. No more so than the shop colleagues themselves.

To many people it may seem a little unrealistic and far-fetched to be talking about shops not being just for selling products; that shops may become more focused on customer hubs, collection and returns and business space.

It may not yet be quite normal to re-design your physical spaces, and divert assortment inventory away from shop space, but what has been started by a few innovative and far-sighted retail businesses, has turned into a steady stream of companies dipping their toes into the opportunities of the retail hub.

The fluidity of shop space

Intelligent fluid architecture allows the flexible allocation of space between different functions. Such innovation is already available in residential properties, through the use of sliding walls, furniture and fixtures that retreat into hidden cavities, floors or ceilings; versatile tables, chairs, floor & wall coverings, and storage that flips for different uses and visual impact.

The retail hub can similarly swap between shopper paradise, collection crossroads, community hubs and business centres. The potential for small spaces to swap space usage is very exciting, as well as hybrid spaces at the centre of larger hubs allowing re-adjustments to the balance of space without a complete change in usage.

Three initiatives are important to facilitate such efficient and productive changes in space usage. Firstly, that product depth and inventory is kept to a commercial minimum to accommodate stock storage space. Inventory levels must also be supported by express replenishment, home delivery, product reservations and click & collect.

Secondly, that shop teams have appropriate training to be able to adapt their roles to suit the demand for selling, inventory management, click & collection and community activities. Finally, that digital screens are used around the environment, that can effectively change the content, mood, and visual communication to support the appropriate use of space.

The creation of space that doesn't exist. Creation through creativity.

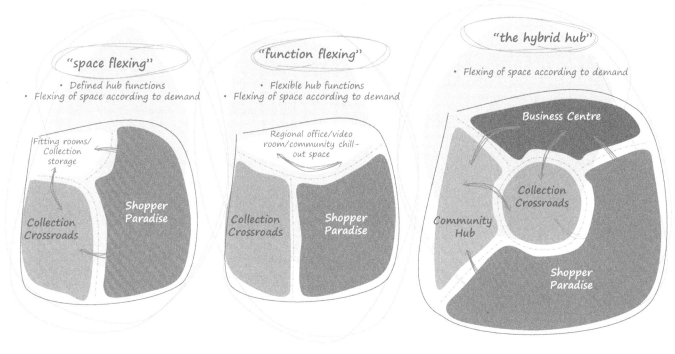

© 2021 vm-unleashed ltd.

Sketch 59 Agile Architecture: The intelligent and innovative creation of space in Retail Hubs

Anonymous: cleaning up your act

I thought long and hard about naming the retailer behind this true story. However, as it actually applies to quite a few retail businesses I resisted temptation. But it is absolutely true.

This retailer had a shop-refurb programme in place. An exercise that required closing shops for two days. The first day the team would clean the shop, make basic repairs, and replace lightbulbs. On the second day they would paint some walls, replace key fixtures and apply new graphics across the shop.

On one occasion the shop colleagues returned after their two days away. They were very pleased at the change and noted that customers were even giving spontaneous feedback on how much better the shop looked. The manager rang the re-furb team manager to congratulate him.

Somewhat surprised he thanked her for the call but explained. The first day went well, but on that evening after a meal together the whole re-furb team came down with food poisoning, so the activities of the second day never actually happened.

Of course, the moral of this story is to never underestimate the importance of keeping shops clean and tidy, making essential repairs as and when they are required, and replacing lightbulbs and cleaning the lightbulb fittings. These are not sexy things to do so they are often neglected.

Their impact on the customer is also very much underestimated, but even if the customer cannot pinpoint improvements specifically, they do feel a general pleasure or unease at the general maintenance and cleanliness of shops.

Cleaning your shops may turn out to be one of the most commercially important tasks you undertake.

Sweaty Betty: fit for community spaces

Across many sectors, retailers are transforming retail shops into 'lifestyle spaces' as they seek to generate meaningful and deeper physical connections with customers. They represent not just superficial interactions but experiences which generate genuine customer relationships.

Sweaty Betty has been specialising in women's active wear for two decades, with the aim to 'inspire women to find empowerment through fitness.' From its core proposition of fitness clothing & accessories, it has evolved into a true lifestyle business where health, wellbeing and fitness are at its heart.

The physical shops have always been a hub for the distinct customer community, often making space on the shop floor, or on adjacent floors for daily fitness, yoga and pilates classes led by local instructors or collaborations with local gyms.

The new flagship shops have taken the lifestyle experience to new limits, with the inclusion of professional gym and exercise studios, cafes & health bars, hair dresses, and beauty services, alongside the retail space. The brand collaborations are carefully selected so that the offers are not just category driven but represent cohesive brand philosophies and commitments to health and well-being.

This sharing of space is not about excess square metres and complementary product categories. It is strategic to create a consistent and collaborative customer experience, based on the awareness that one brand cannot offer all of the pieces of the wellbeing jigsaw. This is brand communities seamless with customer communities.

The Sweaty Betty brand itself uses 'sweat ambassadors' as advocates of the brand, from sports, fitness and media celebrities, but also from the regular customers, to form communities around the shops.

Sweaty Betty also supports vulnerable women throughout the world working with charities such as 'Fallen Angels' – helping addiction through movement, and 'Ditch the label' working against bullying across the globe.

The Z to A of retail disruption

Selfridges: extraordinary spaces

Where to begin with Selfridges, and in particular their shop on Oxford Street in London. It is one of the most extraordinary vibrant and dynamic retail spaces in the world. It is delivered with creativity by highly skilled visual teams, but also planned meticulously in terms of a daily, weekly, monthly retail experiences calendar and driven by a brand ethos that was instilled into the business by its founder, Harry Selfridge.

He imagined a place to socialize, to explore and to enjoy. He also envisaged a place for 'ladies' to socialize, to drink tea together and to relax and stay. He was far ahead of his times, but his ideas have since been universally embraced.

The dynamic of the space is very important to its vibrancy. Any brand strives to be in Selfridges, but the competition is intense and ambitious performance parameters ensure an exciting turnover of new brands, changes to layouts and refurbishments and re-designs to the environment.

In established departments such as young fashion the retailer has used art installations to create dynamic exhibition spaces around the displays. It has introduced skateboard arenas in its youth section, spiral staircases, slides and escalators to add theatre and connections between floors. And it has created a 'Corner Shop' in its highest footfall location where brands deliver their new initiatives on a monthly basis.

However, and despite its obsession with commercial performance per square metre, it has recognized the importance of using space for theatre, to attract footfall. As a result, more of it has been increasingly made into dynamic areas and given over to shop-in-shops, cocktail bars, cafes, restaurants, beauty parlours, fortune tellers, and exhibition spaces and even a luxury digital cinema.

Events are what drives the dynamic of the Selfridges experience, and are what increasingly takes over more of the dynamic and interchangeable spaces in the shop. Whilst Christmas and other seasonal events are spectacular, Selfridges has capitalized on its brand magnetism to generate its own destination events.

These extravaganzas, which last for a month or so, are full of events, demonstrations, collaborations and interaction. Their grand themes have included Bodyzone – a celebration of the human body, Brazil Carnivals, Viva Las Vegas, Project Earth and Good Nature.

Some examples of individual initiatives that these events contained include the Las Vegas wedding chapel with real marriage ceremonies, exhibitions with the science museum on the human body, daily acrobatics down the central escalator wells, the live body casting of Elle Macpherson for her worldwide mannequin design, pop-up cinemas, fitness studios, dance and music shows, and more book signings, personal appearances, demonstrations and beauty makeovers than it would be possible to remember.

Selfridges has also recently introduced a permanent dynamic shop. Its own pop-up shop, or 'corner shop.' This space is in high-demand for a month at a time for brands with new initiatives and brand launches. It is also used by Selfridges for its own marketing and initiatives. A more recent one is a used-wedding shop featuring re-worked and vintage wedding dresses and gowns alongside a repair and adjustments service. Pop-ups within departments within a wonderful retail shop. Truly an extraordinary space.

Selfridges is a retail hub. On an extraordinary scale. It is a shoppers' paradise for sure, but also a worldwide hub for product personalization and ordering, click & collect, and deliveries.

It caters for its communities through its diverse range of specialist services, personal shoppers, hair-dresses, nail bars and beauty salons, hospitality, social spaces and entertainment. It has risen to the sustainability demands of its customers with rental, re-selling and recyclable initiatives.

Unfortunately, my paper space is finite, with no more room to describe the endless stories surrounding Selfridges. Do yourself a favour, and the next time you are in London, pay them a visit.

The Z to A of retail disruption

Google: the mechanics of the digital garage

One of most interesting excursions into physical retailing involved online retail giant Google. In 2017, it announced a new initiative – Digital Garage, with a mission to help 100,000 people in the UK find a job or grow in their careers by offering free digital skills in over 200 towns and cities. It trialed a community technology learning shop in Manchester – the 'Digital Garage.'

The shop was a community hub, designed with a variety of flexible spaces for individual learning, group sessions, demonstrations, workshops and more formal presentations.

The digital skills training centre hosted tens of thousands of successful sessions. The brand reports that 1300 Mancunians took part in the five week 'Start Your Own Business' course, which aimed to grow participants knowledge and confidence in starting their own venture. Meanwhile, 7,900 people took part in the digital marketing course series, whilst more than 1,900 participated in the 'Skills for Work' course series.

The expert coaches at the Google Digital Garage also gave a total of 4,600 one-to-one mentoring sessions: equating to over 2,300 hours or 96 days 24/7 free individual skills coaching.

Google also transformed a traditional double-decker bus into a mobile training hub to visit more remote communities. Over a 12 week period the bus apparently visited 50 locations across Greater Manchester offering free digital skills training.

The format has since closed, however Google will no doubt be assessing both the brand and wider commercial benefits, as well as the social and community impact of such a venture. Expect to see more community involvement and integration from our physical high street spaces and 'retail hubs.'

People often ask why digital pureplay enterprises would ever consider physical retail. The Google garage shows why. It has generated publicity and direct engagement with customers that could not be managed digitally. The intensity of the physical face-to-face interaction is unmatched. Besides, Google also re-thought how to use physical space via a short-term high impact model and the use of a mobile bus training centre. We all need to re-imagine our own 'retail hubs.

Fat Face: sustainable charity in the community

In 2009, the Fat Face Foundation was set up to make a positive and enduring difference to the lives of people in communities where Fat Face sources, manufactures and sells products. Since 2009 it has donated over £1 million to local charities.

As part of the initiative, it has opened Fat Face charity shops in local areas. Their role is to be a physical hub for volunteering, social interaction, and a focus for Fat face within communities. 100% of all profits go to charity and local community projects, generating revenue to be spent in the local area. The projects are the first phase of a larger plan to roll out 'local' support around the country to make a difference in communities in six core strategic areas. Fat Face outlines these.

Firstly, to support hundreds of people by feeding and clothing them throughout the year. To ensure that more young people are given access to work opportunities, completing an intensive personal development course, working with the Prince's Trust.

Supporting local charities such as 'Step by Step' in helping more young people to come off the streets and giving them the chance to turn their lives around. Giving young people more confidence, inspiring the next generation of students to get involved in creative business, working with local sports teams, societies and local schools.

Raising awareness on pollution of the oceans, helping to clean up beaches, through partnering with the Global Ghost Gear Initiative (GGGI), diving specialists Fourth Element and World Animal Protection (WAP.) Helping to restore and conserve local habitats, forests & wetlands, working with partners that are focused on protecting life on land.

Shops should not all be about shopping. They should not all be about making immediate cash profit. A balanced shop estate should have everything from cash-cow sales shops to marketing pop-ups, community hubs and outlets to sell-through excess stock and reduce waste.

The Z to A of retail disruption

BUILD A 'RETAIL HUB' ACTION PAGES

057

CLEAN YOURSELF UP

Customer research & operational processes

We can all search for that magical customer experience in the stars and lights of expensive new shop concepts and sensual product displays. The starting point is generally much closer to home.

How many shops do you go into where the surfaces are dirty, there are boxes and rubbish on the floors, and you enter areas of semi-darkness because lights aren't working?

It's not rocket science. Maybe that's the problem. It is not sexy keeping shops clean and tidy, but it is so important.

Actions

- Assess & analyse the actual situation in your shops
  - Gather images from across your estate
  - Create a database of imagery
  - Feedback from shop colleagues & customers
- Define a 'minimum standards' level for all shops
  - Cleanliness
  - Maintenance
  - Operations
- Instigate self-help initiatives including a 'reporting process'
- Adjust the 'shop maintenance' resources and budgets to achieve acceptable standards
- Re-write shop operations schedules including cleaning, tidiness, shop-floor processes & disciplines
  - Review cleaning contracts
- Plan and begin an ongoing programme of 'soft' shop refreshment for priority locations

058

BRING YOUR SHOPS TO LIFE

Customer analysis, shop feedback & competitor benchmarking

Look around your shops before you look inside. Look at the people that pass by and enter. What do these customers want from you and from your shops? What things will impress them, and which other things will they be blind to?

Head offices are often a long way from shops. It is so important to understand the customer around your shops. Listen to your shop managers and give the customer what they want, not what you think they should have.

Actions

- Instigate a consultation programme across shops
  - Feedback from shop managers on key success drivers in individual shops
    - Promotions and price
    - Shop standards & design
    - Facades and window displays
    - Community & town events involvement
    - Shop colleague training/expertise
    - Services – delivery/collection
    - Competitive advantages
- Cluster shops for 'activation' initiatives
- Define the delivery of several approaches to activate shops
  - Budget, plan & deliver by cluster

059

WHAT IS YOUR 'SHOP OF THE FUTURE?' TAKE A NEW APPROACH TO SHOP DESIGN

Market & customer analysis, competitor benchmarking

We need to bring together the strategy behind the format of shops we want to have, and how we make them 'personal destination retailers.' We've worked this much out.

Probably the core of our estate will be the shop in our community. This is where we need to be smart with different designs. We need to have variations of a core concept. And we need to build in flexibility because the community needs of the shop will vary over time, and even by season, month, week or day.

Our retail hub will be a combination of a "shopper's paradise," a "collection crossroads," a "community hub," and a local "business centre." We need to offer a combination of all four.

First, we need to have an idea of what each part would look like independently and then how it would all work as one, in any combination. We will need a good shop design partner and a lot of liaising to ensure the complexities of the proposition is delivered as a clear and seamless physical concept.

Begin with the most common scenario and shop balance. And then work on variations. Always work closely with the shop manager and team. They will be the ones who make this work.

Actions

- Instigate a major review of your shop estate to identify the different 'omni-channel' roles of the shops you have
  - Leisure shopping Destination
  - Convenience format
  - Click & collection point
  - Warehouse storage
  - Returns point
  - Community centre
  - Social meeting place
  - Working environment
  - Regional managers office
- Define the potential formats for your shops
  - Shopper paradise
  - Collection crossroads
  - Community hub
  - Business centre
- Develop the commercial business case for each
- Define the shop proposition for each type of hub
- Shop layout & design
  - Facilities & services
  - Colleague skills and attributes
  - Product assortment
  - Selling space/storage space/colleague space
  - Delivery requirements – bikes
  - Local partners
  - Community initiatives
- Implement trial shops for each shop format & design
  - Begin with the most common combination of uses
- Adapt, evolve and roll-out

People:
'The shopkeepers of today'

Select any retail business, and you are most likely to discover a culture of colleague collaboration, trust and respect. However, retail has a chequered history of human resource management and interpersonal approaches, to say the least. Even in the best run businesses today there is still plenty of scope for further innovation and disruption to the traditional personnel models.

Overall, there is a growing appreciation of colleagues at every level of organisations, being driven by the new wave of retailers who have a different outlook on how to manage their employees, to nurture loyalty and productivity. And from the evolution of many HR departments who are now introducing different cultures into the traditional retail sector.

Regarding shop personnel there is also a new awareness of the importance of human interactions with the customer. The outpouring of warmth towards 'key workers' and those essential to the fabric of society during the COVID crisis, has been echoed to various degrees by retail boards, and their reaction towards their own 'key-workers.' Those colleagues who kept shops open and stocked in the most difficult of circumstances, and those who kept the brand light shining, even in the most desperate of corporate environments.

For some retailers, the current bar for shop colleague management is set very low, the practices a product of years of personnel neglect and cost-cutting. This does mean, however, that significant gains can be made just from firstly re-establishing good levels of communication with teams and individuals. The setting up of feedback sessions, team building workshops and individual mentoring can go along way to achieving normal relations.

Diversity and inclusion are so important within any business. This book talks about people from cover to cover. The inclusion of everyone within a retailer, from the top executives to the part-time worker, in the decision processes, in implementation and management functions, and through recognition and reward criteria, is essential. Inclusion of diversity across nationality, colour of skin, religion, social background, education, sexuality & gender, politics and opinion and any other artificial segmentation, adds richly and deeply to the working, retailing experience and the quality and meaning of the output for both colleagues and customers. 'Meaning in the Retail Madness' comes only through the inclusion and involvement of everyone.

> *Evolve a culture of treating staff as people, as individuals, as human beings, rather than numbers, positions & costs*

A good HR team, of which there are many, strives to know and understand their colleagues through personal interaction. It is the restrictions to their own resourcing and time availability, that usually limits the level of understanding and empathy.

In head office and in shops, career paths should be the result of consultation and not just internal hierarchies, retirements, and maternity leaves. Good people are adaptable and respond to new responsibilities. Good people bring ideas and enthusiasm to new positions of trust. But good people need to be discovered, through being asked about their ambitions, passions and innovative ideas for themselves and the business.

Beyond the role of HR , the balance and equality within the organisational structure are key to instilling a successful 'people culture.' It is important that every function and team, at every level, are valued as part of the wider corporate approach. What is believed and demonstrated at the top table, for better or worse, usually sets the standards further down the business. The board must be enlightened as to the importance of diversity within the employees of a business.

The improved engagement and mutual appreciation is of course a two-way process. But it is rarely the case that a genuine and considered investment in people is not returned with a positive impact on productivity and profit.

It is rare for colleague focused initiatives, at individual and team levels, not to contribute to a happier working environment. This is always a good place to start for efficiency and productivity.

Evolve

The ongoing process of improvement. People knowledge and skills. Technology applications. Process efficiency.

Areas of consideration:

- Evolve management & employee organisation
- Employ awards for commercial KPIs
- Evolve training & improve career path development
- Consult & communicate across broader issues
- Employ feedback sessions/channels
- Celebrate diversity within your workforce

Summary of opportunities:

- To become better at treating personnel like human beings
- A personal interest in every person in the business
- Equality of importance and treatment
- A commitment to career paths
- Consultation & communication wherever possible
- A meaningful reward initiative
- Feedback encouragement
- To include, stimulate and use the wealth that is diversity

Enrich

Strategic injections modifying and adding scope and benefit to ongoing processes. Introducing different principles, different ways of working, new skill-sets, technology interventions.

Areas of consideration:

- Develop trust building initiatives
- Front line staff re-prioritisation
- Enrich training in product and production
- Integrate customer service across channels
- Performance rewards based on wider social added-value KPIs – and customer satisfaction
- Develop enhanced staff areas
- Enrich the diversity of employees

Summary of opportunities:

- Trust through collaboration, investment, responsibility and the facilitating of the new ways of working
- Front-line shop teams treated as priority with training & rewards and better facilities – treat with respect
- Training in customer service skills, product knowledge
- Dynamic communication apps
- KPIs based on wider performance parameters including social initiatives and community involvement
- A "partnership" reward system
- Involvement in business development ideas schemes
- To enrich diverse thinking and solutions across the business

Expand

Introducing broad strategic initiatives to drive the business in new and profitable directions. Requiring changes to the organisational structure, principles and processes.

Areas of consideration:

- Develop the 'Passion Supply Chain'
- Focus on the financial and mental wellbeing of people
- Become a product & customer focused organisation
- Omni-channel colleague role flexibility from head office to shops and digital channels
- Maximise colleague efficiency and customer reach
- Deliver a diversity & inclusion programme for education and enablement

Summary of opportunities:

- Embrace and nurture people through the supply chain from suppliers to deliverers – Create "The Passion Supply Chain!"
- To give more responsibility to shop managers & teams from assortment allocation, marketing, product development
- To ensure a balance of old & new skills at the top of the business.
- Strategic commitment for the retail business to be essential every person linked to the business – From Boardroom to Stockroom
- A "shares & business partner" related reward scheme
- Sabbaticals related to improving individual and business knowledge
- To generate the most engaged and self-stimulating team with diverse and innovative thinking

Sketch 60 People: Evolve, Enrich & Expand

The COVID-lockdown world resulted in the need for remote working for previously centralized office staff, and the trust that goes with it. It was a long overdue, even if enforced, exercise in what happens when trust and responsibility are given to people.

Every business will have its own view on the benefits and the problems caused, but the likelihood is that remote working will continue going forwards in some shape or form. What was illustrated is that most colleagues can be trusted to work at home, can manage their time, and in many cases increase their output, as well as their input into the business.

Many of us are probably moving towards some form of hybrid working situation. Investments in the required technology to work remotely are generally off-set by the savings in office space, travel expenses and hotel bills. It will be the continued and deeper trust in the workforce and investment in their working conditions, whether at home or in the office, that will engender a fruitful working relationship, whatever the balance of office and home time happens to be.

The outpouring of trust has also reached the management of physical shops. Front-line shop teams are now generally being treated as priority personal with a new impetus for appropriate training, rewards, renumeration, and better facilities. It is a more than worthwhile investment, and again it is well overdue.

This is part of the wider physical shopping picture. Customers have begun again to respond favourably to local shops with their familiar faces and cheerful greetings. In these strange times of distancing in the aisles, the wearing of masks, the appearance of screens, the obstacles seem only to have strengthened the connections between customers and shop workers.

This forgotten bond, of familiarity and intimacy, has seemingly been awakened for customers, for shop workers and for the most senior of retail executives.

The enrichment of shop people

The combination of people and technology is a powerful one. In the correct environments the two can work perfectly together, even in the most physical of places, the shop.

For example, personalised apps, as much as 'in situ' physical managers can train store personnel in service skills, educate them in product, manage and encourage them in their everyday routines. As an extension of the app, the curious relationship of trust and affection seen between people and their Alexa's or Google's, is not so difficult to replicate in the form of a digital support tool for shop workers. Daily roles and regimes, schedules, business news, product information, customer requests and team community apps are all rich content interfaces that can help with the daily shopfloor tasks and the job of converting customers into sales.

Technologies are taking the strain, whilst the structures of physical shop teams are changing with more responsibility and reward to customer facing personnel, and less positions for additional layers of management. The pattern of higher wages for empowered 'sales assistants' and the decreasing increment to shop manager pay, is a testament to the trend of investing in those directly in contact with the customer.

The KPIs that are used to reward personnel across the business are also being reviewed in the aftermath of COVID. The retail brand is a reflection of the people that work for it. Brands with good people have done well from the new reliance of the customer on 'essential retailers.'

The inadvertent advocates

Shop colleagues can shine in many ways. Not only functionally but emotionally. Their personalities, and their social media lifestyles, are potentially an important asset to a business. They are 'inadvertent advocates,' and future considerations when deciding on pay levels, could well depend on social popularity, good works, charitable involvement, community services as much as capability and commercial experience.

Shop teams in general will continue to demand respect and attract a wider appreciation of their value based on their community engagement and individual customer relationships.

Footfall and loyalty will be built more than ever on their familiarity, understanding and empathy with local customers. Individual customers will seek out individual shop managers and individual colleagues.

The personal destination retailer will be built on destination retail personalities

Expanding the role of the 'new shopkeepers'

In a reversal of history, the shop manager and their teams are once again becoming 'The New Shopkeepers' making key decisions in and about their shops. The grip and influence of distant analysts passing down generic instructions to shops will gradually be relaxed as the personal destination shop begins to re-populate the high street and control its own destiny.

Essential retailers must not only be essential to their customers but should learn again to be essential to their shop colleagues. The scales will shift from people looking for shop jobs, to shops looking for valuable colleagues and local advocates.

And whilst the realisation has dawned that these people are important to the customer equation and must be valued and retained, initiatives are also being intensified to ensure that the knowledge and experience of shop colleagues is captured to benefit the wider retail business.

Listen to the shops

The minimum requirement today from internal communications teams is to encourage responsive and organised feedback from shop teams. Colleagues need to feel that their opinions are welcomed, and that those opinions turn into actions.

Imaginative HR departments are using ideas such as inter-shop competitions to harness friendly rivalries, in tasks that encourage shop teams to develop and present ideas to top business executives. Winning entries are then developed in collaboration with the shop team, alongside financial rewards based on the success of the idea.

Investing in shop colleague ideas and enthusiasm can be taken further with training and sabbaticals on offer, allowing colleagues to take paid-leave and be sent on trips to develop their ideas with growers, suppliers and manufacturers at the periphery of the supply chain. Adventures can lead into new product initiatives and process efficiencies.

At the heart of these schemes is the fact that senior executives are willing to invest in, the experience, knowledge and ideas of their shop teams.

Colleague Partnerships

At the summit of retailer employee interaction and collaboration we see retailers entering into a variety of partnerships with employees forging further levels of mutual trust and loyalty. For employers this reduces significantly the hardships of a high turnover of staff, whilst creating job security and career advancement opportunities for employees.

Benefits include of course, price reductions, but also a share in profits at the year end, and more working benefits such as holiday allowances and pensions. Genuine concessions, not vacuous gestures, go a long way to securing loyalty.

Sharing the load, sharing the rewards

Businesses can also offer share options to employees as part of their partnership. The benefit is that a virtuous cycle is created where employee loyalty and commitment contribute to an attractive business proposition, the desirability for investors to buy in, and where employees are rewarded with highly prized shares. Instilling an appetite and an easy mechanism to buy additional shares, can consolidate employee commitment as they become the purchasers of product and the buyers of shares, the recipients of bonuses and the recipients of dividends.

When someone wears their uniform as a badge of honour, with a sense of pride, it is the point when collaboration and reward have created a quite unique bond of loyalty between employer and employee.

The complexity of new retailing will inevitably involve more external partnerships and collaborations with support teams and businesses. Whilst the support partners' wages are not directly paid by the retailer, their impact on the final brand delivery is often critical.

Retail businesses, therefore, need to translate their new commitment to core staff to the staff of their suppliers from warehouse managers, franchise sales assistants to 'peddle-cycle' delivery boys & girls. The strategic objective is to instill in everyone who works in the company's supply and delivery chains, a passion for the retailer they ultimately work for, and who supports their wages. The passion is born out of the way they are treated and rewarded by the retailer themselves.

People through the whole business 'passion chain' are directly and indirectly responsible for the quality of the various customer touchpoints. If that quality is sub-standard, if the ambition to please is lacking, then it is time to investigate the weaknesses in your personnel strategy, improve the levels of expertise, the freedom of responsibility, to restore the passion that makes retailers great.

Promotional misjudgment

Shop managers need to be correctly integrated into the whole of the retail organization and processes.

The retail structure from the CEO to the shop manager needs to be built of mutual appreciation, a clear understanding of each person's value and worth to the business, with each rewarded accordingly.

There is still a widespread view that shop managers and colleagues are somehow second level citizens in the retail business. That they are not worthy of the same respect or rewards as head office management is a mind-set that must change significantly.

Of course, not everyone is equal, contributes equally, or should be rewarded equally, but creating and perpetuating a perceived 'weakest link' in the business is not good practice. Particularly when that 'weakest link' happens to be the one direct connection with the customers whose patronage pays for everyone's wages.

The situation is exacerbated in a culture where good shop managers are rewarded by promoting them out of the shops and into remote central offices. It is worth remembering that for many shop managers, the reason they joined a retail company, probably as a sales assistant, worked their way to being managers or senior shop team members is because this is the job they like, what they excel in, and the interaction with the customers is the thing that they enjoy the most.

The result of 'promotional misjudgments' is unhappy shop managers promoted to unsuitable remote office jobs as a 'reward,' whilst shops are continually stripped of their most valuable and skilled assets.

Shop Manager responsibilities:

- "Specialist"
- Product input
- Shop strategy
- Community initiatives
- Community development

Shop Assistant responsibilities:

- "Generalist"
- Product feedback
- Shop maintenance
- Customer Sales
- Customer relationships

Deputy Manager responsibilities:

- "Expert"
- Product selection
- Shop "experience"
- Customer relationship
- Community involvement
- Community initiatives

Career progression

Shop manager

Deputy manager

Shop assistant

Role progression

"Specialist"

"Expert"

"Generalist"

Local Retail Hub

Local   Regional   Head Office

Company integration progression

Customer sales

Customer relationship

Community involvement

Community initiatives

Community development

Product feedback

Product selection

Product input

Shop community progression

Shop maintenance

Shop "experience"

Shop strategy

Shop involvement progression

Product involvement progression

Sketch 61 Local Heroes: Shop teams spiraling into control

The best solution to gain the most from the skills and experience of shop managers is to support them, and retain them, where they matter most – in shops, and to reward them with higher wages and benefits. Reward them for being in shops, not being in offices!

For the business, it is much better to create and develop shop expertise and to keep it there. Embrace shop managers and their teams. Help them to become better at what they want to do, and where they want to do it. In the shop.

Keeping shop managers in shops does not mean that they cannot engage and participate fully in head office initiatives on how to improve its shops, and the business in general. The important thing is to develop clear communication and feedback conduits and mechanics.

A higher renumeration and better rewards for shop teams may not seem so out-of-line with comparable levels for office workers, if the shop colleagues' wider contribution to shops and the business as a whole, is recognized and communicated effectively within the business.

Spiraling into control

Career progression within the shop, or retail hub, should be meaningful and rewarding.

Meaningful in terms of having a real impact in all aspects of the retail hub from operational responsibilities, management duties, product assortment involvement, inputs into the running and the strategy of the shop, and a progression from building customer relationships into evolving and developing the community involvement of the shop.

The career progression will also mean increasing involvement at a regional level, liaising with regional managers and other shop managers, and then to direct integration with head office activities and executives. Increased integration into the total business is an essential part of the career development process.

Naturally, appropriate training will follow the career development at every stage. Local people with expertise and experience who can progress their skills and have career paths within the retail hub but remain local.

Career progression should not be just linear, about the present, a blinkered approach with no beginning or end. As shop colleagues progress, they should remain in touch with their experiences and the knowledge they have gained and be able to perceive clearly the path ahead of them by learning from those who have made the same journey. They should also have the opportunity to train those below them, on the same learning cycle they have previously experienced.

The progression must be seasonal and annual, spiraling into new responsibilities, skill sets and ways to benefit the customer, the shop, and the wider business. Cyclical shop colleague progression, in tune with the dynamics of 'shop-life.'

The 'Cross-channel shopkeeper'

Many employees still define and identify themselves by channel. It is almost a badge of honour, the Capulets against the Montagues, the Android users against Apple, the Nike advocates against the Adidas, the coffee drinkers against the tea infusers.

If you were to ask retail executives to form two sports teams from a head office workforce, to play an annual challenge match, it would almost certainly be the physical retailers against the digital team. I know where my money would be.

Putting such sporting rivalries to one side, the division is largely non-sensical. There are so many roles within the retail business that can be shared and applied across channels and touchpoints. So many skills that work just as well in the digital world as the physical. So many benefits to a business from integrating these roles more intelligently. So much satisfaction and fulfilment for people allowed to cross the divide.

These roles help to create true omni-channel brands. They are essential to deliver a single product proposition, and a single customer experience across all touchpoints. The cross-channel shopkeepers.

Many retail functions have the need for a structure that completely embraces and managers all channels, with a central head who defines the strategy and development for the whole business by functions across channels and touchpoints.

Customer service, or product category specialists can equally apply their expertise to face-to-face situations in shops, across phone lines, or via 'zoom' demonstrations from remote shops to customers' mobiles.

The cross-channel shop colleague is going nowhere, except everywhere!

The "Physical Shopkeepers"	The "Cross-channel Shopkeepers"	The "Digital Shopkeepers"
Business analyst analysis of physical shop trends	Senior Business Analyst analysis of product performance data	Business analyst analysis of digital touchpoint trends
Shop designer creation of shop concepts	Head of Product Design creation & concept of new assortment	Interface designer creation of digital interfaces
Shop operations manager shop efficiency, maintenance and management	Head Buyer sourcing, manufacture & supplier collaboration	Digital function manager site efficiency, speed and maintenance
Shop merchandiser shop grading, quantifications, product allocation	Head Merchandiser quantification, grouping & channel allocation	Digital merchandiser digital interface grading & product group allocation
Shop distribution manager shop grading, clustering and product story allocation	Central Logistics Manager shipping to warehouse, distribution centres	Digital inventory manager mobile, online, social, editorial, entertainment
Shop visual merchandiser product displays, guidelines, maintenance & moves	Head of Visual Merchandising product story visualization, product descriptions	Digital visual merchandiser page design, architecture & image arrangement
Shop marketing manager graphics, POS & event shop grading, delivery	Head of Marketing calendar development & channel strategy	Digital marketing manager graphics, POS, event interface grading, delivery
Shop communications manager grading/management of content distribution	Information Manager product information, editorial content creation	Digital communications manager content distribution to digital interfaces & media
Shop sales manager re-merchandising guides, promotional delivery	Head of Sales sales analysis, replenishment, promotions	Digital sales manager site & page re-design guides, promotional delivery
Business analyst, Shop operations manager, Shop merchandiser, Sales manager, Shop manager season review	Senior Business Analyst, Head Buyer, Head of Merchandising, Head of Marketing, Head of Sales season review	Business analyst, Digital function manager, Digital merchandiser, Digital marketing manager & Sales manager season review

© 2021 vm-unleashed ltd.

Sketch 62 The Cross-Channel Shopkeepers: delivering a single product proposition,
and a single customer experience across all touchpoints

'We are all shopkeepers'

Every small, medium or large retailer has a community of its own, its workforce. I am sure that the head office community is what many people have missed the most in their period of COVID forced absence. Despite the convenience of home, it is not the same as the engagement and camaraderie of a working community.

I have always subscribed to the view that everyone who works in a retail business is a retailer. Whether you work in finance, or IT, marketing, or the legal team, and of course all those jobs specific to retail, then you are a retailer. You must be a retailer!

Retail is such a unique industry that whatever your role is, if you are managed correctly and with motivation, it is difficult for anyone not to be caught up in the dynamics and energy of the business. Retailing is in our blood.

Richer Sounds: willing the gift of loyalty

Richer Sounds has always been the most admirable of retailers, with an outstanding reputation for the quality and expertise of its customer service. When you're selling expensive hi-fi and sound equipment you need to employ colleagues who know completely and unassuredly, what they are talking about.

It is however no coincidence that the quality of service, the loyalty and longevity of colleagues, are also linked to the way that they are valued and treated by their employer. Therein lays the magic ingredient of Richer Sounds.

The proof, if any were needed, is no less than in the will of the founder & owner, Julian Richer, a former drummer in a funk band. He had always written into his will his plan to hand shares to staff when he died. However, that time came early, as having hit the ripe old age of 60, he felt the time was right, rather than leaving it until his death.

Apparently, more than 500 staff at Richer Sounds were in line for a £3.5m windfall after the retail chain's boss handed them a 60% stake in the business. Each of the 522 employees was to collect £1,000 for every year at the firm, giving an average payout of £8,000. Some longer serving staff were in line to receive more: 39 having worked for the Hi-fi and TV retailer for more than 20 years, including one who had 40 years' service.

If that was not enough, Richer Sounds also donates 15% of profits to several charities, founded, as it is, on the ethical principles of being decent, honest and truthful in everything.

Richer has explained his generosity is linked to his gratitude. He is quoted as saying, 'It's important... my life's work is my legacy, and I haven't got a spoilt child to run the business.'

I heard early on in my career the expression "a fish rots from its head" relating to the ownership of retail businesses. Sadly with bad management the results can be destructive. What better antidote than to consider the values and actions of Julian Richer.

Brewdog: fun & feedback with crowdfunding

Schemes that make colleagues shareholders are one thing but making customers shareholders through crowdfunding represents a different level of opportunity and responsibility, with significant benefits of brand investment & loyalty.

One business that deployed the model is brewery and pub operator Brewdog. Investors do not just expect a return on investment in the traditional sense but instead draw other benefits such as lifetime discounts in Brewdog bars and online, exclusive merchandise offers and invitations to the company's AGMs and live events.

Brewdog has around 180,000 customer investors. The brand turned to them when investment opportunities with traditional banks drew a blank. With a social network for shareholders, concepts can be floated, and feedback can be instant from a wide variety of people. Apparently, investors help the brand to find new bar sites, design beers and develop new approaches to any challenges the business is might be facing.

Having 180,000 shareholders comes with challenges. Keeping everyone in the loop can be tricky but updates are posted frequently on the private Equity Punk forum. Another upside is the annual community AGM, which consists of a lot more beer and music than your average AGM.

However, as I write this final chapter, the warning is there that all members of a brand's community must be considered and treated equally. In the news are allegations from former employees regarding a 'culture of fear' in the breweries. Sometimes it is easy to be distracted from everyone who contributes to the success or your business and the subtle blurring of employees, customers and shareholders.

And there is the moral of the story. Being engaged with only some of the people in your business is not good enough. It has to be across the board. It is apparently also a lesson for new entrepreneurs. Bad management habits are not just historical. People are people, with the same strengths and weaknesses as always. Apparently so.

The Z to A of retail disruption

Loaf: relaxed around people

Loaf is not just a clever name with its implication of relaxation, or its application to product names and its reference to staff as "Loafers," but it is a summary of a state of mind and attitude to its proposition and its customer profile.

When it comes to interaction it is friendly, open, generous and accommodating from its store environment and its store ambassadors through to the curves and comfort of its product to a culture and mind-set that rewards its staff on friendliness and customer satisfaction in addition to sales performance KPIs.

Loaf manages every touchpoint from a customer perspective, ensuring everything is consistent. Its product expertise and passion is matched from the manufacturing process through to the store sales techniques, however priority number one for store managers and staff is to be engaging, fun and friendly, as well as informed.

Apparently, its shop managers are chosen with this same criteria, in a process where years of traditional furniture sales experience may well be a handicap not an advantage to getting the job. The brand works on the premise that people can be trained in knowledge but never in being genuinely nice people.

The touchpoint with staff is exemplified in a business where staff helped select their distinctive blue and white uniform tops, they can then wear their preferred denim jeans and the Loaf business buys everyone their own Converse trainers. You can't buy loyalty, but you can buy the uniform!

Disruption need not always be aggressive and challenging in retailing, and in a category where customer service and generosity of spirit have often been lost in the process of sales commissions, being nice to your staff and your customers can go a very long way indeed.

A hat's off and a big thank you to the former shop manager Kate and the team at Loaf in Shoreditch, London. Wonderful friendly and always informative. Amazing brand ambassadors.

AO.com: social mobility, helping young people.

Social mobility is a topic close to the heart of retail entrepreneur John Roberts, so it is no surprise that AO.com, the electricals e-tailer he founded, is committed to helping young people from disadvantaged backgrounds find employment.

As an online retailer that is benefiting from the surge in digital demand, not only is AO still hiring but it is well placed to help young people get on the first rung of the digital jobs ladder, an area where the market is likely to remain resilient.

AO is one of the founding partners of Fast Futures, a mentoring programme designed to increase employability for 18 to 22 year-olds, and which promotes social mobility at this critical time when many young people may be struggling to find their feet.

Mentors from across AO help equip young people with the skills they need to secure jobs in the digital sector. They give mentees virtual site visits and conduct mock interviews to prepare them.

Roberts is widely reported as saying he believes that 'talent is very evenly distributed, and opportunity is not.' Apparently, something that he says a lot. He believes that those people who have opportunity are often unaware of how unfair society is and how a lot of people just don't have that opportunity.

His philosophy is engrained through the business. Participation in the mentoring scheme is encouraged, everybody has something that they can give, whether that is time, experience, skills, money. Staff are stimulated to consider how they can create an opportunity for somebody, how they can help and inspire the next generation.

If you are interested in hearing more from John Roberts the founder of AO.com then it is always worthwhile. A very charismatic and interesting person. Check out an interview with him in Retail Week "Social Mobility: How AO is helping kids break into the digital economy" October 2020

The Z to A of retail disruption

060

LISTEN

Colleague feedback and consultation

I won't go into the lecture on how many ears and mouths we each have. Needless to say, many retailers have forgotten how to listen. We have all become the experts and the opinion of anyone below us on the dreaded hierarchy is meaningless. Recently, more often than not, at the bottom of the opinion pile has been the shop colleague.

Turn it on its head. Visualise your company organization with the customer on the top, then the shop colleague, down to the board and the CEO. Now you see the priority to listening. Ensure you focus on the people above you in the listening hierarchy. Level by level the CEO will get to know, what needs to be known!

Actions

- Create a chain of 'listening' within your business
  - Begin with the customer and those closest to them
- Plan and deliver workshops and mechanisms for 'listening'
  - Build the mechanisms step-by-step
  - Gathering, assessing and prioritizing
    - Workshops
    - Communication apps
    - Social networks
    - Suggestion boxes
    - Appraisals
    - Consultations
    - Newsletters
    - Reports
    - Presentations
- Create a process of acknowledgement, gratitude, feedback and actioning back down the 'listening chain'

061

LET YOUR SHOPKEEPERS OWN THEIR SHOPS

Internal brainstorming & colleague research

OK, you wouldn't want your shop team to pick up the rent and rates bill. Would you?

But you can make them feel that they really have ownership of their shops. Give them a route to present ideas and a budget to put them in place. From essential repairs, to external flower baskets, window graphics, newly painted woodwork, a hanging chandelier, social media posts, local promotions. Why not even produce a shop décor catalogue and let the shop team decide how they customize and personalize their environment.

Actions

- Re-write the shop manager job description
- Re-define roles & responsibilities, KPIs and reward
- Engender 'shop ownership' and 'trust'
- Support the shop manager with training
  - Personal relationship building
  - Community interaction
  - Social media communication
  - Team building & management
  - Shop performance economics
- Facilitate activities to 'own' the shop
  - Choices of décor/design/uniform
  - Community initiatives
  - Shop social media channel

062

TRAIN CROSS-CHANNEL CUSTOMER ASSISTANTS

Colleague training & operational strategy

We need to get away from our divisive separate channel mentality and operational delivery. If you are in a role, you are in that role for all channels and touchpoints.

That goes for shop colleagues, sales assistants and customer advisers. Everything that is customer facing needs to be customer facing across whichever channel the customer decides to interact with.

We need to train customer assistants on how to communicate and deliver their services across different channels, from face-to-face inside the shop, to a video call, to a phone call.

We need to employ and apply the technologies so that the physical shop can be a place to physically meet and serve customers, as well as a place to carry out a video demonstration, or to take a customer enquiry on the shop floor headset.

It is the same face of the customer. It should be the same face of the retailer.

And please do away with the centralized customer helpline.

Actions

- Define shop catchments/communities in an omni-channel way
  - Physical customers
  - Omni-customers via loyalty programmes
  - Digital customers via CRM data
- Make single 'local' shops the face of customer service across channels for that catchment and any customer in it
  - Shop visits – face-to-face
  - Phone calls
  - Online queries
  - Video demonstrations
- Facilitate through technology and resources the means to interact fully with customers
  - Video demonstration cams
  - Direct phone line
  - Social media site
  - Facility to work from home/remotely
- Resource & train shop manager & colleagues appropriately:
  - Number of staff
  - Product information training
  - Services information training
  - Common Q&As
  - Next step specialist details
- Tell customers about the initiatives
  - Promote the local shop community
  - Make a hero/celebrity out of your shop manager & teams
  - Provide direct communication channels
  - Support fully and intensely the new shop 'face of your business'

Technology:
'The Great Facilitator'

The world, individuals and businesses are dependent, and inter-dependent on technology. It has changed everything, and its applications and intelligence continue to develop at a seemingly ever-quickening pace.

However, it also threatens to overload our capacity as human beings to absorb and apply such amazing potential. It also risks application for applications sake. We do it because we can, not because it improves our lives, our world and our businesses.

> We are alive in a digitally-led world but must not be dead to the possibilities of being blindly-led on a technological journey to nowhere.

No future in isolation

With apparently limitless possibilities available it is important to grasp some important criteria regarding technology in retail.

Firstly, it must be used to bring teams and functions together, and not to separate. The repercussions of creating isolated silos has been an ongoing historical problem for retail. With technology it is a now a live and present danger.

Isolation can happen through incompatible systems, inaccessible data, security firewalls and protocols, or simply from an over-reliance, an obsession with email and app communication, rather than taking the few physical steps to talk, face to face, with a colleague.

It must bring the extremities of our business together, enabling our most far-flung physical shops to be fully coordinated with head office functions, systems and data streams. Technology should allow our digital channels to connect freely with our physical business, our product, suppliers, warehouses and shops.

The future is a balance of technology and people. No hierarchy, no dominance, just cooperation and one 'large human foot' in the world of reality.

Rationalising the technology of yesterday

The reduction of the number of legacy and bespoke technologies that isolate functions, teams and individuals should be a priority. The situation is the result of an aggressive and disjointed IT vendor market, and isolated internal decision making.

This is easily said but complex to do. Thankfully, many businesses are well through the process, although it often seems to be an endless task as new IT acquisitions and bespoke solutions repeat the mistakes of the past.

New retail businesses have the enviable position of being free from such 'legacy-lag.' However, as we have remarked, today is yesterday's tomorrow. Retailers age quickly and so new businesses as well must be watchful not to fall into the technology legacy traps.

Evolve

The ongoing process of improvement.
People knowledge and skills. Technology applications.
Process efficiency.

Areas of consideration:

- Improve technology reliability
- Increase cross-business systems compatibility
- Usability training
- Social media-training
- Roll-out remote working essentials
- Back-up physical shop system essentials
- Evolve operations & training apps
- Supply customer wi-fi

Summary of opportunities:

- The reduce the number of legacy and bespoke technologies that isolate functions, teams and individuals.
- To coordinate software applications across the business allowing fluidity of information and data across all functions
- To facilitate post-lockdown home and distance working
- Ensure that physical shops are technologically supported with broadband width, training apps, payment systems
- Deliver wi-fi for customers to use mobile apps

Enrich

Strategic injections modifying and adding scope and benefit to ongoing processes.
Introducing different principles, different ways of working, new skill-sets, technology interventions.

Areas of consideration:

- Shop colleague automated scheduling
- Individual shop colleague personal tasks, "help" and communication tools
- Multiple customer payment options – mobile, self-checkout, self-scan
- Roll-out digital screens – imagery, video, interactive, demos, colleague training
- Develop rich-media and social media selling
- Colleague customer profile access
- Develop discussion-based search engines

Summary of opportunities:

- Transforming shop operations and working practices through IT enabled teams and task scheduling and operational and comms apps
- Personalising customer profiles for digital and physical marketing
- Creation of content and use of remote and in-store physical screens for marketing, buying, demonstrating and personalised customer services
- Development of discussion-based search engines integrated with shop colleague 'conversation' intelligence
- Fluidity and flexibility of payment systems
- Selling in-shops and digitally direct from rich-media broadcasts.

Expand

Introducing broad strategic initiatives to drive the business in new and profitable directions.
Requiring changes to the organisational structure, principles and processes.

Areas of consideration:

- Embrace digital-first business strategy
- Complete channel & data integration
- AI merchandising, demand planning, availability prediction, allocation
- B&M digital visualisations, supplier interfaces & process streamlining
- RFID supply chain product tracking
- Inter-channel & partner data communication tools
- Personalization of cross-channel touchpoints
- Digital & shop CUI optimisation tools

Summary of opportunities:

- The evolution of artificial intelligence to allow the anticipation and prediction of customer demand at personal/market level
- The application of artificial intelligence to manage supply planning and continuous production management
- Technology in the buying & merchandising process to more accurately design appropriate and produce accurate products to increase sell-through/retail margin
- RFID rollout for end-to-end inventory management
- Extension of inventory and customer profile systems and data flows to suppliers and customers
- Seamless coordination of customer touchpoints

Sketch 63 Technology: Evolve, Enrich & Expand

A major objective is to improve the coordination of software applications across the business, that will allow the fluidity of information and data across all functions. System simplification on its own may help IT departments sleep more easily, but it is the free-flow of information and processes that will allow businesses to re-energise and become productive.

Evolve a logical network

Getting our techno house in order, now extends to getting every one of our employee's techno houses in order as well.

The lockdown which accelerated the move to home working, to distanced working, requires investment in hardware and software to ensure that the new network of fluid information and open communications stretches as far as our employees' geographic spread necessitates.

This wider geographic responsibility must also extend to our physical shops, warehouses and distribution facilities. An omni-channel retailer cannot retreat to the comfort of accessible servers supporting digital retail channels but must also ensure that physical shops are technologically supported with sufficient broadband widths, mobile training apps, reliable payment systems and access to central systems.

Technology for Customers

The technology must also deliver fast and reliable wi-fi for customers. This is wi-fi for customers to use their mobiles, to access the digital sites and apps that the same IT team has invested heavily in to ensure reliable and immersive experiences, that customers can only access through their mobile phones, and fast and reliable wi-fi.

You see my point? We either have a virtuous or a vicious cycle of technology. Shop technology should at the very least provide a virtuous cycle of delivery & accessibility.

Re-scheduling the nightmare

Physical shop operations and management can now move from sporadic injections of technology to fully integrated systems. Staff scheduling, the nightmare of shop managers. A process that involves planning and plotting, whilst considering a variety of staff preferences and working restrictions, requests for holidays, and spontaneous absenteeism, can be re-invented.

AI functionality is having transformative effects on staff scheduling. Not only can it correlate all the above criteria, it can also consider footfall and sales patterns, stock deliveries and merchandising timetables, task manning requirements, an awareness of what each staff member is best at, till work, customer service, and logistics organisation. Within the basics of staffing the shop, technology can place the most appropriate staff, in the best places at the best time, doing the tasks they excel at.

Enrich colleague communications

Communication apps can also be part of the integrated system. Early morning staff meetings are excellent for motivation and the important sales target announcements, but task and responsibility details are not absorbed in such surroundings.

Personal communication apps, via each colleague's mobile and head-set, can deliver a pro-active and reactive experience. The app speaks in a supportive and personal tone, scheduling tasks and reminding the colleague of deadlines and priorities. It highlights new product and sales data information linked to each task, feeds relevant business news, and can even select music of the colleague's taste to pass the time of mundane duties.

Customer personalisation

AI, of course, is at the bottom of the amazing customer personalisation work being carried out using sales data, browsing histories and social media profiling. As far as each customer wants to progress with this, the accuracy and relevance of the process will allow the proactive anticipation of customer needs as well as intelligent reactive suggestions.

A seamless customer profiling system will feed the loading of web and mobile pages and will be available to educate and coach shop colleagues, at the till or on the shopfloor.

As with all the best of things, such systems will be circular, allowing shop colleagues with person-to-person interaction to update observations about customers to add further richness to the profiling. Shop and digital customer service colleagues also have the opportunity to blend their skills and knowledge of products and customers.

Cross-channel services

The use of technology can allow in-store demonstrations and specialist knowledge to be streamed live to online customers in one-to-one video calls. Whilst customers in-store can talk face-to-face with customer service teams in head office, for more product information or questions about payments, deliveries and returns.

The fluidity of payment systems will continue to be accepted and accelerated across retailers, allowing a seamless experience for customers. The COVID experience has brought home the benefits of cashless payments, even the downsides of physically touching keypads, and overcome a lot of customer concerns about using technology to make their purchases and take their money.

The development of discussion-based search engines for digital selling will continue to improve, replacing static product hierarchies with intelligent and responsive customer questioning. As the repository of digital journeys builds, the same logic and question sequences will be introduced into the physical world, through colleague training workshops, and then via personalised head-set guidance, akin to news broadcaster feeds.

Add to this, the more immersive use of rich-media technologies both online and in-store, social media sales channel developments, and direct to buy capabilities on music and sports broadcasts, in shops and online, and you can see the opportunity for technology to enrich the customer experience, is still only at the foothills of the exciting journey ahead.

The expansion of the applications and the benefits of Artificial Intelligence will soon be integrated into retail on an industrial scale.

The customer journey interface

It is no surprise that a lot of technology and new thinking is being applied to the customer journey, the product interface, the search, browsing and purchasing processes.

Because the customer is remote from the product when buying digitally, this is an important focus for technology investment.

The bonus is that the thinking behind the technology, and certainly the learnings from implementing digitally, can be applied to physical selling as well. The media may be different, but the principles of good selling are remarkably similar.

Understanding the customer journey is essential to both the physical and digital journeys. The solutions mirror each other.

- Responsive site menus and fluid navigation is being replicated in shops with more free-flow and intuitive navigation.
- Conversational search is echoed with conversational speech.
- Enhanced visualization can now be transferred across channels, with digital screens and visual merchandising coordinated. Product information in the form of visuals and verbal communication works equally in the physical and digital worlds.
- Enhanced visual fitting rooms in physical shops can integrate with the virtual fitting rooms in the home or on the move.
- Feedback and recommendations, good and bad, are transversal across all touchpoints.

© 2021 vm-unleashed ltd.

Sketch 64 Customer Interfaces: Acceleration, Accuracy and Agility.

The shop colleague 'influencer'

Video customer service experts have an opportunity to shine. On a one-to-one level they are beginning to command respect and becoming figures of authority and trust. They can become valuable assets to retailers and rewarded accordingly.

For those with personality, and "star-quality" the possibility arises of being internal advocates and influencers.

The personal service relationship can be transformed into the social advocate relationship. Instead of retailers needing to pay for expensive 'celebrities' with a modicum of knowledge in what they are selling, much better to encourage and mentor your experts to become 'celebrity experts.'

Bloggers doing the business

However, not all colleagues need to be celebrities to influence customers. Their important role of being enthusiastic and loyal about their businesses is finding a route to customers via a number of apps. The apps create social media brand advocates from colleagues, by helping them to participate in posting across their social media platforms.

The app feeds shop colleagues company content to re-post, recommends messages to send with prompts and reminders. It also awards and rewards the most prolific and successful colleagues, in terms of posting and re-posts, friends and followers.

Specialist shop colleagues promoting and recommending shop services across digital touchpoints, in beauty or home décor, are also being rewarded through an uplift in appointments, and a bonus for building brand loyalty. The retailer and the colleagues receive constant feedback on the impact on sales, as the balance of content is continuously evolved and improved.

Video retail

Brands such as Zoom, the bastion of virtual business meetings, are becoming portals for a wide selection of retailers to communicate directly with potential customers, explaining and selling their products.

Envisage a 'dragon's den' scenario where brand salesmen pitch their product in a personal, conversational way, to a potential client. The conversation software then facilitates a direct purchase.

This is the digital version of the door-to-door salesman, except no one is allowed in without an invitation, and it's much easier to pull the plug than to remove a size ten jammed in your door.

A new way to shop has already emerged via Zoom. So called, "Squad Shopping" digitally replicates the shopping trip.

"Squad Shopping!"

COVID lockdowns have inspired friends to use the technology to go shopping as a group, chatting as they travel around e-commerce sites, visiting cafes, using the screen share facilities to get feedback on possible purchases before they buy.

It is yet another extraordinary twist in retailing, that the touch-point again becomes the retailer, the customer becomes the shopkeeper, and the retailer becomes the supplier. In this modern world who is the retailer?

Expand intelligent supply chains

Considerations on seasonality, weather patterns, social mood, economic stability, local, national, and international events are all being correlated for accurate daily, weekly, and seasonal time frames.

These predictions are being integrated with supply planning and demand availability, speeding up and slowing down production rates, switching between product lines, coordinating the balance between local and international suppliers, value or added-value products, product types, sizes, colours and product design. The assortment opportunities are limitless.

Technology will also impact in more significant ways the buying & merchandising process to more accurately design and produce appropriate and accurate products. AI will analyse historical patterns of design, colour and materials and reference against current best seller attributes to allow more certainty to commercial buying order commitments.

Customer profile databases will harness the power of loyal customers to preview potential products before order commitments. Advanced 3D visual rendering, and physical 3D printing, will present lifelike prototypes for customer previews, and ensure a 'real' template for the production process. Increases in sell-through, and reductions in waste, will drive the benefits of producing accurate products.

Efficiency will be ensured through the widespread adoption of RFID technology to label products consistently from factory to the customers door. End-to-end inventory monitoring and management will be the norm. To facilitate this, there will be an extension of system and data sharing flows from suppliers to customers, giving the customer the ability to access stock availability data and lead-times by touchpoint, and to live-track their order, even from the factory direct to their door.

Anyone who has been able to return goods simply by handing over the product has been experiencing first-hand the benefits of RFID technology. No receipts, no paper, no cards or cash or payment machines. This is not just remote invisible technology but with applications that are real and instant.

> *Live tracking of products crossing the globe will not just be for Santa Claus, and Christmas, but be a part of our everyday 24/7 lives.*

The limitations of technology

Ultimately, perhaps ironically, technology will become more under the control of people. The period of new technology saturation in the race to get ahead, and not be left behind, will evolve into a rationalisation of the benefits of specific uses of technology.

Technology will also know its limitations. Or rather people will know its limitations. Distribution centre robotics have proven their worth, with outstanding efficiency and productivity in delivering directly to customers – under normal market circumstances.

COVID showed us that increasing capacity quickly can only be achieved through the employment of more people, to drive, to sort, to pack and to cycle. It was somewhat reassuring from a 'luddite' perspective that the solution to a human disaster was found through humans 'rolling up their sleeves' in a physical endeavour of 'blood, sweat and tears!'

And whilst human beings do experience burnout, and the occasional meltdown at work, it is a pretty rare occurrence for us to burst into flames and burn down part of a state-of-the-art-factory. You may need to research that reference.

> '*The unlocking of human potential sometimes out trumps the potential for more robotic procreation.*'

Technology will take the pole position behind the scenes, but more of a back-seat in the public arena. Its immense power will drive the wheels of retail businesses, but people will emerge again as the face of physical retail shopping, and through interactive communication tools, will also be a popular interface for digital channels.

Outstanding retail experiences will not be exclusive to either physical or digital channels and touchpoints. Just as the COVID lockdown accelerated a move to digital commerce, it also stimulated a need for physical human contact and interaction in physical shops. Neither trend will disappear.

> *Technology is the 'great facilitator.' It will become the 'greatest facilitator.' But its androids will be confined to the micro-distribution centre, not rolled-out to the corner shop.*

Amazon Go: Alexa dash cart technology

Amazon's forays into physical retail may be short-lived and sporadic to-date, but they are always innovative. Its "Fresh" supermarket has incorporated elements such as checkout-less payment options including a Dash Cart trolley, drive-thru collection and customer advice through Alexa devices.

The Dash Cart, which apparently uses computer vision algorithms and sensors, allows customers to sign in using an app or QR code, purchase automatically and then pay on-the-move whilst leaving through a special lane without stopping.

Customers can also access their Alexa shopping lists and Echo Show devices to answer questions such as "where can I find the hot sauce?" or "how much is a watermelon?" …

Some features will die, but many will become mainstream across many retailers such as the payless exits and digital shopping assistants, that feel like they were born to shop.

Co-op & Starship: rolling out the robots

The collaboration first teamed up in 2018, using robots to offer emission-free online home deliveries in Milton Keynes and surrounding areas. Starship Technologies' robots use sensors, AI and machine learning to travel on pavements and navigate around obstacles. They are also battery powered, therefore helping to reduce pollution.

The Co-op has said the number of deliveries completed by robots in Milton Keynes tripled during the pandemic, as elderly and vulnerable customers opted for the contactless method of online food shopping. The Co-op has ambitions to use 300 of Starship Technologies' robots by the end of 2021.

The Z to A of retail disruption

Peloton: boutique technologies in your home

For the unsuspecting, and for the compliant, retail technologies are entering every part of our lives, and our homes. Peloton is a stella example of such a brand.

The Peloton bike is a high-end indoor exercise machine with a Wi-Fi-enabled, 22-inch touchscreen tablet. The screen is located on the handlebars in front of the rider's face. The screen is the ultimate touchpoint taking your mind and imagination directly into the world of Peloton, whilst your body engages with the machinations of the physical cycle.

The screen streams live, and on-demand classes and allows the rider to compete with other participants via a live leaderboard that ranks riders based on "output," or the total wattage of energy expended. The most popular on-demand classes have tens of thousands of rides completed. Special live rides have been known to pull in nearly 20,000 riders at one time.

The bike is a re-invented and re-imagined version of an exercise bike, but the technology behind the screen is the exciting part as it links to unique content, and also to like-minded people. The smart move is that activities carried out in isolation allow the rider to "like" and communicate with riders on the same ride and to develop chats and friendships with them. The exercise evolves into social media on wheels, with liking, chatting and Peloton community building.

The personal 'icing on the Peloton cake' are the instructors, who attain celebrity status as your guides, buddies, brand advocates and influencers. The relationship with the brand that the technology allows creates strong customer loyalty. New and dedicated races and race locations, exercise music downloads and exercise wear are all available to buy and download. Immersive retail in action.

Yet again we see it is the process that is the USP and not the physical product. Whilst Peloton has adapted the screen for use on other exercise equipment such as treadmills, it is in all cases the digital interface, the classes and the community that make Peloton unique to its customers.

John Lewis: 100 virtual experiences

Consumer went 'creative mad' during the various COVID lockdowns, trying all kinds of new activities to fill their home leisure time, and re-kindle long lost hobbies. The John Lewis Partnership launched 100 new virtual experiences to keep the nation entertained during the UK's Covid-19 lockdowns.

Examples of experiences offered by John Lewis and Waitrose included pancake cooking classes for kids, knitting workshops, batch cooking tips for people working from home, sewing machine classes, advice on dressing for a Zoom date, inspiration to keep the kids busy, help tidying the home, planning an upgrade to your workout wardrobe or tips on preparing a baby's nursery.

The people behind many of the videos were sales assistants & specialists from the John Lewis shop floor, from home décor advisers to beauty consultants. Video interfaces gave their experience and skills new purpose.

Dobbies: bringing the garden into the home

Dobbies the DIY & garden retailer produced a series of exclusive virtual events hosted by their horticultural director Marcus Eyles, apparently live from his own garden, including tutorials and live demonstrations across a variety of topics.

Events covered filling pots and planters with springtime blooms, developing healthy soil and edible crops, cultivating garden wildlife and maintaining a lush lawn. The workshop sessions also enabled viewers to interact and ask questions.

Dobbies' virtual events follow a successful programme of Facebook Live sessions in 2020 and provide a virtual alternative to the regular 'Grow How' events previously hosted in-store.

The Z to A of retail disruption

Zara & RFID: single inventory position

Whilst there is much fanfare surrounding the use of technology in the customer interface, and the coordination of the experience across channels and touchpoints, that isn't necessarily the most crucial injection of technology for a retail business. And despite the shift to services and subscriptions as revenue drivers, the physical product still makes the dollars.

To sell it you need to know where it is. That is the key to commercial performance, and RFID is the technology that is on everyone's lips.

Zara has invested heavily in the product tracking system, with the majority of its shops now capable of using the technology. RFID allows Zara to build a 'single inventory position,' integrating all its stock into the same system. In any retail landscape where inventory needs to be flexible across channels, available across locations, and visible before, during and after the sales transaction, tracking is essential.

RFID allows Zara to know what options are available, for re-ordering and re-freshing. It allows them to know where the options are so that it can move them to where they will be sold more easily, or indeed to customers who have already bought them. This flexibility of movement alone means that more products are sold at full price & margin.

RFID also paid dividends during the coronavirus crisis, where Zara's single view of stock meant it was able to fulfil 'a big part' of its online order backlog by selling products located in closed stores. Managing what would have been largely dead-stock, effectively turned empty shops into micro-fulfilment centres.

Moving forwards, RFID will allow Zara to make more money from less inventory through fully integrating with its supply chain. Ordering lower inventory initially, shipping it to the correct locations, achieving full price, and moving ever on.

JD: seeing the potential of digital screens

'My word!', what a lot of misguided effort has gone into the use of digital screens in shops. Even today there are few exponents who truly gain the full potential of them.

JD Sports are one of the best employers of digital screens in shops. The reason is that the business is content focused and not screen technology focused, therefore every size screen and its location has a reason. In fact, the gem of JD sports usage is that any number of screens can have multiple purposes, depending on the scenario they find themselves in.

JD uses large screens high up on the walls, suspended from ceilings, behind tills and in waiting areas to set the atmosphere and the 'design' of the environment, and it employs tablets for interaction, either carried by colleagues or set in terminals. But it is the use of its middle-sized screens that really gains impact and advantage. These portrait screens find themselves on walls breaking up product displays, on pillars, or in sequence on free wall space adjacent to customer flows.

Marketing has a big say in their content. It would seem the screens are programmed to switch automatically in loops between series of static promotional images, brands, products, promotions, events and loyalty benefits. Every so often the pace is changed with the injection of a short, dynamic video, a brand advertisement of sports action. Content details & changes programmed according to customer patterns and commercial stimulation.

Many of the screens can also instantly change to product webpages with interaction and payment facilitation, literally at a touch. Combine this with customer analytics, interaction analysis, and demographic profiling, and we can see how screens truly begin to pay back their investment and fulfill their overdue potential.

The big message. Find the reason for digital screens and put those in charge of the content on them, in charge of the physical screens themselves.

The Z to A of retail disruption

063

GET RID OF LEGACY

Internal analysis & IT strategies & operations

There you go in four words. "Get rid of legacy." The curse of modern business. Too many disconnected and bespoke technologies that make modern working painful. Of course, it is a massive task (or can be) but it must be done. You're competing against new tech-savvy businesses with super smooth systems. They are not going to wait for you.

Actions

- An internal, or external assessment of the systems, compatibility and friction points in the business
- A budgeted plan to replace or integrate all existing systems
- A list of prioritisations
- A correctly resourced internal team, or external partners and contractors
- An experienced project manager
- Default fines for contractors missing dead-lines and going over budgets

064

PUT FAST BROADBAND WI-FI IN EVERY SHOP

Shop analysis and IT roll-out

Your shops are not on the edge of your universe. They are at the very centre of your universe. Just ask your customers and ask your colleagues.

Footfall is difficult enough to achieve without putting a big sign on the entrance 'No wi-fi in hear!' or even worse 'Ne FREE wi-fi in here!" It's a small investment that will pay for itself many times over. Don't be one of those mean hotels that charge their customers for anything other than the most painfully slow wi-fi option. They just blackmailed themselves out of customers.

Your shops need to be wired up for store operations, multiple customer payment options, centrally controlled digital screens, inventory management data, sales data, product information, subscribed customer profiles, security, video analytics & customer wi-fi. Don't short-change them and leave them in the lurch. Give them unbelievably fast broadband. Surpass their expectations.

Actions

- Make an assessment of the current capability of every shop
  - Operational capability
  - Customer w-fi capability

- Allow free customer access immediately where possible
- Communicate in-shop windows, inside and on mobile that free wi-fi is available
- Develop a priority action plan to widen the broadband where required across shops to facilitate acceptable operational capability and offer customer wi-fi
- Resource and action
- Make an assessment of phone charging capabilities in every shop
  - Allow and communicate the service and facility where immediately possible
  - Action a plan for phone charging in every shop
  - Communicate in shop windows, in shops and on mobile apps.

065

TRAIN IN SOCIAL MEDIA

Competitor benchmarking, tech operations, marketing & PR

Your colleagues are your advocates in so many ways. Shop managers, of independent retailers and multiple chain shops, should be their own advocates building up loyalty through their personalities, through their conversations.

Formally and informally an employer base can have a big influence on the wider customer perception. Use it. Train your workforce in social media. For LinkedIn, for Facebook, for Instagram, for twitter. Feed them content if you want. Train them in business and personal profiles. That's important.

Actions

- Facilitate each shop to have the most appropriate official social media platforms
  - Websites
  - Facebook, twitter, Instagram...etc.
- Train shop colleagues on how to communicate locally with customer communities across social media
- Set-up an internal scheme where all employees across the business can post and become influencers for the business across social media platforms
  - Train in setting up profiles
  - 'tone of voice;
  - 'do's and don't's'
  - Feed daily information and communication suggestions
  - Reward schemes for most influential employees
  - 'Celebrity' status

066

AUTOMATE SHOP STAFF SCHEDULING

Shop analysis, operations & HR, research and IT roll-out

In a nutshell. This is a nightmare task. The worst ever to do manually. Virtually impossible. There it is.

There are several excellent automated solutions so invest in one for the sanity of your shop managers. And why not invest in one that doesn't just fill holes in the schedule but takes account of colleague personal commitments and lifestyle, role and task preferences, sets 'live' working schedules by individual by shift, adjusts jobs, tasks and priorities in real-time as the shift evolves. Simple!

Actions

- Research and tender for partners to install and manage a state-of-the-art staff scheduling system
- Train your shop managers thoroughly in its use
- Update your colleague preference profiles
- Ensure the 'live' schedule is available to all colleagues
- Keep adding to the system
  - Colleague personal assistants
  - Live feeds
  - Personal communication tools

067

ENSURE THAT DIGITAL SCREENS IN SHOPS ARE OWNED BY THE CONTENT PLANNERS AND CONTENT PRODUCERS

Strategic ownership & responsibility

Why oh why do shops fill themselves with digital screens, very expensive screens, when they have not fully thought through what they will do with them?

Digital screens are an excellent innovation and inclusion in any shop. They save money over time in comparison to printing endless paper messages, they help to reduce paper use and wastage and they allow for full multi-media immersion and communication dynamics.

Let the content planners and content producers be in charge.

Actions

- Make a comprehensive and compelling business case for investment in digital screens in shops.
- Business case to be written & presented by content producers & users
  - Marketing
  - L&D, colleague training
  - Omni & digital content owners
  - Shop analytics
  - Shop operations/communications
- Encourage participation from multiple users to maximise ROI
- Agree investment budgets and testing of ROI
- Agree investment stakeholders
- Clarify ownership after implementation by user group
- Ensure efficient maintenance responsibility of IT/operations

068

DON'T BE DAZZLED BY TECHNOLOGY

IT responsibilities & roll-out

It is so easy to be dazzled by new technologies and to fill your procurement basket will all kinds of smart and useful software, systems, apps and gadgets. I've been to those shows as well.

What the company needs should be driven by what the customer needs. Technology is the facilitator. Before you invest in technology applications make sure you have a customer driven need and an ongoing project to deliver that technology.

Happy customers and colleagues can be dazzling, as well!

Actions

- Carry out due diligence and analysis for every new technology application
- Ensure technology investment is led by internal needs & requests based on business efficiency and customer experience.
- Do not allow IT directors and teams to select and buy IT products, systems and vendors without full consultation with the users. The user directors to have the final say on the most appropriate solution.

Ethical Values: *'Performing on a different level'*

The COVID crisis gave everyone a chance to reassess their values in life. After the shock and the anxiety, the lockdown resulted in a change in priorities for many, an appreciation and gratitude for people and not for possessions.

Those fortunate the be with families and loved-ones, re-discovered friendship, and kindness, those lucky to re-discover the environment around them, the countryside, and the peace, realised that the way things are currently needs to change. On a personal level, but also on a fundamental level for society.

That reflection and the changes in values have persisted for many people. The outpouring of that reflection was initially as individuals. But individuals run businesses, made of many other individuals, whilst groups of individuals become customers, consumers and footfall.

As employees, and customers, we have begun to speak with our feet. We have changed the shops and shopping locations we visit, and we have put our feet up and browsed the internet. As employees we have stayed at home, and as retailers we have gone with the flow. Retailers have largely had no choice. But now retailers do have a choice.

The leaders of retailers are also reflecting on COVID, and the customers' reaction to COVID, the lockdowns and the relaxation of isolation measures. The conclusion of many is that COVID hasn't changed anything, other than it has accelerated dramatically the wider feeling that our values towards consumerism and business need to change. There is more to life than owning things. There is more to retail than making money.

Growth and success have traditionally been measured purely in financial terms. As individuals the size of our pay-check, size of house, our brand of car, trump everything else. As retailers our volumes of sales, our margins and profit have been our only considerations. There is space for movement in our values.

Evolving our perspectives

Big profit, big success. Respect? Not necessarily any longer.

The concept of growth, business growth is being re-evaluated by the individuals who shop, the individuals who work within retail, and the individuals who run retail businesses. New KPIs of growth are emerging. Familiar but forgotten parameters such as happiness, fulfilment, contentment, quality of life, authenticity, craftmanship, gratitude, honesty.

Business growth cannot just be measured anymore in sales, margins and profit, but the quality of its products, the quality of its people, the quality of its relationship with its customer. Growth is no longer just being measured in volumes of product, volumes of money in the bank, but volumes of energy savings, volumes of recycled materials, volumes of happy customers.

The KPIs of success are also changing. If everyone associated with a business is happier, more contented, from the shareholders to the customers, from the boardroom to the stockroom, then the ostensibly 'fundamental' measures of success such as profits, will largely look after themselves. Assuming you have a sound strategy and compelling proposition, of course.

> *Look after the people, and the profit will look after itself.*

It has become ethical to communicate frankly and frequently with your workforce. More accurately it is now unethical not to be open and honest with them. Corporate communications that work both ways allowing feedback and facilitating conversations go along way to creating a contented workforce.

Smart owners and executives should also feel a sense of re-assurance and self-confidence in their strategies and decisions if they have been fully discussed and approved by the people who will be required to deliver them.

It is hard to be ethical whilst isolated. Ethical actions by definition will effect others. Only by embracing those others in the day-to-day running of a business can leaders claim genuinely to be acting in an ethical way.

Evolve

The ongoing process of improvement.
People knowledge and skills. Technology applications.
Process efficiency.

Areas of consideration:

- Achieve KPIs in non-exploitative ways
- Efficiency over cost reduction for profit gain
- Add KPIs other than financial performance
- Ensure fair wage/rewards for all employees
- Achieve Buying/Initial margins honorably
- Re-invest % of profit into employees
- Apply sustainability considerations

Summary of opportunities:

- To define what growth & success should be
- To change the business model from volume to added-value through a realistic progressive process with many ethical steps
- Treat employees with new respect and value, ensuring fair wages and working conditions, and re-investing in training and well-being
- Ensure that negotiations with suppliers are non-exploitative and suppliers pay their employees well and treat them well.
- Set new KPIs as targets – reduction of waste, volumes of unsold stock, amounts of materials recycled, air-miles reduced

Enrich

Strategic injections modifying and adding scope and benefit to ongoing processes.
Introducing different principles, different ways of working, new skill-sets, technology interventions.

Areas of consideration:

- Review performance KPIs of all job functions to reflect added-value measures
- Prioritise full price sales
- Reduce volumes of unsold product
- Match supply in-line with demand
- Manage use of resources/waste recycling
- Drive loyalty through added-value products
- Fair employee & supplier wages, conditions and standards
- Initiate supplier charters

Summary of opportunities:

- Re-prioritise corporate KPIs, and re-appraise KPI targets and rewards for all employee roles, as measures of success, % full price sales, recognising final margins, % sell-through, % recycling, carbon footprint
- Adjust assortment volumes in-line with demand forecasts
- Initiate ethical charters with suppliers, and partners on working conditions and pay, and on sustainability objectives
- Set objectives as a business for energy use, % of sustainable energy, air-miles, sustainable transport use
- Develop career paths and training for employee roles
- Develop wellbeing support services, flexi-hours and remote working

Expand

Introducing broad strategic initiatives to drive the business in new and profitable directions.
Requiring changes to the organisational structure, principles and processes.

Areas of consideration:

- Develop a sustainable Business Model
- Commercial growth via Business growth
- Set Growth KPIs across wide social and ethical parameters
- Circular model, re-use, re-pair, re-cycle
- Work with natural resource capacities, not resource intensification.
- Commit to ethical partnerships
- Commit to investing in local shop communities

Summary of opportunities:

- Develop a Sustainable Model for Profit with plans and objectives across employees, supply chains, sustainability, ethical behaviour
- Set growth targets, action plans and timelines for non-profit KPIs
- Set targets for re-use, re-pair and re-cycle as % of assortment
- Develop a community plan to facilitate and fund initiatives by shops with their local communities including "Secret Millionaire"
- Commit to only collaborating with, being supplied by, and investing in, equally ethical businesses.

Sketch 65 Ethical Values: Evolve, Enrich & Expand

Ethical customers

Retailers continue to adjust to what is expected of them in the new disruptive markets. It is time to explore in which place in the spectrum of the post-COVID mind-shift your customer is sitting. Wherever it is, they will be impatient. It is the time to realign your strategic values with theirs. To make them happy, contented and re-assured to shop with you.

As a fundamental starting point. How much is your customer looking for your business model to evolve from product volumes and low costs to responsible volumes and added-value products? In doing so, whether they expect you, as a business, to be treating employees with new respect and appreciating their worth, ensuring fair wages and working conditions, re-investing in training and the physical and mental well-being of the workforce.

The Re-awakening of the customer conscience

Be aware. The public awareness of the retail supply chain has reached an all-time high, following high profile documentaries and exposés. For many, some of the practices are no longer acceptable. Negotiations with suppliers must be seen to be non-exploitative with the onus of responsibility falling on the retailer to ensure that the suppliers pay their employees well, treat them well, and do not pollute or exploit the environment where those same employees must live.

Other documentaries have highlighted the extreme pollution caused by plastics from products and packaging. For many, rightly or wrongly, plastic pollution has become the symbol of the age of exploitation.

Within any customer group, there cannot be many who are still oblivious, never-mind un-concerned, about un-recyclable products and packaging, and the irresponsible brands whose corporate identities now 'literally' litter the oceans and the countryside.

> *The corporate reputations of consumer brands now pollute the oceans and litter the countryside.*

Staggering facts about the daily volumes of clothes being put into landfill have created an uncomfortable murmur in the industry and beyond. Many of the clothes were never even worn. Many of the clothes were never realistically intended to be worn.

It is now expected by many customers that retailers should adjust assortment volume orders in-line with demand forecasts. That they should begin to turn their backs on long lead times, and fleets of ships transporting onions, and socks halfway around the planet to a customer that is turning its back more and more on such incredulous practices.

Reports of stockpiles, and the destruction and burning of unsold items to keep prices high will be met increasingly with disdain by more and more potential customers.

The public will expect to be able to scrutinise ethical charters initiated by retailers and agreed with suppliers, covering everything from working conditions and pay, raw material sourcing, codes of conduct, worker security, pollution limits and action plans for water and energy consumption reductions.

Expanding the power of the people

The COVID lockdowns have certainly shown us the destructive impact on the retail economy when many people, in this case through lockdown restrictions and enforcement, stop shopping.

That power is a warning. The same reaction of the customer to certain retail brands, albeit caused through voluntary choices and not judicial legislation, would be just as catastrophic for businesses. That drip-feed of sentiment is growing.

Sadly, retail bankruptcies are now not uncommon. They have been caused partly by customers being barred from shops by lockdown law. The same outcome will occur if staying away from shops is driven by customer choice!

Employees also have opinions on the type of retailers they work for, and increasingly how those businesses should be run. It will be expected by many more employees themselves, that their own individual performance and reward KPIs should be changed to reflect the new added-value parameters.

Performance and pay will be increasingly linked more directly to positive parameters such as % full price sales, higher achieved final margins, higher % of sell-throughs, higher % of excess stock recycled, less miles travelled by each product, less meetings, smaller carbon footprints and more local suppliers.

Less carbon emissions and less hot air would suit well many business boardrooms.

Doing the right things, and making those things commercial, should make both owners and employees happy, and proud to be part of the business. Taking the money is one thing, but taking the plaudits as well, is everything.

ESG is the new buzzword in retail boardrooms and beyond. 'Environment, Sustainability and Governance' directors are being appointed, watchdogs are being formed. Whether by choice or commercial prudence, managing every area of a retail business from an ESG perspective makes absolute sense. How the times are a changing.

Caring for employees

Prospective employees will also be looking to see more developed career paths, supported with specialist training, and certification. The onus to provide better working conditions and wellbeing support services, and the acceptance of flexi-hours and remote working will be the new minimum expectations for many employers and employees.

Excellent people, will increasingly not want to join a business that will not make them happy, or contented. Who wants be in an office, or a factory full of unhappy people? Who wants to be in an office or a factory as we have known them? Of course, many employees will return to the office, but most probably different kinds of offices. We are a gregarious species. We learn our trade and we learn to socialize. And we are learning to expect more from many of our employers.

Caring for local communities

Customers have certainly re-discovered local. Travel restrictions, and a nervousness with crowds forced many people to explore their local shops, and what their local communities had to offer.

Far from freezing in the unaccustomed headlights of customer traffic, many local retailers have risen to the challenge of popularity.

The customer has been pleasantly surprised. Community spirit has gathered around retailers as new centres of the community.

Retailers will need to take an active involvement in the communities that their shops serve. Whether independents, or parts of a large retail empire, each must develop a community plan. Chains need to facilitate and bankroll initiatives by their shops, in their local communities, including 'Secret Millionaire' funding for social initiatives and individual customer causes.

At every level, the customer will be scrutinising the retailer. The retailers must be just as watchful, and responsive. This may well begin as a ritual dance of suspicion but will ultimately lead to a virtuous cycle on approval and collaboration.

The routes to customer happiness, employee happiness and enlightened ownership must now come together to form the new Business Model. Retailers will need to underscore their commitment to change, by measuring appropriate and alternative growth parameters, other than just financial. They will need to consider 'success' well beyond immediate sales and profit. They will need to consider success in how happy they make their colleagues and their customers.

Some customers undoubtedly remain happy with their current lot, but a growing number are feeling unhappy about what they are buying, how it was produced, and who they bought it from.

Customers will hold to account retailers without a genuine ambition to change, and those who fail to deliver that ambition. 'Greenwashing' will be the new dirty laundry of the retail industry.

People are increasingly seeking out new retailers who wish to make money, but in a responsible way, to please their customers, please their employees, and not simply to please themselves.

The majority of course will rise to the challenge. Many have already done so and will continue to develop more initiatives to balance the need to make commercial profit, whilst doing so in a responsible and a collaborative way.

Making profit is good, it is profiteering that is unethical.

Is being ethical as simple as putting people first? The more people you consider and the better you treat them makes you more ethical? It is not a bad place to start for sure. If we are thinking about our employees and colleagues, our customers, our suppliers and our shareholders first when we decide and when we act then those decisions tend to be good ones.

Even the wider decisions on the environment and sustainability are ultimately people focused. They effect citizens in our local communities and those thousands of miles away. We are all citizens of the earth. Environmentalism, it can be argued is not about saving the planet, it is about saving humanity. Humanity begins at home, in our own back yard, but in a globalised industry our ethical decisions and actions can be for the benefit of humanity worldwide. Surely that is ethical?

Pandora: the ethical value of diamonds

Occasionally, the weight of public pressure can change the supply chain and point of origin of a product. The move away from real fur to man-made substitutes would be a valid example. Whilst some may still crave, and seek out the real thing, commercial common sense is at least one good reason to follow the crowd, notwithstanding our ethical objections.

Are we about to see the same shift in the jewellery industry, and particularly the lucrative world of diamonds? Whilst the objections are not as defined, the imagery not so shocking as the killing of wild animals, there is growing disquiet regarding the jewellery mining industry from both ethical and environmental standpoints.

Diamonds are mined in some of the most beautiful places in the world, by some of the poorest communities in the world. Destroying mountainside forests, and reports of accidents and miner's deaths has shifted the sentiment of the younger generations specifically.

Probably, no surprise then that the adored 'charm' jewellery retailer Pandora has launched a lab-created diamond collection as it looks to transform the market for diamond jewellery with affordable, sustainably and ethically produced products. Going forwards, the brand has made the definitive commitment that mined diamonds will no longer be used in Pandora's products.

According to Pandora, the lab-created diamonds have been grown with more than 60% renewable energy on average, whilst greenhouse gas emissions from non-renewable energies are being offset through the Carbon Neutral certification.

When Pandora launches globally next year, the diamonds will be made with 100% renewable energy. In a demographic market where beauty is as much in the eye of the ethical storm, as the beholder, Pandora may just be the first of many.

Joules: investment in 'doing the right thing'

Sustainability and ethics have been gaining in importance for both customers and retailers over recent years. Now it seems that investors are getting on board with ethical financing deals.

Fashion retailer Joules has reported updated funding arrangements with Barclays Bank, which include a £9m loan. The interest on the loan is linked to sustainability targets including carbon emissions and employee engagement.

It is a watershed moment. Rates and financial conditions are being provided on terms that reward corporate responsibility. It is already a long way from the purely performance-based criteria that might have been applied recently.

Many other retailers' commitments to environmental, social and governance (ESG) standards may be coming under similar scrutiny. Businesses who unlike Joules, do not put sustainability commitments as central to their business purposes.

Tesco: sustainably-linked supply chains

In a case of 'poacher turned gamekeeper' Tesco is applying similar ethical and sustainable standards to the terms and conditions of its supplier relationships.

It has become the first UK retailer to offer sustainability-linked supply chain finance to its partners. The scheme, in partnership with Santander, provides Tesco suppliers with preferential financing rates to encourage them to commit to "science-based emissions reduction targets".

The 'ethical supply-chain' is on the move, with sustainable and renewable energy. And some of the biggest players in the retail industry are putting their considerable weight behind it.

The Z to A of retail disruption

069

SET NEW TARGETS FOR GROWTH

Customer research & Business strategies

Let's be clear there's no taking your eye off the ball when it comes to being commercially successful. Those KPIs for sales and profit are still essential.

But there are any number of KPIs that go together to achieve those big commercial figures. Re-align sales and profit KPIs with KPIs on sustainability, carbon emissions, colleague and customer contentment. The two are increasingly commercially compatible, not mutually exclusive.

Actions

- Re-assess KPIs across the business
- Re-focus on 'soft' customer focused KPIs
- Research the KPIs that your customers care about the most
- Analyse and explore the relationships between 'Soft KPIs' and commercial KPIs
- Plan the communication and publicity of the different KPIs strategically for each audience
  - Investors
  - Colleagues
  - Collaborators
  - Customers

070

MAKE IT EASY TO BE "ESSENTIAL"

Strategic brainstorming

Whether it is ethically correct to make people like you or not, it is actually good for business as well.

We've seen the power of the customer in their retail allegiances, and increasingly the power of employees as brand advocates. On a brand, operational and individual level consider what is good for the people around you. Consider that making money and making friends are not mutually exclusive. It has not always been that way in retail.

Why not re-examine your responses to the previous 69 'astute strategy' actions in this book, and see if you can't add in some ethical additions to make your business essential to everyone?

Actions

- Ensure you know what your customers, employees and stakeholders want from you across every interaction with your business
  - Product
  - Price
  - Touchpoints
  - Convenience
  - Experience
  - Services
  - Communication
  - 'Tone of voice'
  - Sustainability
  - Ethics
- Don't leave any stone unturned, because your eager customers will probably look under it.
- Simply don't give your customers or your employees any 'easy' reason to be dissatisfied with you.
- Don't risk becoming 'non-essential!'

The Brave New World

The proud status of retail, as being the country's favourite leisure activity, is being challenged by immersive digital experiences, video, photo and editorial. Retail is becoming the secondary activity to more important and personal passions.

The gamechanger is that the passion is now leading directly to the product. 'Passion itself is the product.' The retailer is easily eliminated, except to the roll of supplier. The retailers who will survive and flourish will be those born out of a passion, a lifestyle, a pastime, where the product is a secondary event in the customer's journey. Where the product is a secondary event in the retailer's journey. The first point of call is 'passion.'

It is the passion generator, that is required to build the required authority and inspiration. It is their touchpoints that deliver the customer experience. To become a 'real & realistic' retailer the 'Passion generator' must then partner with an "End-to-End Channel Facilitator."

In this new model for retailing, we are looking at 'Passion Generators' and 'End-to-End Channel facilitators'

Full-Circle to a New Retail Order

New retail brands are more likely to originate from a passion and a vision. A passion and a vision from outside the retail industry. It is difficult to say that anyone is born today with a passion for retail, but a passion for life which is rich for retail.

The new breed of 'accidental' retailer is already close to the Passion Generator model. The end-to-end facilitation in the hands of a third party.

These new models are ironically replacing what has been lost from traditional retailing. Where the pursuit of scale and growth have quickly engulfed and smothered the original vision, and where the driving passion behind the brand has become the obsessive perpetuation of the performance economics of the supply chain itself.

In a world where customers are now embracing emotional connections with brands, demanding a product that has differentiation and purpose, the new retail brands are simply filling the void that has been created by soulless retail.

Where does that leave the traditional retailer in the new retail order? When your passion is mis-placed only in the buying data, it is hard to re-direct and re-develop a customer facing passion.

Passion with product

As we have seen, technology is allowing the development of a wide variety of customer touchpoints, outside the normal parameters of physical and digital shops. Retail brands are going to the customer in every possible sense, with services, community initiatives, competitions, advice, support.

Brand touchpoints are coming from the digital screen and out into the physical world. The only limitation is what is appropriate to your brand and relevant to your customers.

We can take whatever passion we want to the customer. Wherever and whenever the customer wants it.

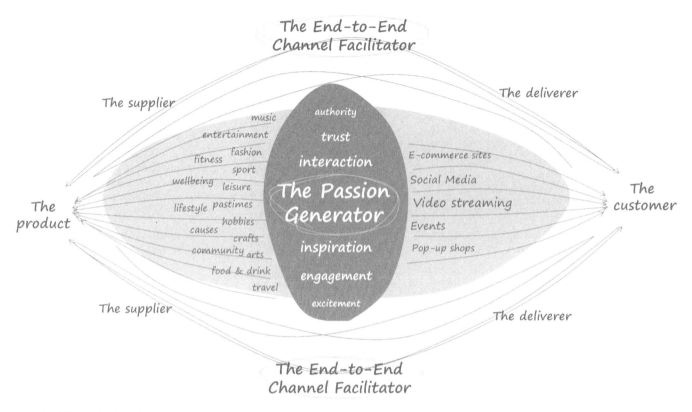

The End-to-End
Channel Facilitator

The supplier

The deliverer

The product

music
entertainment
fashion
fitness
sport
wellbeing
leisure
lifestyle pastimes
hobbies
causes
crafts
community arts
food & drink
travel

authority
trust
interaction
The Passion
Generator
inspiration
engagement
excitement

E-commerce sites
Social Media
Video streaming
Events
Pop-up shops

The customer

The supplier

The deliverer

The End-to-End
Channel Facilitator

© 2021 vm-unleashed ltd.

Sketch 66 The Passion Generator & End-to-end Channel Facilitator

For such a potentially disruptive force, the principle and structure of the relationship is simple, even familiar.

We go back to the fundamentals of bringing together the customer and the product. Channels are irrelevant.

We go back to the past. We re-discover the virgin market when life was so exciting for the customer and the retailer.

The centre of the customer relationship is 'Passion!'

The connection is the 'End-to-end Facilitator!'

Many new retail services are new evolutions of historical ideas. Ideas that come from a time when retail brands went the "extra mile" to peoples' homes. When retailers did have a genuine passion, for delivering their product, and for pleasing the customer.

Along the way many lost that perspective. They decided that customers had to make the sacrifice of time to come to the shop. Critically they forgot the importance of being with the customer in their homes.

Retailers became players that
never played away from home.

Amazon: the whole world in their hands

We all need to learn from Amazon. It serves no purpose to cry 'foul' and wallow in our self pity. Amazon never had any unfair advantage, it was born from nothing a few decades ago, from some innovative ideas and a vision. But the past is not the issue, it is the future strategy of Amazon which we need to consider, because this is where elements of our own strategy should also be facing.

We are talking about how 'retail' is transformed in the eyes of the customer. All things are changing. The product is passion, the retailer is the deliverer, the logistics company the retailer, and so on. What is clear is that what we need are two elements – the 'passion generator' and the 'end-to-end facilitator.'

We have been considering two entities coming together, but what if that was just one entity. This is the strategy for Amazon. They strive increasingly to create the passion and combine it with their incomparable logistics capabilities. And for a company that began with a traditional physical product – the book, their product is increasingly seen as the third element. Product, at a commodity level, can be made and sourced relatively easily today. It is the passion that stimulates the desire for it that is key.

As I write this book the news is about Amazon acquiring MGM. That is MGM 'film studios' which has a huge archive of entertainment content, as well as new hits such as 'The Handmaid's Tale.' This is where the passion is coming from, and Amazon is all over it.

Commanding content on any subject from sci-fi to gardening, travel to steam trains, where passions can be stirred and where the need and desire for physical products fall naturally from the passionate engagement and experience.

Amazon is increasingly much more about passion generating products, than products generating passion.

Vans: the passion of playing

Amongst the passion behemoths of Amazon there will still be plenty of room and opportunity for passionate retail brands to be successful and profitable.

The 'corporate's' passion will fail to stir any favourable emotions in many customers who prefer their experiences to be more genuine, local and personal. However, the ingredients required are still the same. The gradual shift from products with passion to passions with products will continue, with the need to end-to-end facilitate.

The 'end-to-end' is the open opportunity. Sitting in front of a screen is one starting point, but there are many other more active and social starting points. In many ways the lockdown has stimulated renewed energy in these 'new' entry points.

Consider 'The House of Vans', located under the arches of Waterloo Station. This starting point aims to celebrate creative expression – inside visitors can find an art gallery, a live music venue, a cinema, bars and a cafe. 'House of Vans' also contains its very own artist incubator space – VansLab. This is a free workspace for budding artists. There is the space and facilities to indulge your passion, and then the opportunity to showcase the results in the art gallery space.

The Vans experience also has two indoor skate parks to stimulate a more active passion for what after all is a famous street wear brand. It does us no harm to be reminded of the 'passion of the streets' the energy and enthusiasm of the streets, as the stimulation for buying the iconic Vans product.

Mega-events such as the Olympics are also now bringing the excitement and 'passion' of skateboarding to a whole new market. A perfect circle of digital and physical stimulation is adding new value to the Vans product.

Passion before product stays with us, even as we sit in front of our Amazon screen to select our next sneakers purchase.

The Z to A of retail disruption

Retail: the making of us all

The things you need to be a successful and fulfilled retailer at any level, are not that dissimilar. Looking, listening, and learning are important in any job. They are important in any business.

I always judge a good day as one where something good exists at the end of it that did not exist at the beginning. That could be something you have created, a report, a design, a product display, a product design, a product idea, a full stockroom, an empty stockroom, a happy customer, another happy customer, a happy colleague, an idea, or two. But it can also be knowledge in your head. If you look and listen, you will have learnt many good things by the end of the retail day.

Do not be afraid to try new things, take the till, man the customer services desk, give shop announcements, dress a mannequin, make an audit. If colleagues from head office arrive, ask them questions, absorb their experience. Never waste the chance to talk to anyone in your company. Never think of them as too important, or not important enough.

Take advantage of internal learning facilities, work your way through online modules and exercises. Develop an appetite for information and knowledge, read all the product, marketing and financial updates. Take any help, subsidies, bursaries offered by your employer to study for industry qualifications. Always fill in feedback forms and enter internal suggestion competitions, be positive, constructive, give ideas, and always put your name and number on your work.

Experience as many roles as you can and develop a plan to get to where you want to be in the business. Do not set the bar too low. There is no fulfilment in achieving below your capabilities. Do not set the bar too high. There is no achievement in being deflated and disappointed.

Many 'successful' people point to someone they have met in their working lives who has had a profound impact on their career and has given them the confidence to get to where they want to be in their retail lives.

That helping hand may have held open the odd door or two on the way, but what they really gave was the chance to be with inspired people, to watch them work, to listen to their words, carry out their instructions, face their wrath, and bathe in the glow of their gratitude. What they gave you was a chance to be part of an exclusive school of retail life that opens its door only once or twice in everyone's lifetime.

When you see the door open, grasp it, embrace it, and take it with you on your individual retail journey. Should you ever be fortunate to be in the position to give others a chance, to inspire others who are following you on the same journey, then do so, for the good of the business, for the benefit of others, for the love of yourself, and for the love of retail.

The makings of a community

Adversity brings people together. The COVID pandemic, the lockdown of friends, the opening of essential shops, all created adversity in retail business communities that had never been witnessed before.

The reaction of enlightened CEOs and senior executives showed each retail business, and each individual, in their true colours. There were some remarkable responses, generous, and supportive, that set the highest of standards for how we, as 'shopkeepers,' should manage ourselves and our businesses.

There has been a return to managing people instead of just employees. Sacrificing commercial returns to ensure that colleagues are first and foremost safe and secure. Many have invested in counselling services, and wellbeing support for those most effected.

HR teams have taken on the responsibility for personal development as well as professional enhancement. Training people to be confident as well as competent. The channels of communication have been permanently accessible, the virtual door always open.

Senior executives, and team leaders have taken on the true responsibility of leadership, as sources of positivity and strength for colleagues trying to navigate through each day, and week of work. New service initiatives, brand collaborations and product developments have been accelerated to give a purpose and focus for work, for the future.

The best CEOs have retained a sense of calmness, that has filtered through to the rest of the company. Communication has been clear and transparent, honest but reassuring. Leadership has been welcomed and appreciated.

These examples, and the lessons we draw from them, should hopefully be a benchmark, a catalyst for how we should always behave and mentor our shop colleague teams.

It is still an uncertain time, it is a worrying time, but it is also a time not to let go of the momentum that has built. Built for a better retailer environment, competitive but compassionate, and a new retail community, both diverse and inclusive.

Gymshark: we're in it together

It is normal to talk about Gymshark's meteoric rise as a manufacturer and retailer of gym & sportswear. However recent times have shown us that its new approach to retail is as much about its ethical and compassionate behaviour, as it is about its product processes.

It approached the COVID lockdowns as an opportunity to be more people focused than ever. The brand realized that open and honest communication channels were essential and developed regular and direct conversations with its teams. It talked about the things they wanted to hear about such as the business's financial buffer and the risk of redundancy.

It made the decision not to furlough staff, even those in the physical retail space, but to redirect them to volunteering for the NHS and other services. It valued its employee's physical and mental wellbeing over logical financial decision making. That philosophy now continues, as it allows individual teams to decide their own working practices and locations as the potential to office work opens up.

It continues to put 'people' first across its business, with traditional hierarchies secondary to its ethical values.

Retailing: A maze of people. Amazing people.

Retail has always been built on the shoulders of people. Such a diverse group of people as could ever be imagined.

From precious designers in rooms full of sketches, to the seamstress immersed in the folds of her fabric. From the farmers in seedling fields, to the white coated operators in deafening factories. From one computer terminal to the next, to the next, along a digital chain of orders and payments. From the creative drawing boards and the photographer's studios, to the dazzling colours on the digital screens of mobile phones and the facades of metropolitan cityscapes. From the crowded, chatter filled buses and trains to the stream of customers snaking their way past the window cleaners of the waking world. From the sales assistants searching for shop door keys, and the delivery drivers revving the cold choking engines of their scooters.

And from the retail executive at his high glass window surveying his estate from afar, to the shop manager basking in the heart of his pristine shop, open for business and ready to serve.

We are all shopkeepers.

We keep shops alive, and in many changing guises, channels, and incarnations we always will. Because buying things is essential. And shops both physical and digital will always be essential. Not just for necessities, but because we need the anticipation and the expectation, the social enjoyment and personal fulfilment.

We need the life, and the soul, of shopping. We need our essential retailers.

The Z to A of retail disruption

The Z to A of retail disruption

Businesses that are successfully disrupting the traditional ways of doing retail are creatively and commercially diverse, emerging from the worlds of imaginative new enterprises, and re-energized classic retail brands.

This book contains around 90 specific insights on how 'doing things with meaning' is now the only way to be 'essential' to customers in this brave new retail world.

Action Pages

How to make yourself into an 'Essential Retailer'

With such a myriad of opportunities available to join the retail revolution, it can be difficult to know where to begin and how to proceed.

This book contains 70 Action Plans, linked to every area of retail innovation and evolution, outlining the reasoning behind every disruptive initiative and offering step-by-step guidance on how to achieve your goals.

Acknowledgments, notes & sources

I always imagined the notes & sources section at the back of non-fiction books to be full of the titles of other reference books looking at the same or related issues. In fact, these notes do contain a few excellent books that I would recommend to anyone. I have read them and found them valuable background material and inspiration for this book.

However, reflecting on the content of this book, I find that I have acquired many more insights, opinions and ideas in a more organic way, from a wide variety of sources, and significantly from first-hand interaction with retailers. I think this reflects some of the key messages of this book.

That retail businesses are much more open to scrutiny and transparency than ever before. That many of them publish more material and data about themselves than ever before, from formal accounts to press releases, social media feeds, blogs and interviews. That retail business colleagues from shops to head offices are becoming honest advocates for their businesses and are happy to share their knowledge & experience with anyone with a genuine interest. That retail content, knowledge and expertise are available to anyone who wants to take the time to form relationships on LinkedIn or via the array of blogs, newsletters and feeds that are freely available.

Retail news, as with all topics in the media, is best acquired and absorbed from as wide a variety of sources as possible. The more people are talking about something the more reliable is the news itself.

Read with your two eyes, listen with your two ears and think deeply about what you learn.

Firstly, thanks to all those retailers who speak openly to the world about their businesses. Through news feeds and social media channels, blogs, magazines, LinkedIn sites, and their websites and mobile sites. This book is sprinkled with facts and anecdotes from many of these retailers. Their stories are fascinating to follow, and inspirational in the process of extrapolating and imagining future trends across the retail sector.

I would advise everyone in retail to stay close to their favourite retailers, the businesses who have the same philosophies and brand values as their own...and to a few who haven't.

Thank you to all the engaged and inspired shop colleagues it has been my pleasure to meet and discuss their businesses and personal retail experiences with. It is refreshing to be able to walk into so many shops, as a genuine customer, or consultant, and be able to engage in intelligent and inspirational conversations.

As you will see from the retail insights in this book, I am lucky enough to call London my home city. I always take the opportunity to walk its streets and visit retailers new & old. I have learnt so many important lessons directly from those who walk their shop floors and engage directly with customers.

My particular stars from the retail galaxy. The shop team at Loaf in Shoreditch, the Lush team on Oxford Street, Dark Sugars in Brick Lane, the shop managers in the Conran Shop in Marylebone, Selfridges customer services team, John Lewis retail experiences in London Westfield, the West Elm Team in Tottenham Court Road, the Schuh regional manager on Oxford Street, the shop manager at Timberland on Carnaby Street, the staff in any Sweaty Betty, but particularly Carnaby Street, the White Company in Sloane Square, Fortnum & Masons, the team at Hotel Chocolat in Soho, Whittards in Covent Garden, House of Hackney in Shoreditch...and many other encounters.

Many thanks to the best of colleagues, and the best of friends. **Luca Peruzzi** at **Ispira** in Italy, **Carlos Dominguez** at **MHE Consumer** in Madrid, **Stephanie Sergeil** at **Tisserlis** in France.

Fiona Gunn, one of those career defining people that I talk about in the book. A wise and generous lady who physically and metaphorically opened so many doors for me.

My thanks to **Luis Leal, Maria, Lucia, Beate, Scott, Freya, George, Will** and to **Edward Whitefield**, my mentor at Management Horizons Europe. A man who showed me the passion in retail.

Mike Booth at ClaroBlue without whose help, and very good taste, I may never have finished this book. A new special friend.

Mike MacMillan for his professional inspiration in retail technologies, and his kindness to my family.

Stephen Springham, long time collaborator and perpetual source of retail wisdom, currently to be found as Partner and Head of Retail Research at Knight Frank.

Tom Hesse, owner of **Congress Incentive Reisen GmbH** in Germany, without whose encoragement, I would not have discovered so many amazing retail people in my own city.

David Dalziel, founder & owner of **Dalziel+Pow**, world renowned Retail Design Agency. A long-time collaborator, and a man who drips retail inspiration.

To my English teacher, **Mr Lumb** at **Wath-upon-Dearne Comprehensive**. I didn't go the usual route, but I have written my book. This book rewards your faith and inspiration.

To all the colleagues I have worked with through the years. For all the fragments of retail inspiration and knowledge that have embedded themselves inside me...

Primark, Walgreens, Boots, Adidas, AllSaints, Ferrari, Luxottica, Ray-Ban, Nespresso, Bata, Halfords, Carrefour, Camper, Jack Jones, Marks & Spencer, Cortefiel, Sainsbury, Continente, Sonae, Otto Versand, BonPrix, World Duty Free, Sprinter, La Caixa, National Geographic, Real Madrid, KappAhl, Flex, Gruppo Vestebene, Alessi, Eroski, Gruppo Coin, OVS, Carrera, Aena, Heatons, Bally, Portaventura, Sony, Clarks, Benetton, Imaginarium, Dublin City Council, Porcelanosa, Northumbria University, Bialetti and Baltika...

Inspirational reading

Retail Week as the best-ever source of retail news. A magazine that has become an absolute retail beacon through the COVID pandemic and beyond. If you are interested in retail, anywhere in the world, then make sure you subscribe.

Smart Retail: Richard Hammond – Pearson
It has been my pleasure to work with and share a conference stage with Richard. His classic book – Smart Retail – should be an inspiration to all retailers, with its down-to-earth approach to improving retail performance.

Retail's Seismic Shift: Michael Dart/Robin Lewis – St Martins Press
An absolute powerhouse of a book if you want to understand the economics of retail and commerce. Unlike many futurist books, which seem to live on some vague future timeline, this book is relevant for now. All the points made are backed up with a myriad of third-party research and statistical evidence. This is very impressive. A huge amount of authority.

Cradle to Cradle: Michael Braungart – Vintage
A book before its time, updated for the 21st century, that shows the alternative way to destructive consumerism. A must read for all those that do believe in sustainability in retail, and even more so for those that don't.

How to Thrive in the Next Economy: Designing Tomorrow's World Today: John Thackara – Thames and Hudson Ltd
This book is extraordinarily optimistic about human change and explains new ways to design, produce and sell products, with many examples from across the globe.

The Retail Revival: Doug Stephens – Wiley
My first retail read. Taught me the important lesson that retailers are a product of the times in which they live.

The Invincible Company (The Strategyzer Series): Alex Osterwalder, Yves Pigneur et al – Wiley
An excellent insight into some of today's most powerful consumer facing businesses. The book that showed me that communicating business need not to be dull and monotone

Printed in Great Britain
by Amazon